my friend leonard

also by james frey

a million little pieces

riverhead books

my friend leonard

james frey

a member of penguin group (usa) inc. new york 2005

Some names and identifying characteristics have been changed.
Some sequences and details of events have been changed.

RIVERHEAD BOOKS
Published by the Penguin Group
Penguin Group (USA) Inc., 375 Hudson Street, New York, New York 10014, USA
• Penguin Group (Canada), 10 Alcorn Avenue, Toronto, Ontario M4V 3B2, Canada
(a division of Pearson Penguin Canada Inc.) • Penguin Books Ltd, 80 Strand,
London WC2R 0RL, England • Penguin Ireland, 25 St Stephen's Green,
Dublin 2, Ireland (a division of Penguin Books Ltd) • Penguin Group (Australia),
250 Camberwell Road, Camberwell, Victoria 3124, Australia (a division of
Pearson Australia Group Pty Ltd) • Penguin Books India Pvt Ltd, 11 Community
Centre, Panchsheel Park, New Delhi–110 017, India • Penguin Group (NZ),
Cnr Airborne and Rosedale Roads, Albany, Auckland 1310, New Zealand
(a division of Pearson New Zealand Ltd) • Penguin Books (South Africa) (Pty) Ltd,
24 Sturdee Avenue, Rosebank, Johannesburg 2196, South Africa

Penguin Books Ltd, Registered Offices:
80 Strand, London WC2R 0RL, England

Library of Congress Cataloging-in-Publication Data

Frey, James, date.
My friend Leonard / James Frey.
p. cm.
ISBN 1-57322-315-8
1. Frey, James, date.   2. Recovering addicts—United States—Biography.
3. Ex-convicts—United States—Biography.   4. Male friendship.   I. Title.
HV5805.F73A3   2005   2005042139
362.29'092—dc22
[B]

Printed in the United States of America
20 19 18 17 16 15

Book design by Stephanie Huntwork

While the author has made every effort to provide accurate telephone numbers
and Internet addresses at the time of publication, neither the publisher nor the
author assumes any responsibility for errors, or for changes that occur after
publication. Further, the publisher does not have any control over and does not
assume any responsibility for author or third-party websites or their content.

beginning

my cup runneth over.

psalm 23:5

On my first day in jail, a three hundred pound man named Porterhouse hit me in the back of the head with a metal tray. I was standing in line for lunch and I didn't see it coming. I went down. When I got up, I turned around and I started throwing punches. I landed two or three before I got hit again, this time in the face. I went down again. I wiped blood away from my nose and my mouth and I got up I started throwing punches again. Porterhouse put me in a headlock and started choking me. He leaned toward my ear and said I'm gonna let you go. If you keep fighting me I will fucking hurt you bad. Stay down and I will leave you alone. He let go of me, and I stayed down.

I have been here for eighty-seven days. I live in Men's Module B, which is for violent and felonious offenders. There are thirty-two cells in my module, thirty-two inmates. At any given time, there are between five and seven deputies watching us. All of us wear blue and yellow striped jumpsuits and black, rubber-soled slippers that do not have laces. When we move between rooms we walk through barred doors and metal detectors. My cell is seven feet wide and ten feet long. The walls are cement and the floor is cement and the bed is cement, the bars iron, the toilet steel. The mattress on the bed is thin, the sheets covered with grit. There is a window in my cell, it is a small window that looks out onto a brick wall. The window is made of bulletproof glass and there are bars on both sides of it. It affords me the proper amount of State required sunlight. Sunlight does not help pass time, and the State is not required to provide me anything that helps pass time.

My life is routine. I wake up early in the morning. I brush my teeth. I sit on the floor of the cell I do not go to breakfast. I stare at a gray cement wall. I keep my legs crossed my back straight my eyes forward. I take deep breaths in and out, in and out, and I try not to move. I sit for as long as I can I sit until everything hurts I sit until everything stops hurting I sit until I lose myself in the gray wall I sit until my mind becomes as blank as the gray wall. I sit and I stare and I breathe. I sit and I stare. I breathe. I stand in the middle of the afternoon. I use the toilet and I drink a glass of water and I smoke a cigarette. I leave my cell and I walk to the outdoor recreation area. If the weather holds, there are prisoners in the area playing basketball, lifting weights, smoking cigarettes, talking. I do not mingle with them. I walk along the perimeter of the wall until I can feel my legs again. I walk until my eyes and my mind regain some sort of focus. Until they bring me back to where I am and to what I am, which is an alcoholic and a drug addict and a criminal. If the weather is bad, the area is empty. I go outside despite the weather. I walk along the perimeter until I can feel and remember. I am what I am. I need to feel and remember.

I spend my afternoons with Porterhouse. His real name is Antwan, but he calls himself Porterhouse because he says he's big and juicy like a fine-ass steak. Porterhouse threw his wife out the window of their seventh floor apartment when he found her in bed with another man. He took the man into a field and shot him five times. The first four shots went into the man's arms and legs. He waited thirty minutes to let the man feel the pain of the shots, pain he said was the equivalent to the pain he felt when saw the man fucking his wife. Shot number five went into the man's heart. From three o'clock to six o'clock, I read to Porterhouse. I sit on my bed and he sits on the floor. He leans against the wall and he closes his eyes so he can, as he says, do some imagining. I read slowly and clearly, taking an occasional break to drink a glass of water or smoke a cigarette. In the past twelve weeks we have worked our way through *Don Quixote, Leaves of Grass,* and *East of Eden.* We are currently reading *War and Peace,* which is Porterhouse's favorite. He smiled at the engagement of Andrei and Natasha. He cried when Anatole betrayed her. He cheered at the battle of Borodino, and though he admired the Russian tactics, he cursed while Moscow burned. When we're not reading, he carries *War and Peace* around with him. He sleeps with it at night, cradles it as if it were his child. He says that if he could, he would read it again and again.

I started reading to Porterhouse the day after he hit me with the tray, my second day here. I was walking to my cell and I had a copy of *Don Quixote* in my hand. As I passed his cell, Porterhouse said come here, I wanna talk to you. I stopped and asked him what he wanted, he said he wanted to know why I was here and why a County Sheriff would give him three cartons of cigarettes to beat my ass. I told him that I had hit a County Sheriff with a car going five miles an hour while I was drunk and high on crack and that I had fought several others when they tried to arrest me. He asked if I had hit the man on purpose. I told him I didn't remember doing it. He laughed. I asked him why he was here and he told me. I did not offer further comment. He asked what the book was and I told him and he asked why I had it and I told him that I liked books. I offered to let him have it when I was done with it and he laughed and said I can't read motherfucker, fucking book ain't gonna do me no good. I offered to read to him. He said he'd think about it. A couple of hours later he showed up and sat on my floor. I started reading. He has been here every day since. At six o'clock, I walk with Porterhouse to dinner, the only meal of the day that I eat. It is usually foul, disgusting, almost inedible. The meat is mush, the bread stale, potatoes like water, vegetables hard as rock. I eat it anyway. Porterhouse eats seconds and thirds and fourths, which, by long-standing arrangements, he takes from the trays of other prisoners. He offers to get food for me, but I decline. When I am finished eating, I sit and I listen to Porterhouse talk about his upcoming trial. Like every other man in here, regardless of what they might say, Porterhouse is guilty of the crimes that he has been accused of committing. He wants to go to trial because until he is convicted, he will stay here, at county jail, instead of doing his time in state prison. Jail is a much easier place to live than prison. There is less violence, there are more privileges, most of the prisoners know they are getting out within the next year, and most sooner than that, and they want to be left alone. Once they're gone, they don't want to come back. In prison, there are gangs, rapes, drugs, murder. Most of the prisoners are in for long stretches and will most likely never be free. If they are ever free, they will be more dangerous than they were before they were imprisoned. They could give two fucks about rehabilitation, they need to survive. To survive they need to replace their humanity with savagery. Porterhouse knows this, but wants to remain human for as long as he can. A guilty verdict is coming his way, but until it does, he will stay here, and he will remain a human being.

After dinner I go to the payphone. I dial a number that was given to me by my friend Leonard. The number allows me to make free long distance phone calls. I do not know where Leonard got the number, and I have never asked him. That has always been my policy with Leonard. Take what he offers, thank him for it, do not ask questions. Leonard is what I am, an alcoholic and a drug addict and a criminal, though he is not currently incarcerated. He is fifty-two years old and he lives in Las Vegas, where he oversees an unnamed organization's interests in a number of finance, entertainment and security companies. When we talk we do not discuss his business.

I always call Lilly first. Lilly with long black hair and pale skin and blue eyes like deep, clean water. Lilly whose father deserted her and whose mother sold Lilly's body for drugs when she was thirteen. Lilly who became a crackhead and a pillpopper and hitchhiked across the country on her back so that she could escape her Mother. Lilly who has been raped and beaten and used and discarded. Lilly who is alone in the world except for me and a Grandmother who has terminal cancer. Lilly who is living in a halfway house in Chicago while she tries to stay clean and waits for me to be released from this place. Lilly who loves me. Lilly who loves me.

I dial the number. I know she's sitting in a phone booth in the halfway house waiting for my call. My heart starts beating faster as it does whenever I see her or speak to her. She picks up on the third ring. She says hello sweet boy, I say hello sweet girl. She says I miss you and I say we'll see each other soon. She asks me how I am and I tell her that I'm good. She's upset that I'm here and I don't want her to worry, I always tell her things are good. I ask her how she is and her answers vary from day to day, hour to hour, minute to minute. Sometimes she says she feels free, which is a feeling she has rarely felt but has always sought. She says she feels like she's getting better and healthier and can put her past behind her. Sometimes she says that she feels fine, that she is getting by and that is enough, that she's off drugs and has a roof over her head, she says she's fine. Sometimes she's depressed. She feels like her Grandmother is going to die and I am going to leave her and she is going to be alone in the world, which is something she says she cannot handle. She says there are always options, she'll weigh them when the time comes to weigh them. Sometimes she feels nothing. Absolutely nothing. She doesn't talk she just breathes into the phone. I tell her to hold on, that she'll feel again, feel better again, feel free again, I tell her to hold on, sweet girl, please hold on. She doesn't talk. She just breathes into the phone.

I met Lilly and Leonard five months ago. I was a patient at a drug and alcohol treatment center. I checked in after a ten year bout with alcoholism and a three year bout with crack addiction, which ended when I woke up on a plane after two weeks of blackness and discovered that I had knocked out my front four teeth, broken my nose and my eye socket, and torn a hole in my cheek that took forty stitches to close. At the time, I was wanted in three states on drug, drunk-driving and assault charges. I didn't have a job or any money and I was nearly dead. I didn't want to go to the treatment center, but I didn't have any other options. At least not options I was ready to accept.

I met Lilly on my second day. I was standing in line waiting for detoxification drugs and she was standing in front of me. She turned around and she said hello to me and I said hello to her and she asked what happened to my face and I shrugged and told her I didn't know and she laughed. I saw her and spoke to her later that day and the next and the next and the next. The treatment center had a policy against male/female relationships. We ignored the policy. We talked to each other, slipped each other notes, met each other in the woods that were part of the center's grounds. We helped each other and understood each other. We fell in love with each other. We are young, she is twenty-four and I am twenty-three, and we fell in love. Neither of us had felt anything like what we felt for one another and we agreed that we would stay together and live together when we left the treatment center. We got caught with each other and we paid for the violation of the center's rules. Lilly left the center and I went after her. I found her selling her body for crack and I brought her back. I left a week later and came here. Lilly stayed for nine more weeks and has been at the halfway house in Chicago for a month. When I leave here, I am going to meet her.

I met Leonard three days after I met Lilly. I was sitting by myself in the cafeteria eating a bowl of oatmeal. He came to my table and accused me of calling him Gene Hackman. I didn't remember calling him Gene Hackman, which made him angry. He told me that if I called him Gene Hackman again, there was going to be a problem. I laughed at him. He did not take kindly to my laughing and he threatened me. I laughed again,

7

called him an old man, and told him if he didn't get out of my face, I was going to beat his ass. He stared at me for a minute. I stared back. I stood up and told him to get the fuck out of my face or prepare to get his ass beat. He asked me my name and I told him. He told me his name and asked me if I was fucked-up. I said yes, Leonard, I'm fucked-up, I'm fucked-up real bad. He offered me his hand and said good, I'm fucked-up too, and I like fucked-up people, let's sit and eat and see if we can be friends. I took his hand and I shook it and we sat down and we ate together and we became friends.

Over the course of the following two months, which is how long I was at the treatment center, Leonard became my closest friend. When I walked out of the center shortly after finishing the process of physical detoxification, Leonard walked out after me. I told him to leave me alone, but he wouldn't do it. He followed me. I knocked him down, and he got up. I knocked him down again and he got back up again. He told me that he wasn't going to let me leave, and that if I tried, he would have me found and brought back. He told me it didn't matter how many times I left, he would have me brought back every single time. I looked into his eyes and I listened to his words. He is thirty years older than me but he is what I am, an alcoholic and a drug addict and a criminal. His eyes and words held truth, a truth that I knew and trusted more than institutional truth or medical truth or the truth of people who haven't seen the shit that I've seen. I went back to the center and I stayed at the center. I was leaving because I wanted liquor and I wanted crack and I wanted to die. I went back because of Leonard.

For whatever the reasons, and I do not know all of them, whenever I needed something or someone, Leonard was there. He watched over me and protected me. He helped me reconcile with my family. He gave me the best advice that I was given while I was at the center, which was to hold on. No matter how bad or difficult life becomes, if you hold on, hold on to whatever it is you need to hold on to, be it religion, friends, a support group, a set of steps or your own heart, if you hold on, just hold on, life will get better. He encouraged me to be with Lilly. He told me to forget about the fucking rules, that love doesn't come around that often, and when it does you've got to take it and try to keep it.

After Lilly left, she needed money to come back and stay at the center.

Her Grandmother didn't have any more money. She had spent what she had to put Lilly there the first time, and Lilly didn't qualify for any of the financial aid programs. I didn't tell Leonard about Lilly's problems and I didn't ask him for help. He had done enough for me.

The morning he was leaving he asked to speak to me. I went to his room and he handed me a card. It had five names and five phone numbers on it. All of them were his, he said he used different names in different places. He said call if you need anything, doesn't matter what it is or where you are, just call. I asked him why there were five numbers and five names on the card and he told me not to worry, just call if I need anything. After he gave me the card, he said he had something he wanted to talk to me about. I said fine, talk. He looked nervous, which I had never seen before. He took a deep breath. He said Kid, I have always wanted to be married and I have always wanted to have children. More specifically, I have always wanted to have a son. I have been thinking about this for a while now and I have decided that from now on, I would like you to be my son. I will watch out for you as I would if you were my real son, and I will offer you advice and help guide you through your life. When you are with me, and I plan on seeing you after we both leave here, you will be introduced as my son and you will be treated as such. In return, I ask that you keep me involved in what you are doing and allow me to take part in your life. If there are ever issues with your real father, I will insist you defer to and respect him before me and over me. I laughed and asked him if he was joking. He said that he wasn't joking, not even close. I warned him that I tended to cause a lot of problems for the people in my life, and that if he could deal with that, I'd be happy to be his son. He laughed and he hugged me. When he released me he said he wanted me to go to jail and do my time and protect myself. He said not to worry about Lilly that she was going to be taken care of, that her financial issues had been resolved, that he hoped someday she would be better, that someday we would have a life together. I tried to object, but he interrupted me. He said what is done is done, now say thank you. I said thank you and I started to cry. I hoped that someday she would be better, that someday we would have a life together.

I talk to Leonard every two or three days. I call him if I can't get hold of Lilly, or I call him when I'm done talking to her. He always asks the same two questions: are you okay, do you need anything. My answers are always the same: yes I'm okay, no I don't need anything. He offers to come visit I tell him no. He asks when I'm getting out, I always give him the same date. He wants to have a party the day of my release, I tell him I want to see Lilly, I want to be alone with her. When we hang-up he always says the same thing: look 'em in the eye and show no fear.

When I'm done with the phone, I go back to my cell. I do a hundred push-ups and two hundred sit-ups. When I am done with the push-ups and sit-ups, I walk to the shower. Most of the Prisoners shower in the morning, so I am usually alone. I turn on the heat from multiple faucets. I sit down on the floor. The water hits me from multiple directions it hits my chest, my back, the top of my head. It hits my arms, my legs. It burns and it hurts and I sit and I take the burn and I take the hurt. I don't do it because I like it, because I don't. I sit and I take the pain and I ignore the pain and I forget the pain because I want to learn some form of control. I believe that pain and suffering are different things. Pain is the feeling. Suffering is the effect that pain inflicts. If one can endure pain, one can live without suffering. If one can learn to withstand pain, one can withstand anything. If one can learn to control pain, one can learn to control oneself. I have lived a life without control. I have spent twenty-three years destroying myself and everything and everyone around me and I don't want to live that way anymore. I take the pain so that I will never suffer. I take the pain to experience control. I sit and I burn and I take it.

I finish my shower and I go back to my cell. I sit down on the floor and I pick up a book. It is a small book a Chinese book. It is a short book and a simple book called *Tao Te Ching*, written by a man named Lao-tzu. It is not known when it was written or under what conditions, nothing is known about the writer except his name. Roughly translated, the title means The Book of the Way. I open the book at random. I read whatever is in front of me. I read slowly and deliberately. There are eighty-one simple poems in the book. They are about life and The Way of life. They say things like in thinking keep to simple, in conflict be fair, don't compare or compete, simply be yourself. They say act without doing, work without effort, think of the large as small and the many as few. They say confront the difficult while it is easy, accomplish the great one step at a time. They say let things come and let things go and live without possession and live without expectation. These poems do not need, depend, create or define. They do not see beauty or ugliness or good or bad. They do not preach or implore, they do not tell me that I'm wrong or that I'm right. They say live and let live, do not judge, take life as it comes and deal with it, everything will be okay.

The lights go out at ten o'clock. I stand and I brush my teeth and I drink a glass of water. I lie down on the concrete bed and I stare at the ceiling. There is noise for about thirty minutes. Prisoners talk to each other, yell at each other, pray, curse themselves, curse their families, curse god. Prisoners cry. I stare at the ceiling. I wait for silence and the deep night. I wait for long hours of darkness and solitude and the simple sound of my own breath. I wait until it is quiet enough so that I can hear myself breathe. It is a beautiful sound.

I do not sleep easily. Years of drug and alcohol abuse have sabotaged my body's ability to shut itself down. If I do sleep, I have dreams. I dream about drinking and smoking. I dream about strong, cheap wine and crack. The dreams are real, or as real as dreams can be. They are perverted visions of my former life. Alleys filled with bums drinking and fighting and vomiting and I am among them. Crackheads in broken houses on their knees pulling on pipes with sunken cheeks screaming for more and I am, among them. Tubes of glue and cans of gas and bags filled with paint I am surrounded stumbling and huffing and inhaling as much as I can as fast as I can. In some of the dreams I have guns and I'm playing with the guns and I am debating whether I am going to shoot myself. I always decide that I am. In some of the dreams I am being chased by people who want to kill me. I never know who they are, all I know is that they want to kill me and they always succeed. In some of the dreams I keep drinking and smoking until I am so drunk and so high so goddamn fucked-up that my body just stops. I know that it is stopping and I know that I am dying I don't care. I reach for the pipe and I reach for the bottle. My body is shutting down rather than suffer the continued consequences of my actions and I don't care. I never have good dreams or happy dreams or dreams in which life is good. I have no memories of good dreams or happy dreams or dreams in which life is good.

When I don't sleep, I lie on my bed and I close my eyes. I think about Lilly. I think about where she is and what she's doing. One of the requirements for her residency at the halfway house is that she have a job. She works the nightshift doing laundry at the hospital where her Grandmother is dying. She washes dirty sheets and dirty towels, used gowns and stained scrubs. On her breaks, she goes to her Grandmother's room. Her Grandmother has bone cancer, and it has spread throughout her entire body. She can't move without pain and she hasn't left her bed in two months. Her doctor has said that she will be lucky to live for another month. Lilly tells me she's on a morphine drip and she's incoherent and she doesn't know Lilly's name anymore and she doesn't remember anything about her life. Her mind has been consumed by her cancer as much as her body has been consumed by her cancer. It has overwhelmed her and there is nothing left. Just a shell of pain and morphine. Just a shell of what was once a life.

Lilly sits by her side and holds her hand and talks to her. It doesn't matter that she doesn't understand anything, Lilly sits and holds her hand and talks with her anyway. She tells her about the halfway house she hopes that it's working she can't wait to get out. She tells her about the job it isn't so bad she's certainly done worse. She tells her about me she misses me and she wishes I were there, she hopes I still love her. She tells her about the hope for a future with me and without drugs and with a sense of freedom and a sense of security. She tells her Grandmother about her fears. About the loneliness she's been alone forever she doesn't want to be alone anymore. About a return to her old life she would rather die than sleep with men for money. About me she's scared that we won't survive in the world away from institutions she's scared I'm going to leave her like everyone else in her life has always left her. About what life will be like when her Grandmother dies. She's scared because her Grandmother is the only person Lilly trusts and the only person that she is secure with and she can't imagine living without her. Sometimes Lilly can't talk anymore and she sits with her Grandmother and she holds her hand and she cries. She's scared and she can't imagine living without her. She cries.

I am leaving here in three days. I will have served my time, paid my debt to society. As I lie here in bed listening to the sound of my own breathing as I lie here fighting off dreams and drifting through the deepest night, I think about what I am going to do when the steel-door slams shut behind me. I am going to Chicago. I am going to Lilly. I love her and I want to be chicago

Lilly's Grandmother died two nights ago. Lilly found her when she went to visit during one of her breaks. She looked at Grandmother's chest it wasn't moving. She looked at her lips they were blue. She reached for her hand and it was cold. Lilly started screaming. When the doctors came and the nurses came she wouldn't let go of her Grandmother's hand. They tried to sedate her. She wouldn't take the drugs she just held her Grandmother's hand and cried. When the body was wheeled from the room, Lilly walked with it. Hand in hand all the way to the morgue. She sat outside the morgue for the next twelve hours. Crying.

I talked to her the next night. She was hysterical. She was sobbing and heaving, begging for me to come to her. I told her I would be there as soon as I could, I would be out in twelve hours. She said please James I need to see you, I need you right now, please, please, please, I need you right now. I said I'm in jail Lilly, I can't do anything here but talk to you. I'm being released in the morning and I'll be with you tomorrow night. She said I need you now James, I'm so scared and lonely, please. She started crying harder harder harder. I tried to talk to her, but she couldn't talk to me. I told her I loved her and I was coming as soon as I could, that she'd be okay that we'd be okay that everything would be okay once we were together. She cried and I told her I loved her. She cried and I told her I loved her.

Her crying slowed and her breathing became normal. I asked her if she was all right and she said no. I asked her if she would be okay until I got there and she said hurry, please hurry. We said I love you, we both said it. We hung up the phone I wanted to say I love you one more time. I hope she'll be okay.

I have been sitting on the floor waiting for morning. I have been sitting on the floor waiting to be released from this place. I have stared at the wall and I have watched it turn from black to gray to white. When I hear noise the noise of other prisoners up and around, awake and starting their day, I stand and I walk to the sink and I brush my teeth and I wash my face. I finish and I take a deep breath, it has been a long night I'm worried about Lilly. I know there's nothing I can do until I am out of here. Nothing.

I sit back on the floor. I wait. A second a minute five minutes ten they are all a fucking eternity, it is taking too fucking long. I wait. Once the doors open I have an hour before the deputies come to get me and thirty minutes of release administration. I hope she's okay.

A buzzer. The day begins, the door opens. I stand and I pick up my books. I leave my cell and I walk to Porterhouse's cell, the door is open he sees me coming he stands to greet me. I ask him if he's ready to finish. He says yes. He sits on the floor and I sit on the edge of his bed. I read the last fifteen pages of *War and Peace*. When I am finished I close the book. Porterhouse opens his eyes and nods his head and says that is one good motherfucking book. I smile and say yeah. I stand and I set the book on top of the other books, which are stacked next to Porterhouse's door. I start to walk out. He speaks.

James.

I stop, turn around.

Yeah?

Thank you.

No problem.

I stand outside of his cell and I look at my friend. He looks at me. He is going to spend the rest of his life in prison. He knows it and I know it. We will never see or speak to each other ever again. He knows it and I know it. He speaks.

Be good, motherfucker.

You too.

He smiles and he nods and I smile and I nod back. I turn around and I walk away. I walk to my cell and I sit down on the floor. I wait. I hate waiting, I hope they hurry, I sit and I wait. I do not wait long. Maybe fifteen minutes, which seems like fifteen hours. Two deputies show up and I greet them and I invite them in and they inspect my cell for general cleanliness and good order. They check to make sure that I haven't broken anything or altered anything or given anything away or stolen anything. They have a clipboard with a checklist. Sink, check. Toilet, check. Pillow, check. Towel, check. When they are finished checking, they shackle me and they walk me to Intake/Release. They stand with me while a clerk looks at his computer and makes sure that today is my release date, that this is not a mistake. The computer tells him that today is the correct day and the guards remove my shackles and I walk through a steel door. Another clerk meets and hands me a box with my belongings. I open the box. There is a pair of jeans a pair of wool socks a pair of scuffed black boots a white t-shirt a black hooded sweatshirt a wallet thirty-four dollars a pack of stale cigarettes a lighter a set of keys. I sign a piece of paper acknowledging that all of my possessions have been turned over to me. I step into a small room and I take off my jumpsuit, fuck that jumpsuit. I put on my clothes and I step out of the room and I sign another piece of paper and I'm done. A large steel-door opens and I step through it. I step through another, another. I step through another and I am outside and I am free. I take a deep breath. It is the middle of February the air is cold and clean. I take a deep breath, as deep as I can, I'm fucking free. I walk across a short expanse of concrete. I stop at a gate, which is part of a fifteen-foot razor-wire fence that surrounds the jail. I wait for the gate to open. It is moving too fucking slowly, I'm in a hurry. As soon as there is enough space, I step through the opening and start walking down the street. It is a barren street. No houses, no trees, no other buildings besides the jail. There are fields on both sides of the street with dead yellow scrub and drainage ditches. There is a lot of mud.

I walk as quickly as I can down the street, I walk jog run walk as fast my lungs allow. Before I came here and surrendered to the proper authorities, I went to North Carolina, where I lived before I went to the treatment center. I picked up my truck, my old blue battered truck and drove to a friend's house, a friend who was a professor of mine while I was in school. My friend makes moonshine in his basement and we used to drink the shine and smoke crack and get fucked-up together. He watched me get arrested on more than one occasion. He was happy when he heard I was coming back to serve time, happy that I was attempting to straighten out my life. Part of my sentence was a permanent revocation of my driving privileges in the state, permanent meaning for as long as I am still alive. If I get caught driving, it will be a violation of the conditions of my release and I will serve three to five years in state prison. He said I could leave my truck with him and he would drive me out of the state when I was ready to leave. I'm going to need someone to drive me out of here. I hope he's home. He better be fucking home.

Trees start appearing, an occasional house, a school, a gas station. My lungs hurt. I think about Lilly I hope she's okay. I look for a payphone the one at the gas station didn't have a receiver. I hurry to my friend's house I hope he's home I'll use his phone. I don't want to call my family or friends there will be time for them later. I want to call Lilly, I hope some-one answers the phone I hope she's there. Tree lawn house fence barking dog rusty swing set car on blocks fast food heaven convenience store church. They are all a blur I'm moving as fast I can. I look for the correct street-sign I hope I'm going the right way. Continental Avenue. Brookside Lane. Cloverdale Street. Cherry Valley Road. I'll know it when I see it. He better be fucking home.

I come around a corner and I see my truck sitting in a driveway. I start running. Up the front walk front porch knock on the door look through the window nobody's home. I think about what to do. I don't want to wait. I don't want to wait. I don't want to fucking wait no no no no no I'm not going to fucking wait. If I'm careful I'll be fine. I'll drive cautiously, drive the speed limit, I'll be fine. Fuck it, I'll be fine.

I reach for the door. It's unlocked. This is a small town people still feel safe. I walk into the house, through a hall, into the kitchen. There is a phone on the wall. I pick it up and I dial. It starts ringing. I wait for some-one to answer there must be someone at that fucking halfway house who will answer the phone. Nothing. Ringing, ringing. Nothing. I want to talk to Lilly before I leave, I want to tell her I'm on my way. I want to hear her voice, make sure she's okay. I want to tell her I love her.

I hang up the phone try again. Nothing. Try again. Nothing. I look for a piece of paper and a pen I find them on the counter. I write a note it says Thank you for taking care of my truck, I'll be in touch soon. I leave the note in the middle of the kitchen table and I walk out of the house.

I walk to my truck. I take the key out of my pocket, open the door, sit down in the driver's seat. There's another pack of smokes on the passenger seat, I don't know if I left them or my friend left them, either way it's a beautiful thing, I can save what little money I have to spend on something other than smokes. I put the key in the ignition, turn it, the engine starts. I look at the dashboard clock it is eleven A.M. Chicago is five hours away. I told her I would be there by dark, I'll be early. The earlier the better. I hope she's okay. I want to hold her hand and tell her everything is going to be okay.

I back the truck out, start driving through the town. The highway isn't far, I know my way. I drive just above the speed limit. I know that if I drive too fast I draw attention, if I drive too slow I draw attention. I'm not nervous about driving. I know the risk I am taking sitting behind the wheel. I am making a decision to take the risk because it is worth it to me. If I sit here and wait I will go fucking crazy with worry. I want to get to Chicago as fast as I can. If I get caught, I get caught. I will deal with it if it happens. I roll out onto the highway. It is not crowded. I pull into the right lane behind a large tractor/trailer. I turn on the radio. I find a station that has the news twenty-four hours a day. I haven't looked at a newspaper or watched television in three months. I have no idea what is going on in the world. I listen for a few minutes. Same bad news. I turn it off. I stare at the road. Time moves slowly when you want it to move quickly. Each minute is ten, each ten a thousand. I stay behind the tractor/trailer, drive three miles over the speed limit. I smoke my stale cigarettes one after another after another. I think about Lilly. I think about what it is going to be like when I see her again. I think about what it is going to be like when I stand in front of her door. Despite the circumstances, I know I'll have a big smile on my face. I'll knock and she'll say come in and I'll open the door and I'll step into her room. Hopefully someone will have been sitting with her, helping her, holding her hand, Lilly will pull away and come to me. She'll come into my arms. I'll close them and I'll hold her. She'll start to cry and I'll say I love you. I'll hold her for as long as she needs to be held. We'll deal with her Grandmother and her Grandmother's death. We'll get Lilly out of the halfway house and out of her job at the hospital. We'll find a place to live it doesn't have to be a palace, just has to be a place for us. We'll get jobs, make some money, be together, stay together, live together, deal together, just be together. We'll grow old together.

I cross the border of Indiana and Ohio. I smile. I'm safe now, I will not be back in Ohio for a long fucking time. I put my foot down, my old blue truck jumps, we go from sixty-three to eighty-three. I keep it at eighty-three because I know that if I get caught going eighty-five or higher, twenty-five miles or more over the speed limit, there's a chance that I will get arrested for reckless driving instead of speeding. Part of being arrested for reckless driving is that the trooper has the option of putting the offender in jail. If I go back to jail, even if it's for a couple hours, I'm fucked. I could give a shit if I get a speeding ticket. I'll tear it up and throw it out the fucking window as soon as the trooper who writes it is out of eyesight. I drive eighty-three.

The miles start to add up. I see signs that have the mileage to Chicago on them. One hundred twelve miles. Eighty-eight miles. Sixty-three miles. Thirty-nine miles. I smoke my cigarettes and I smile I am almost there I smile. I turn the radio back on and I find a station that plays light hits, cheesy romantic ballads, lovey-dovey love songs. I sing along if I know the words. If I don't know the words, I make up my own. I'm getting closer sweet girl I'll be with you soon big kisses on your face my heart goes boom, forever and ever, oh yeah, oh yeah.

I cross the border into Illinois. The highway becomes bigger and more crowded. Smoke stacks and oil tanks dominate the land, the air smells like sulphur, gasoline. The sun is starting to drop, the sky is the menacing gray of deep winter. I should make it before it is completely dark. I should be there soon. I have the address of the halfway house and I have a general idea of where it is, somewhere on the north side of the city. Near downtown. It is a major street I should be able to find it without a problem. I start to get more excited. I smile. If I got in a wreck right now, I would do it with a smile. If someone shot me, I would take the bullet with a smile. If I got in a fight, I'd smile as I threw my punches. I am almost there, almost there. I love you, Lilly. Almost there.

I cross a large bridge I'm closer. I get off the highway I'm on a smaller road that runs along the edge of Lake Michigan. The lake is frozen. The ice is dirty and black. I can hear the wind screaming, I can feel it pushing my truck. My truck is a good truck a strong truck an old friend of a truck. My truck laughs at the wind, says fuck you wind, we've got somewhere to be, someone is waiting for us.

I take a ramp off the road into the center of the city. Towers of steel and glass on every side, crowded streets, horns. Pedestrians are heavily dressed, they lean slightly forward as they walk, they hurry to escape the bitter, bitter cold. I move inland, north and across the Chicago River. There are icicles hanging from the iron rails of the bridge, smoke and steam drifting through the girders. I look for Dearborn that is the name of the street. Dearborn. She's on Dearborn.

I see it and I turn and I start scanning the buildings for an address. I start to get nervous, excited, scared. My hands start quivering trembling shaking. I can feel my heartbeat increase, it starts pounding, pounding. The last time I saw Lilly we were in a hallway at the treatment center. It was the day I was leaving. We stood in the hall and we held each other and we kissed each other and she cried and told me she was going to miss me. I told her to be patient that I would come to her as soon as I could. We said I love you, we held tight, we didn't want to let go. I walked away and Lilly stood and cried. I told her to be strong that I would come back to her.

I find the neighborhood, which was once the most glamorous in the city, fell into disrepair, and is now coming back. I see the building. It is a large stately home. Four floors, white columns, tall framed windows, a grand entrance. It is ragged, but still gorgeous, as if in a previous life it was an embassy or the home of a corporate titan. There is a small subtle sign in the front yard that has the name of the treatment center and in smaller letters reads Residential Extended Care.

I see an open parking space about half a block away. I drive down the street, pull into the spot. I see a florist at the end of the block. I fumble with the keys, my hands are shaking, I get out of the car. I walk to the florist and I open the door and I step inside. There is a woman behind the counter. She has gray hair and brown eyes, she is wearing a bright red turtleneck. She smiles, speaks.

Cold, isn't it?

Miserable.

You should wear warmer clothes.

I would, but I don't have any.

As I look around, I take a deep breath through my nose. I let it out, speak.

Smells nice in here.

Good. I'd be worried if it didn't.

I smile.

I need some flowers. I've got thirty-four dollars in my pocket. What can I get?

What would you like?

I don't know shit about flowers.

She laughs.

What's the occasion?

Reunion.

What type?

I smile again. I can't help it. Lilly is down the Street.

I just got out of my jail. My girlfriend is in that halfway house down the street. Her Grandmother just died, and I want to give her something that will make her feel better.

The woman nods.

You want to cheer her up, and you probably want to show her that you love her.

I smile.

Yeah.

The woman steps from behind the counter, leads me toward a cooler. The cooler is filled with flowers sitting in white plastic buckets and arrangements sitting on shelves. She opens the cooler and she reaches into a bucket and she pulls out about twenty red roses, she pulls out every rose in the bucket. She closes the cooler. I speak.

I can't afford all of those.

She smiles.

I'm having a sale. How's thirty dollars sound?

I smile.

Thank you. Thank you very much.

Do you want them wrapped?

Is that what you do?

Yes, it is.

I smile again. I can't stop smiling.

I'd love to have them wrapped.

The woman steps back behind the counter. She reaches for some white paper, pulls it from a long roll, tears it along a sharp edge. She sets it on the counter in front of her and she sets the roses the beautiful red roses on top of it. I turn and I walk to the window. I look down the street toward the halfway house. It is almost dark, there are lights in the windows, on the front porch, along the front walk leading to the porch. Lilly is in there, in that house, I will have you in my arms soon. Beautiful Lilly, beautiful Lilly. I have missed you so much. I will have you in my arms soon. I have missed you so much.

I'm finished.

I turn around. The woman is holding the roses wrapped in paper, baby's breath surrounding them. I step toward her, reach into my pocket.

Thank you.

I set the thirty dollars on the counter, take the flowers. The woman smiles.

Have a good night.

Thank you. Thank you very much.

I turn around and I walk out of the shop. I'm smiling still smiling. I start walking down the street. It's cold, but I don't feel it. I start running, gradually faster, as fast as I can, I'm running and smiling. I turn up the walk, I'm on the front porch, I open the door, I step inside.

A simple foyer. Dark carpet, beige walls, a worn wooden desk, a cheery landscape on the wall behind. There is a woman sitting at the desk smoking a cigarette. She looks up at me. Her eyes are red and swollen.

She speaks.

Can I help you?

I step forward.

Is Lilly here?

She stares at me for a moment. Her upper lip quivers, she looks like she's about to break.

Who are you?

My name is James.

She looks at me, bites her lip. She takes a deep breath and stands.

Just a minute please.

She steps from behind the desk, walks to a door, opens it, leaves. I stand with my flowers and my smile and my pounding heart, my pounding heart.

The door opens and a man steps into the room. He's in his late thirties. He has short dark messy hair, wears baggy jeans and a wool sweater. He has bags under his eyes, which are also red and swollen. He speaks.

James?

He reaches out a hand. I shake it.

I'm Tom. I'm the director of this facility.

What's up, Tom?

Would you mind coming back to my office?

Why?

I need to talk to you. I'd prefer to do it in private.

Where's Lilly?

Why don't you come back to my office.

I want to see Lilly, Tom.

Please, James.

I'm not going back to your office, Tom. Just tell me where the fuck Lilly is.

He looks at the floor, takes a deep breath. He looks up at me.

Before I tell you, I just want you to know that Lilly loved you very much. She talked about you all the time and . . .

What the fuck is going on here?

He looks at me. He doesn't speak. His eyes are wet.

Tell me what the fuck is going on here.

He looks at me, bites his lip, takes a deep breath. My heart pounding.

Lilly.

His voice breaks.

Lilly.

His voice breaks again.

Lilly passed away this morning.

I stare at him. I am holding her roses.

What?

My heart pounding.

Lilly died this morning.

My heart pounding.

What happened?

Pounding.

She took her own life.

I stare at him. My heart, my heart, my heart. He stares at me, speaks.

I'm so sorry. I'm so, so sorry.

Her flowers slip from my hand.

What happened?

My heart.

We don't know. Her grandmother had just died. She was very shaken. We found her hanging from the shower faucet. She didn't leave a note.

I turn around.

I walk out of the House.

My heart.

My heart.

My heart.

No no no.

Suicide.

It is dark and it is cold.

No no no.

Suicide.

I start walking toward my truck.

No no no.

Suicide.

My legs start shaking. Yes, suicide. My chest starts shaking. Yes, suicide. My arms start shaking and my hands are shaking. Yes, suicide. My face is shaking. Yes, suicide. I take a step and my knees buckle. I try to take another, my legs won't support me. I fall, fall to the sidewalk. I try to get up, but I can't, yes suicide. I look around me. I'm on a street I don't know in a city I've been in twice. Yes, suicide. I came here for Lilly and she's dead, hanging in the shower, she's dead. Yes, suicide. She was supposed to wait for me. I told her I would be here she was supposed to wait. Yes, suicide. She hung herself in the shower, I can't believe this is happening. She's dead. She killed herself. I can't believe this is happening. She's dead.

I start crying. I sit on the sidewalk and I cry. It feels like there's a hole in my chest, it feels like everything has become a deep dark horrible fucking hole. There are tears, I shake. I lose my breath. There's a hole and I can't get out of it, I can't escape. I'm falling deeper, deeper, deeper. I cry, I can't breathe. I bury my face in my hands I feel tears dripping from my eyes and my nose, streaming across my cheeks, running down my neck. I was coming I got here as fast as I fucking could. She didn't wait for me. She went into the bathroom and she tied a knot a strong knot. I want out of this hole I want out I want to stop crying. She put her neck in a noose she knew I was coming to her she knew what she was doing to herself. She put her neck in the noose. Please please please let me out of this please. She strung herself up. She let herself down. She lost the ability to breathe. No, I can't believe this is happening, no. She put her neck in the noose and she hung herself and she couldn't breathe and she didn't stop, she didn't stop, she didn't stop. Why she didn't stop. Why didn't she fucking stop. I came here to help her I came here to give her everything. She hung herself. I can't stop crying I want to stop crying I can't stop. Hang, my beautiful Lilly, hang. I would have done anything for you. Hang my beautiful Lilly, hang. Let me out of this fucking nightmare please let me wake up, let me wake the fuck up. She stopped breathing. I'm not waking up. She stopped seeing thinking feeling she stopped breathing. I can't get out. She hung herself and she's dead. She hung herself and she's dead.

There is a church on the next block. I can see the steeple and I can hear the bells. The bells ring every hour. I can hear them above the wind.
The streets are empty. It's late and it's dark and it's cold as hell.
I am sitting on the sidewalk. I am crying. I have been here for hours. Just sitting and crying. The crying comes in waves. Tears, sobs, screaming. The crying hurts. Hurts my chest and my faces, hurts the things inside that do not have names. Tears sobs screaming. Everything hurts. The same word over and over.
No.
No.
No.
Crying.
Sobbing.
Screaming.
I can't stop.
I can't stop.
The bells are ringing.
The wind is screaming.
Nine times I hear the bells.
And it starts to slow.
Gradually slow.
Slow, slow, slow.
I stop crying. I stand. My legs hurt and my chest hurts. My face hurts, my eyes and lips hurt. I am cold. I am shaking. It's dark and I am cold and my entire body is shaking. I can see the building down the street. The building where Lilly lived. The building where she was supposed to be getting better. The building where she was waiting for me, the building where we

were supposed to meet. I can see the building. The building where she killed herself. The building where she killed herself.

My lips quiver. A chill shoots down my spine. I can see the building. I turn away and I start walking down the street. I stop at my truck. I take my keys out of my pocket. I open the door, climb inside, shut the door. It is warmer inside, but not much. I put the key in the ignition and I start the engine and I turn on the heat and I wait and I start to cry again. I start to cry. I want to stop, but I can't stop. I want to take a deep breath and tell myself that everything is okay, but I'm unable to do so. I have no control over myself. I have no control over my emotions. I have no control over my body's need to express those emotions. All of the time I spent sitting alone in my cell trying to teach myself how to regulate my behavior is worthless, irrelevant. Lilly killed herself. Hung herself in the shower. She's dead. She's fucking dead. It doesn't matter that I don't want to cry. It doesn't matter that I want to stop. I can't do anything. I have no control.

I cry and I wait for the heat. The heat comes and I sit in front of the vents and I stop shaking. The inside of the truck becomes warmer and warmer and I stop crying. My body needs a break, needs to rest, needs to try to let my mind and my heart accept what has happened. They don't want to accept it. They know one word. No. They keep telling me that I'm going to wake-up and find her waiting for me. No. They keep screaming she's not dead, she's not dead, she's not dead. No. She is the only person I have ever truly loved. She is the only person who made me want to live. She is the only person on Earth who could hurt me. She killed herself this morning. Walked into the bathroom and tied a knot and hung herself from the shower. It didn't matter what I felt, how much she meant to me, how much I loved her. It didn't fucking matter. She hung until she stopped breathing. She's dead. My mind and heart don't want to accept it. No.

I reach for my pack of cigarettes. I take one out and I light it. I take a deep drag, hold it in, exhale. I stare out the window. I feel empty. I feel like my heart has been ripped out of my chest. I feel disconnected, as if my body and mind are no longer part of the same vessel. I am exhausted. As I lift my arm to bring the cigarette back to my mouth, my arm is heavy, my hand is heavy, the cigarette is heavy. Everything I do takes great effort. I inhale slowly. I feel the smoke traveling through my throat and into my lungs. I exhale slowly, feel the smoke coming back. I am so tired. What the fuck am I going to do. Somebody please help me.

I finish the cigarette, put it out. I look into the rearview mirror, see the house down the street. I want to be away. I put my truck into first gear. I want to be away from that House. I pull out of my parking space. I want to be away from that fucking house. I start driving down the street. I have no idea where I am and I have no idea where I am going. I just want to be away.

I drive. I smoke another cigarette. I turn on the radio and I turn off the radio. The neighborhoods all look the same. Row after row of brown-stones. Tree-lined streets with sidewalks and overhead lights. I see churches and schools, fire stations and playgrounds. I see all sorts of small shops; shoe shops, clothing shops, candle shops, art and sculpture shops, real estate shops, book shops, garden shops. I see grocery stores and restau-rants, convenience stores and gas stations. I see bars and liquor stores. On almost every block, I see either a bar or a liquor store. Beautiful bars filled with people drinking. Beautiful liquor stores devoted to alcohol. Beautiful establishments where I can make this nightmare go away. Beautiful bars and beautiful liquor stores. On almost every block.

I feel the urge. Drink. The instinct begins to assert itself. Destroy. My old friend the Fury starts to rise, it says kill what you feel, kill what you feel. The Fury rises it says kill.

My hands start shaking. I can feel my heart beating. My teeth chatter. I take a deep drag of my cigarette, it doesn't help. I am an alcoholic and a drug addict. I have used substances to control and to kill my emotions and my insecurities and my rage for my entire life. I have spent the bulk of my existence using alcohol and drugs to destroy what I feel so that I wouldn't have to feel it. I have never felt like this before. Never even close. I know death, I have seen it and been close to it, but not this type of death. I know grief and sorrow and sadness, but I have never felt them so deeply. I know horror, but I have never cringed before it, I know self-destruction, but it has never made me shake. I don't know what I am going to do. There are beautiful bars and beautiful liquor stores on every block. I can make this all go away, the Fury says kill kill kill, it is time to destroy. I am an alcoholic and a drug addict. I can't deal with my feelings.

I pull over, park. I turn off the engine take out the key turn out the lights. I look up and down the block. There are two bars within eyesight, one liquor store. I have four dollars in my pocket and I have three reasonable options. Go to the most crowded of the bars and take half-finished drinks from tables when people stand and leave. Go to a less crowded bar and find a drunk. Drunks are stupid with their mouths and stupid with their wallets, and if I find one, I can probably get them to buy me a drink or several drinks. Fuck the bars, go to a liquor store. If they sell what I like to drink, which is cheap, strong, gutter wine, I could probably afford a bottle. I need something now. I need to make this go away.

I open the door. Step outside. Close the door. It's cold, I look around me, I start shaking. The wind is screaming. I start walking. I walk toward a corner where there is a bar across the street from a liquor store. I can see people through the windows of the bar. They look young and happy. They are jumping up and down, dancing, moving to the beat of some cheery music. All I want is a drink, two drinks, as many drinks as it takes to make it all go away, to send me hurtling toward oblivion, to destroy. Fuck those happy people. Fuck that cheery music.

I walk toward the liquor store. It is on the opposite corner. It is a small store. It has a bright neon sign hanging above the door that reads Liquor, the windows are filled with bright posters of bikini-clad women holding beer cans. Behind the posters I can see rows and rows of bottles. Beautiful bottles filled with alcohol.

I open the door and I step inside. It is warm and bright with fluorescent light. There is a counter along the front wall, a man stands behind it. There are cigarettes above the counter and candy bars below it. There is a television behind the man. It is broadcasting images of the store taken by cameras in each of the corners. I am the store's only customer. I can see myself on the television and I can see the man behind the counter on the television. He is staring at me. I ignore him. I start walking down one of the aisles.

The man watches me as I walk, I stare at a set of coolers along the back wall. The shit I drink is always in a cooler along the back wall, always hidden away so that respectable customers don't have to see it. It is of the lowest class of alcoholic beverages. Produced by liquor companies for poor drunks who need a strong, quick charge. Though it is called wine, it doesn't resemble real wine in any way. It is much cheaper, much more powerful. It comes in thick, squat bottles that are effective weapons when empty. It tastes like grape juice mixed with rubbing alcohol. Long term users of it often die from the effects that it has on one's internal organs. It burns holes in the stomach. It eats away the lining of the intestine. It causes cirrhosis of the liver. It is liquid death. Available in a pint or a quart. Sometimes a liter. Always in a cooler along the back wall.

I find four different types lining the bottom shelf of the corner cooler. I am familiar with all of them, have experienced the horrors of each. The worst of them, and the one I enjoy the most, is known as the rose. Its label calls it a fruit-flavored, ethanol-fortified dessert wine. I call it a quick ride to hell. It is available in one-liter bottles. At the height of my drinking, I could down three of the one-liter bottles before losing consciousness. At this point, having not had a drink in almost six months, one bottle will do everything that I need it to do. I need it to kill. I need it to kill.

I open the cooler pick up a bottle look at the price. Just under three dollars. With my remaining dollar I can get myself a bag of potato chips. This is not what I expected to be doing here. Getting drunk and eating chips on my first night of freedom, my first night in Chicago. Were it up to me, I would be with Lilly. Were it up to me I would be asleep in her arms. She's dead, in a cooler in some fucking morgue, and I'll never sleep in her arms again. The thought of it makes me sick, and it makes me want to join her. The rose will help me. It is time to start the killing. Time to fucking start.

I walk to the front of the store. The man behind the counter watches me the entire time. As I pass a rack of chips, I reach out and I grab a bag. I don't look at the flavor because the flavor doesn't matter. All I'm going to taste is the rose. I arrive at the counter and I set my wares down in front of the man and as he rings them up, I take the four dollars out of my back pocket. I set the money in front of him and he takes it and puts it in his register and he hands me a dime. I have ten cents to my name. Ten cents and a bottle of wine and a bag of chips and half a pack of cigarettes and a beat-up truck. The chips and the wine will be gone in twenty minutes. The cigarettes will be gone tomorrow. I'm starting to think I will follow them.

I walk out of the store. It's cold, the wind, the motherfucking wind. I walk to my truck, I open it, I get inside. It is still warm. I climb into the passenger's seat. I know that if I get caught drinking in the driver's seat I can be charged with Driving Under the Influence. It doesn't matter if the car is moving or not, I can still be charged under the laws of every state in America. In the passenger's seat they can charge me with open container in a motor vehicle, the equivalent of a parking ticket.

I settle into the seat. I light a cigarette. I open the chips put a few in my mouth chew. I set the bottle in my lap. I take it out of the brown paper bag that is holding it. I stare at it. My hands start shaking and my heart starts beating faster. Like Pavlov's dog I react when alcohol is in front of me. I smoke with one hand, hold the bottle with the other. I have a decision to make. Yes or no. The Fury is screaming drink, motherfucker, drink drink drink. The grief I feel says I will leave you if you feed me. My heart and my hands are shaking like dogs they want the taste. I know if I open the cap and put the bottle to my lips, pour and swallow, I will be taking a road from which there is no return. I know that once I have it in me again I will use it until I die from it. I was almost dead six months ago. Dead from the damage that hardcore drug and alcohol abuse cause to the body, dead because I didn't want to live anymore. I chose life because of Lilly and Leonard and because once I tasted life again it tasted good, good enough to try to live it. Lilly is dead now. Dead by her own hand. The how and why don't matter. All that matters is the end result. Death. I can't believe I'm here. I can't believe I'm in this position. What the fuck am I going to do.

I stare.

I have no money.

I stare at the bottle.

I have no job, I have nowhere to live.

I stare at the bottle.

I am an alcoholic and a drug addict. I have been incarcerated for the last six months of my life in a treatment center and in a jail.

The bottle.

I am shaking. The Fury is screaming. The grief is overwhelming me please please please. I can make it all go away. I can kill it. Killing it will be the first step toward killing myself. Everything I have dreamed about and hoped for and wanted and expected is gone. It's dead and it's not coming back. There is no nightmare to wake from, this is my fucking life.

What am I going to do.

The bottle.

I start to cry.

What.

Cry.

There is sun streaming through the front window of my truck. It is bright, but it is not warm.

It is early morning and I am waiting. The bottle of rose is sitting on the seat next to me. It is still full.

I spent the night crying, staring at the bottle, smoking, cursing. I cursed God that motherfucker. I cursed myself I should have gotten here earlier. I cursed everyone I saw, I screamed at them and I cursed them. I cursed my truck it didn't do anything I cursed it anyway. I cursed the ground the sky the night. I cursed the bottle in my hand I cursed the parts of me that wanted it. I cursed them and I defied them and they cursed me and they tried to defy me. I cursed my shaking hand and my beating heart, I cursed myself, I should have known, I should have stopped her. I cursed the dime in my pocket. I cursed the potato chip bag. I cursed Lilly. I cursed Lilly how could she have done this to herself. I cursed and I cried. How could she have done this to herself.

It is early morning and I am waiting. The bottle of rose is sitting on the seat next to me and it is still full. I am going to keep it. I am going to keep it so that if I decide to use it, it will be within reach. I made it through last night, but that does not mean I will make it through today or tomorrow.

I am waiting. I am waiting for the sun to move above me. I am waiting to hear the bells ring ten. I am waiting to call my friend Leonard. He told me that if I ever needed help he would give it to me I need help now. I have no money and no job and nowhere to live. I am waiting to call Leonard. I need help now.

I start the truck. I pull out of my parking space and start driving back toward the house. If I get hold of Leonard and he helps me, I will need to be near the house. The people there will know where Lilly is and who has

taken her. I want to see her again before she is gone. I want to see her
again.

I find my way back I see the house. I pull over and I park. I get out of the
truck look around me. I see the flower store. I see the steeple that holds
the bells. I see a park, the park is empty. I see a bank and a shoe store and
a diner. I start walking toward the diner.

I open the door, step inside. It is warm and loud. It smells like bacon and
eggs. There are people at every table eating, drinking coffee, talking. There
is a short hall in the back of the diner I can see two bathrooms and a
phone. I walk toward the phone, reach into my back pocket. I take out my
wallet and I take a card from my wallet. The card has five names on it,
five numbers. They all belong to Leonard.

I pick up the phone and I dial zero. I speak to an operator. I give her my
name and the first number. I tell her I need to make a collect call. She puts
it through, no one answers. We try the second number. No answer. We try
the third, the call is denied. We try the fourth I hear Leonard answer.

Collect call from James?

Fuck yeah.

Thank you.

The operator hangs up.

My son.

What's up, Leonard?

You're out of jail and you're in Chicago. That's what's up.

Yeah, I'm here.

How is it?

Not good.

What happened?

I start to break.

I don't want to talk about it.

What's wrong?

I need your help, Leonard.

What happened?

I need help.

What do you need?

I need thirty thousand dollars.

What?

I need thirty thousand dollars, Leonard.

What the fuck is going on there?

You told me to call you if I ever needed help. I need fucking help. I need thirty grand.

Are you drinking?

No.

Getting high?

No.

What the fuck is wrong?

I start to break.

I need money.

He does not speak.

Please, Leonard.

He does not speak.

Please.

I hear him take a deep breath.

Where are you?

In a diner.

How do you want me to get it to you?

Thank you, Leonard.

You're my son. I'm going to take care of you.

Thank you, Leonard.

Now tell me how you want me to get you the money.

I give him the address of the house. He tells me that it will be there in an hour. I thank him, thank you, Leonard. He asks me if I want him to come to Chicago and I tell him no. He asks again if I'm drunk or high he wants to make sure and I tell him no. He says that though he does not need to know right now, at some point he'll want to know why I need so much money. I say fine. I thank him again and he says don't worry about it and I say thank you again and we hang up. Thank you, Leonard. Thank you. I walk out of the diner and I walk back toward my truck, toward the house. As I get closer, my heart starts beating faster. I think about what happened in the house, the images in my mind are clear. Hanging hanging hanging. I try to push the images away, but they remain, hanging hanging hanging. Every step is harder, every step is heavier. I start up the walk that leads to the door. Every step. Hanging.

I open the door step into the foyer. I want to leave, the images are clear. The same woman is sitting behind the desk. There are some red roses in a vase next to her. She looks up at me and I say hello and she says hello and she motions toward the roses and she tells me that she saved them for me. I thank her and I ask for Tom. She says he's out can I help you. There is a chair across from her I sit down. I want to leave, the images are clear. The bathroom where Lilly hung is in this house. I look at the woman and I speak.

I need some information.

I keep the flowers. They were for Lilly, not for the house. I keep them in water and I will use them. They were for Lilly.

I give all of her clothing to an organization that helps the poor. She did not have much, but maybe it will help someone.

I give her books to a library. She wanted to go to college and she had been studying for the entrance exams. She had seven books, all textbooks.

What little money she had was in a box beneath her bed. I give it to a homeless woman who is sitting alone on a bench. The woman tells me it is enough to get her a place in a shelter for two months. I hope that time makes a difference.

She had a plastic Superwoman watch. I always thought it was funny that she wore it. I find it on a table next to her bed. When I find it, I cry. I hold it to my heart and I cry. I keep it in my pocket.

She had a hairbrush, a toothbrush. A tube of toothpaste and a bottle of shampoo and a bar of soap. I leave everything in the bathroom.

She had a simple silver necklace. It held a platinum cross. Her Grandmother gave it to her, it was her most cherished possession. I find it on a table next to her bed. When I find it I cry. I want to give it back to her. I want to give it back.

I don't have any photographs of Lilly. I don't have any photographs of the two of us together. The only documentation I have of our relationship is a large stack of letters, some written by me, some by her. This lack of documentation has made seeing her more difficult. Tom helps me. He speaks to an assistant medical examiner, he speaks to the medical examiner. He confirms that Lilly did not have any family aside from her Grandmother, who is in the morgue with her. He confirms that I was her boyfriend, and that I am the only person who is likely to claim her body. He helps talk the Medical Examiner into letting me see her. Just once, by myself. I am going to see her.

I walk down a hallway. A bright clean sterile hallway. At the end of the hallway is a large metal door. A man is standing in front of the door. He is wearing a white lab coat and latex gloves, an air filtration mask hangs at his neck. As I approach, he says hello and I say hello and he opens the door and he gestures me inside and I walk through the door and he follows me. The door closes behind us.

I am in a large open room. Along one wall there is a bank of stainless steel cabinets. Along another are three sinks and a large stainless steel countertop. Along the back wall there are four rows of doors, each with a handle like the handles on large refrigerators. There is a stainless steel table in the middle of the room, a halogen lamp above it, a drain below it. There is a body on the table. A body that is covered by a white sheet.

I turn to the man.

Can I be alone?

Yes.

Thank you.

He motions toward a counter near the cabinets.

There are gloves and masks over there if you want to use them.

Thank you.

He turns and he leaves. I turn back to the body. I stare at it. I am scared. My heart starts pounding, pounding to the point that it hurts. I am scared. I take a deep breath. Part of me wants to run. To get the fuck out of here, that is her body, her dead body beneath that sheet. Part of me knows that I need to do this. I have to see her. I have to see her. I have to see her.

I step forward, once twice, heart pounding. I step forward I am next to the table. I stand and I stare at the sheet she is beneath it. I place the palm of my hand in the center of the sheet. My heart is fucking pounding. I softly press so that I can feel beneath the sheet, my hand is somewhere on her stomach. I start moving it along the top of the sheet, along the contour of her body. She's beneath the sheet and I can feel her body. The body I once held, the body I loved, the body that loved me. I run my hand up the curve of her neck, over her chin. I move it to the edge of the sheet, I put my other hand with my first. My heart is fucking pounding. My hands are shaking.

I start to slowly pull the sheet. I see her hair jet black so black it is almost blue. I slowly pull I see her skin, it was pale like porcelain in life, it is pale gray now. I slowly pull. I see her eyebrows black I see her lashes black. I see her eyes closed they were blue in life, beautiful clear deep-water blue in life, they are closed and I will leave them closed. I pull the sheet slowly her cheekbones strong and defined I pull past her nose I pull down and across her lips. Full and red they are still full. They are also quiet, calm, still, at rest. I pull the sheet down across her chin and off her face. I pull the sheet from her neck. She has a deep blue bruise around her throat. Whatever she used was thick, maybe a towel, I don't know, I don't want to think about it. I pull the sheet to her shoulders she is not wearing a shirt. I will not expose her naked flesh I will respect her in death as I respected her in life. I let go of the sheet and I set it just below her shoulders. I stare at her. She is quiet, calm, still, at rest. I love her now as I did before I love her now. In death and in life. My heart is pounding and my hand is shaking. I love her.

I stare.

I run my hands along the top of her head and through her hair.

I cry.

I feel the contours of her face.

I kiss my fingers and I press them to her lips.

I cry.

She is quiet.

Calm.

Still.

At rest.

I take her hand beneath the sheet. It is stiff and cold. I take her hand.

I am with her.

I hold her.

I love her.

She's at rest.

Cry.

They sleep in peace.
They sleep in peace.

Grieve.

I grieve alone.

Grieve.

I call my friend Kevin. Kevin is an old close friend, one of the closest friends that I have had in my life. We met at school and we lived together while we were there and he watched me as I fell apart and helped me as I started to pick up the pieces of my shattered life. He knew I was coming here, though he did not know exactly when I would arrive. He says welcome to Chicago and I say thanks and he asks me how I'm doing and I say fine and he asks me how it was he is aware of what I was doing in Ohio and I tell him it was fine. He knows about Lilly and he asks me how it's going with her and I tell him bad and he asks me what happened and I tell him I don't want to talk about it. He asks if I'm okay. I tell him I don't want to talk about it. I ask him when he'll be off work and he tells me seven and we agree to meet at his apartment.

Kevin lives on the north side of the city. His apartment is on the first floor of a four-story brownstone on a street lined with four-story brownstones. The neighborhood is full of people in their twenties working their first or second professional jobs, the streets are lined with suits and skirts and loafers. I find the building easily, park in front of it. I can see through the windows, I see a group of people smoking cigarettes and drinking. I get out of my car and I take a deep breath. I don't want to do this to see a group of people I'm nervous and scared I am used to being alone. I know I need to break the solitude to spend time among the living. I push the buzzer walk through the door into the hall he is waiting for me. He is smiling. He steps forward and he gives me a hug and he speaks.

It's good to see you, Buddy.

You too.

We separate.

Who's inside?

Some people who wanted to see you.

Who?

Come in and see.

You won't tell me?

Just come in.

I take a deep breath. I know I need to try and move forward with my life. I step inside.

I see people I know, people I am friends with, people I am surprised to see. Adrienne and Ali. Two friends great friends, for several years we drank together and smoked together and laughed together and sometimes cried together. Erin and Courtney they were her friends, someone I was with in a different life. They were her friends and they became my friends. I don't know if they see her or speak to her and I don't care, it was a different life. David and Scott, older than me I used to drink and smoke and snort with them they are bankers now buttoned up and prim. Callie and Kim, they live with Kevin I used to sell them drugs, occasionally I used drugs with them. All of them know that I recently came out of a drug and alcohol treatment center, only Kevin knows about jail. They all seem happy to see me, they also seem scared to drink around me and smoke around me and be themselves around me. They ask me tentative questions. How are you is everything okay is it all right if I have this drink around you are you comfortable like this. I tell them I am fine. That the alcohol does not bother me, that they should be at ease. I keep a calm face and a relaxed demeanor. Inside I am not calm, this is all overwhelming. All the noise all the faces all the words. I have been alone for a long time. Alone and unsocial. This room is full of people I know and I like and who have come here to see me and it is overwhelming.

We go to a bar. All of us together we go to a bar. I shoot pool and smoke cigarettes and drink soda water. My friends shoot pool and smoke cigarettes and get drunk. As the night moves deeper I speak less and less. As the night moves deeper my friends lose the ability to speak. I do not judge them. I did what they are doing now every night for years. Got drunk and stumbled and slurred my words. I do not judge them, I am happy to see them.

We stay at the bar until it closes. We leave I say goodbye to everyone thank them for coming to see me walk back to the apartment with Kevin and Callie and Kim. They go to their rooms and they go to bed. I find some blankets in a closet and I go to the living room and I clear a space on the couch and I lie down.

I stare at the ceiling.

I start looking for an apartment. I look through the classified sections of the paper, I walk the streets and I look for rental signs, I go to local real estate offices and I look through the listings. I don't want much and I don't need much. Almost all of the money is gone. I want something simple and small and clean. Somewhere for me to sit and sleep and read. Somewhere for me to be alone. Simple and small and clean.

I find a place on my second day. It's on a small street only one block long. At one end of the street there are two giant steel giraffes on opposite corners, they're ridiculous and they make me laugh. At the other end there is a delicate little restaurant, its menu is written in Italian. Trees line both sides of the street, and though I know nothing about the neighborhood, it feels like somewhere that I could live for a while.

The apartment itself is in a large five-story building shaped like a U. It is a one-room apartment on the first floor. It has one brick wall, plain wood floors, an oven and refrigerator. There are three windows, all of them are barred, there are two doors, the doors are in opposite corners. One of them leads into a hall and the other to an alley where there are several large dumpsters.

I meet the building superintendent. His name is Mickey and he is about thirty. He is thin and effeminate and he has blond hair and blue eyes and he wears pajamas. He says he is a painter who is working as a super because he gets free rent, money and lots of time to paint. As he reads my application, I see him occasionally glancing up at me. He finishes and he tells me that he isn't usually allowed to rent apartments to people without jobs. I tell him that I intend to find one. He asks if I have any references and I say no. He says he'll need to check with his boss and I take all of the remaining cash that I have and I place it in front of him.

That's a deposit and two months' rent and a bit extra for you.

He looks down at the money, back at me.

How much extra?

Another month.

He looks me up and down.

You seem nice.

I chuckle.

And you seem like you won't be much trouble.

I laugh again.

He reaches out his hand.

Welcome to the building.

I shake his hand, smile.

Thank you.

We let go of each other's hands.

When do you want to move in?

Right now.

You're in a hurry?

I need somewhere to live.

He reaches into a file and takes out a lease. He asks me some questions, fills in the answers, I sign the lease. He hands me the keys.

Thank you.

You're welcome.

I stand.

I'll see you around.

He nods.

You certainly will.

I turn and I leave. I walk to my truck, which is parked on the curb outside the building. I get my clothes and my bottle and I walk back to the apartment. I open the door and I step inside. I set my clothes in a pile on the floor. I hold the bottle in my hand. I have taken it with me almost everywhere that I have gone in the last few days. I keep it with me as a test of my strength. I keep it with me in case I change my mind.

I feel like I want it now the rose. I feel like I want it all the time but more now more. I set it on the floor in the middle of the apartment. I open the door I am going to walk, walking calms me.

It is cold outside. The wind screams through the streets like a whip. It lashes at my face, penetrates my clothes, stings me shakes me hurts me. I start to walk. No agenda nowhere to go no idea how to get there. I just walk.

I pass the giraffes I say goodbye friends. I walk down a street called Broadway lined with pawnshops, no dreams coming true here. I walk past Wrigley Field it's a baseball stadium dead in winter, old and silent and noble and dark. I walk under the elevated train tracks the ground shakes beneath them every five minutes the ground is shaking. I walk past people some I can't see they are hiding from the winter. I walk past store after store after store selling things I don't need. I walk past apartment buildings light and warm and offices light and warm and schools light and warm. I walk past a hospital. A police station. A firehouse. I just walk. For whatever the reason, it helps me forget. For whatever the reason, it brings me calm. As the day fades the temperature drops, the light disappears. I have been walking for hours, I make my way back to Kevin's apartment. I see him through the window drinking wine his roommates are smoking. I hit the buzzer go inside sit with them as they drink and smoke. I tell them about my apartment they want to celebrate.

We go back to the same bar we were in last night. We meet most of the same people. I sit with them as they drink and smoke. I have a glass of water. I want to drink, part of me wants to drink, one drink two drinks five drinks twenty. I want to drink because I know drinking will make it all go away. The pain I feel the sadness and sorrow and grief that are with me all day every second in every breath and beat of my heart in every thought in every step in everything I see and hear there is nothing but pain and sadness and sorrow and grief and I know drinking will make it go away. I also know it will kill me if I do it. Maybe not today or tomorrow but it will kill me. If I start I won't be able to stop. There is pain and sadness and sorrow and grief. I have a glass of water. I sit with my friends as they drink and smoke.

When it is time to leave I go back to Kevin's apartment with him. I borrow three blankets and a pillow. I walk back to my new apartment. It is bitter fucking cold and as I walk I wrap myself in the blankets and I clutch the pillow against my chest. I am tired. I don't know why I'm here or what the fuck I'm doing. I need a job and I need some money. I am lonely I miss Lilly so much, so much. It is the dead of night and it is bitter fucking cold and I don't know what the fuck I'm doing.

51

I find the giraffes I say hello. I find my building and I open the door and I find my apartment and I open the door. I step inside. I don't turn on the light and I don't take off my jacket or my boots. I lie down on the floor. The blankets are wrapped around me and I'm clutching the pillow.
I want to drink, but I know drinking will kill me.
I want Lilly, but I know she's not coming back.
I am tired and I want to sleep.
Sleep is not coming.
I lie on the floor.

I need a job and I need some money.

I find a paper and I look through the classifieds. I write down addresses and walk around the city. It's cold and the wind is a whip but the walking calms me. I apply for several jobs. Two at bars working as a doorman. One at a clothing store working in the stock room. One at a coffee shop serving the coffee and working the register. Two at gas stations pumping the gas. I shake hands and I smile and I am told to wait. I give them Kevin's phone number. I wait.

At the end of the day I meet Kevin. He takes me out for pizza. I didn't eat today I'm flat fucking broke. After we eat, we meet our friends at the bar. They drink and smoke and I drink water and smoke. We shoot pool and talk and laugh, I am starting to be able to laugh again. I stay late sitting watching laughing smoking. I don't laugh much, but every now and then is fine.

The night ends and I walk back to Kevin's apartment with him, check the messages, nobody's called me. I walk home. It is home for at least the next two months I have nowhere else to go. I lie down on the floor and I wrap myself in the blankets and I clutch the pillow.

Sleep does not come easily.

Seconds become minutes become hours.

Hours.

I lie on the floor and I clutch the pillow.

I miss her.

I'm alone.

I miss her.

Dark becomes light.

I lie on the floor.

At last I sleep.

I sleep.

Sleep.

I hear my door open. I'm not sure if what I hear is a dream or not. I hear footsteps across my floor. I'm awake I know it's not a dream. I hear voices. Words being whispered someone's in my apartment. What the fuck is going on here. I hear words someone is in my apartment. I'm awake. This is not a dream. Someone is here.

I crack my eyes, look through the slits. My heart starts pounding. I see two pairs of leather shoes, expensive shoes. Who the fuck is here. I try to place the shoes, I can't. I try to place the voices, I can't hear them well enough to place them. I crack my eyes more, look up without moving my head. Why the fuck would someone be in my apartment. Cabinet doors start opening and closing. I look up more, more, more. I see the backs of two heads. I see a familiar bald spot. I open my eyes and I sit up and I speak.

Leonard.

Leonard turns around. He's wearing a black trenchcoat and black suit and he's holding a bag of coffee.

My son.

What are you doing here?

You remember Snapper?

How did you find me?

Had someone look. Wasn't hard.

How'd you get in here?

He motions to the man next to him.

Had him open the door. That wasn't hard either.

I look at the man, who has turned around as well. He's tall and thick and has short black hair and is also wearing a black trenchcoat and a black suit. I met him when he picked Leonard up from the treatment center. He's an intimidating man, a man who looks more like a bear than a person, a man I would avoid were he not with my friend.

How you doing, Snapper?

I'm okay, Kid.

I look back at Leonard.

What are you doing here?

Come here.

How'd you get in my apartment?

Just come here.
I stand.
What?
He motions me forward.
Come here.
I step toward Leonard, he steps toward me. He opens his arms and he
puts them around me.
I'm sorry for your loss.
I start to speak, but I can't.
I'm so sorry.
I start to cry.
He hugs me.
I start to cry.

I cry.

In the shower.

As I brush my teeth.

As I get dressed.

Cry.

I've never experienced anything like this, nothing else comes close. Grief, sorrow, sadness, pain pain pain. A hole in my chest that cannot be filled. A wound that is leaking. A break that I can't repair, I'm broken and I can't repair myself and there's nothing I can do.

I cry as I get dressed.

I cry.

I take a deep breath, compose myself. I step out of the bathroom. Leonard and the Snapper are waiting for me. We leave the apartment and I lock the door and we walk to their car, which is sitting at the curb. It's new and large. A white, four-door Mercedes-Benz with black one-way windows. From what Leonard has told me, it is the only type of car that he will own, ride in or drive. He opens the front passenger's door and climbs inside. Snapper opens the driver's door and sits behind the wheel. I get in the backseat and Snapper starts the engine and we pull away from the curb. We drive out to the lake, head south down Lakeshore Drive toward the center of the city. I stare out the window, the lake is frozen, the trees without leaves, the wind strong enough that I feel it pushing the car. Leonard turns around, speaks.

You hungry?

I look at him.

Yeah.

You look thin.

Jail food, and I haven't been eating much since I've been here.

I hate fucking jail food.

Snapper speaks.

Me too. That shit sucks.

Leonard speaks.

I always try to pay someone to bring me real food.

Snapper speaks.

Sometimes it works, sometimes it doesn't.

Leonard speaks.

I should have done that with you. Paid some motherfucker to bring you a Big Mac.

I laugh.

It's not funny. You're too thin. You look sick. We're going to fatten you up while we're here.

I smile.

Okay.

When we get where we're going, I'm going to order you some bacon. A big plate of nothing but bacon.

Okay.

And then we'll get a big lunch.

Okay.

And then we'll get a big dinner. A huge fucking dinner. Steaks, spinach, cake, all kinds of tasty shit.

I laugh.

And you can bring your friends. However many you want. Everybody's welcome.

Laugh again.

It's good to see you laughing, my Son. It's good to see that. I'd be very scared if I couldn't make you laugh.

No reason to be scared, Leonard.

You just had a fucking bomb dropped on you. You seem okay, but that doesn't mean I'm not scared.

I'm fine, Leonard.

You keep saying that to yourself and eventually you will be fine, but don't try to lie to me about it now. I know you're not fine, and you shouldn't expect to be, and that's okay.

I look at him.

It's okay to be fucked-up, James.

And it all comes back. I look down, bite my lip, try to stop myself
from crying.

It's okay.

I nod, try to hold back the tears. I turn away from Leonard, look out the
window, he leaves me to myself. I try to hold back the tears, but I can't.
We drive south toward the city. The lake is frozen. I stare out the window,
the tears run down my cheeks.

We reach a sweeping turn in the drive there is frozen beach on our left,
we take a right into a mass of steel and stone and glass. We start to drive
down Michigan Avenue, skyscrapers line both sides of the street. The sidewalks are crowded, people bundled and warm, nobody here is bothered by
the cold. The Hancock lies ahead of us, grows larger as we approach, wide
and strong a majestic tower of black steel, I try to follow it with my eyes
it stretches beyond my line of sight. I look straight up. It rises higher.

We take a right off the avenue, Snapper pulls up in front of an elegant entrance with a red carpet and a black canopy. He stops the car, two uniformed bellmen open the side doors, a valet rushes to the driver's door.
Leonard and I get out of the car. Snapper waves off the valet and pulls
away. I ask Leonard where he's going and Leonard says that he's parking
the car. I ask why he doesn't let valet do it, he says it is safer that way, nobody can access the car if the Snapper parks it. I sometimes forget who
Leonard is and what he does for a living. Snapper parks the car.

We walk under the canopy, doors are held open for us. We enter a small
oak lobby. We stand in front of an elevator and we wait for it, when it arrives we step inside. It is also oak, its carpet thick and deep, blood red. It is
as nice an elevator as I have ever seen. Its control panel only has one button. Leonard pushes it and up we go very quickly my ears pop.

We stop. The doors silently slide open. We step into another lobby this
one huge with soaring ceilings, expensive furniture, a subtle reception
counter, three well-dressed concierges. We walk through the lobby toward
a restaurant on the far side, it sits in front of a huge bank of windows with
a view of the city and the lake.

We stop at the hostess stand. Leonard says hello, the hostess smiles and
asks if he would like his usual table. He says of course, Madam, and there

is no need for you to escort us. She laughs and we walk to a table for four near the windows. We sit down. A waitress comes she says hello to Leonard she seems to know him too. She offers him a menu and he says no thank you, I already know what we would like. She says okay and he orders a plate of bacon, a big plate of nothing but bacon. He orders a plate of sausage, a big plate of nothing but sausage. He orders blueberry pancakes, Belgian waffles, scrambled eggs, fried eggs. He orders a pot of coffee and a pitcher of water and three glasses of milk. He orders three omelettes, one with cheese, one with steak, one with spinach and tomatoes, and he orders corned-beef hash and hash browns and roasted potatoes and four types of toast. The waitress is laughing and so am I and Leonard looks at the ceiling and starts scratching his chin. He asks himself if he forgot anything and he thinks for a moment and he says ha, I did forget a couple of things. He orders a basket of scones and a basket of muffins. The waitress asks if that is all and he says yes, for now. She laughs again and she walks away.

The Snapper joins us. He sits next to Leonard, across from me. Leonard looks at him and the Snapper nods. Leonard turns to me, speaks.

Time to talk.

Something wrong?

I'm not sure, that's why we need to talk.

Okay.

Leonard looks in my eyes.

You drinking?

I shake my head.

No.

You doing drugs?

No.

After what's happened, I'll understand if you are.

I'm not.

And I'd rather have you be using, than have you lie to me.

I'm not lying to you, Leonard.

You sure?

Yeah.

Leonard looks at Snapper. Snapper reaches into one of the side-pockets of

his trenchcoat and draws out my bottle of rose. He sets it in the middle of
the table. Leonard looks back at me.

Care to explain?

I laugh.

It's not funny.

First you break into my place, and now you're stealing shit from it.

Yeah.

I shake my head.

That's fucked up, Leonard.

Why do you have it?

Because I've been thinking about it. I keep it on hand in case I decide I
want it.

You don't want it.

We'll see.

Trust me, you don't want it.

We'll see.

No, we won't see. Drinking is not an option for you.

That's for me to decide, Leonard.

You want to die?

No.

That's what'll happen if you start again.

I know.

Do you think that's what she would want for you?

I haven't thought about it.

Maybe you should.

Maybe you should leave it alone.

She wouldn't want you drinking.

Shut the fuck up, Leonard.

She couldn't do it, but you know she'd want you to.

Shut the fuck up, Leonard.

Didn't she used to say that a second of freedom is worth more than a lifetime of bondage?

Yeah, she did. Now change the fucking subject.

She wasn't strong enough, James. She couldn't do it over the long term.

Shut the fuck up, Leonard.

But you can, and she would want you to, and you should remember that.

Fuck you, Leonard.

I reach out, take the bottle, set it on the floor next to my chair.

I appreciate the sentiment, and I'm not going to fucking talk about it anymore.

The food arrives. We eat in silence. The bacon is hot and crispy, the sausage thick and juicy, the pancakes with syrup sweet. I drink one two three cups of coffee. I look at my food or out the window, I do not look at Leonard or Snapper. The bottle is at my feet. The decision is mine.

I hear Leonard set down his fork and his knife, take a deep breath, let out a long sigh. He speaks.

James.

I look up.

Yeah?

You promise me two things and I won't bring that shit up again.

What?

Promise me you didn't spend the money I gave you on drugs or liquor.

I didn't.

And promise me if you do decide to drink, you'll call me and talk to me before you do it.

I can promise you that.

Leonard turns to Snapper.

You heard him, right?

Snapper nods.

Yes, I did.

Leonard turns to me.

You're going to have to deal with Snap if you break the promises.

I laugh.

Fine.

You laughed. That's good. I came here to have some fucking fun, and I want you laughing, and I want you having fun It'll help.

I nod.

I know.

I want you to stay in the hotel with us tonight. I got you a room right next to our rooms.

You didn't need to do that.

I know I didn't need to, but I wanted to, and I already did. And feel free to

61

take whatever you want from the mini-bar. The chips are tasty and the
cola is cold.

I laugh again. Leonard keeps talking and we eat. We finish eating and we
stand and Leonard leaves a hundred-dollar bill on the table and we walk
to a bank of elevators in the lobby. We step inside Leonard hands me a
key. The doors close and we move up quickly and silently. The doors open
and we step out the hall is quiet and the walls are perfectly painted the
lights dim the carpet thick. We walk to the end of the hall there are three
rooms in a line. Leonard speaks.

You want to go down to the pool?

I speak.

I'm going to take a nap.

Take a nap? It's not even ten o'clock.

I'm tired.

Leonard looks at Snapper.

He's tired.

Snapper speaks.

So what, let him sleep.

Leonard looks at me.

How long you want to sleep for?

An hour or so.

We'll come get you in an hour. We'll go down to the pool, do some swimming, maybe some Jacuzzi.

Okay.

Leonard points to a door.

That's your room. I'm in the middle. Snap's over there.

I walk to my door, open it.

See you in a while.

I step inside, close the door, walk down a short hall. I pass a large bathroom and I walk into a large open room. There are three large windows
across one wall I can see the skyline I can see the lake it is still frozen.
There is a large oak cabinet against another wall. I walk to it and I open it.
There is a large television sitting on a shelf in the upper half, a mini-bar is
built into the lower half. Sitting against the third wall is a giant bed. There
are nightstands on both sides of the bed, there are phones on both of
them. I walk to the bed and I pull the sheets down they are white and

clean and soft, I kick off my boots and I sit down on the bed and I take off
my socks. I climb under the covers, put my head on a pillow, close my
eyes, clutch myself clutch myself.

The bed is soft and warm.

I think about Lilly.

Miss her.

Hate that I am here without her.

She would have loved this place.

This room.

This bed.

This comfort.

This warmth.

She never knew anything like this.

Never knew, never got the chance, never had a chance.

I wish she were here.

Would give whatever, everything.

For five minutes.

One smile.

One laugh.

One kiss.

Just one.

Alone.

I clutch myself.

Sleep.

Knock. I open my eyes. Another knock. I sit up, get out of my bed, walk
toward the door another knock. I open the door. Leonard and Snapper are
standing in the hall. Both of them are wearing thick white bathrobes.
Leonard is holding a small box. He speaks.

Time for the pool.

He hands me the box, steps past me. Snapper follows him.

Go put that on. We'll wait for you.

They walk into the room, I walk into the bathroom. I close the door, open
the box. I take out a small bathing suit. It is a bikini bathing suit, small and
thin with black and white stripes. I open the door, walk into the room.
Leonard and Snapper are looking out the window, have their backs to me.

Leonard.

They turn around. I hold up the suit.

What the fuck is this?

Leonard smiles.

Your bathing suit.

I'm not wearing this.

Why not?

You've got to be fucking kidding me.

What's wrong with it?

It's a fucking bikini bottom, Leonard.

He laughs.

Not it's not, it's a Speedo, it's a fine swimsuit.

What are you wearing?

He smiles, opens his robe. He's wearing the same suit.

What's Snapper wearing?

Snapper opens his robe. He's wearing the same suit. I laugh, shake
my head.

No way, Leonard. I'm not wearing it.

Competitive swimmers wear them.

I'm not a competitive swimmer.

Europeans wear them.

I'm not European.

Motherfuckers with style wear them.

I'm not a motherfucker with style.

He looks at Snapper.

He doesn't want to wear it, Snap.

I heard him.

What do you think about that?

He ain't a swimmer and he ain't European and he ain't got no style. Why
should he wear it?

Leonard turns to me.

Let's go. And bring your robe.

Where we going?

Snap and me are going to the pool. You're going to the gift shop to find
another suit, then you're meeting us at the pool.

Okay.

Leonard and Snapper walk past me and out of the room. I grab my robe

and follow them. We ride the elevator down and Leonard and Snap get
out before me and I go further down and I go to the gift shop and I return
the striped Speedo and I find a nice large, normal American bathing suit. I
try it on it's two or three sizes too big. I have to tie it tightly tie it to keep
it from falling down. It's just my size, just the way I like it. I walk to the
counter and a woman behind the counter asks for my room key and she
charges the bathing suit to my room.

I go to the elevator, the pool. There are gray marble floors simple white
walls. There are simple wooden lounge chairs along a wall and there is a
Jacuzzi built into the floor at the far end. It is warm, and the crisp clean
smell of chlorine is strong. Leonard is swimming laps in the pool and
Snapper is sitting in the Jacuzzi. I walk toward the Jacuzzi. Snapper looks
up, speaks.

Nice suit.

Thanks.

Fits nice.

I laugh, look toward Leonard.

What's he doing?

Swimming back and forth.

Why's he doing that?

He's been exercising like fucking crazy ever since he got out of the
drug place.

Fuck that.

That's what I say. I go with him, but I don't do it.

Leonard stops at our end of the pool.

Nice suit.

Thanks.

You coming in?

No

You're skinny, but you're in bad shape. You should exercise.

No thanks.

I'm going to do some more laps.

Go ahead.

Leonard turns and starts swimming, back and forth, back and forth. I get
into the Jacuzzi it's hot. I close my eyes and lean back and let the heat
soak in it feels good, relaxes me, calms me. When Leonard finishes his laps

65

he gets into the Jacuzzi and me and him and Snapper sit and relax. It feels good.

When we've had enough we get out and we put on our robes white and thick and we go to the restaurant. People stare at us. Most of them are well dressed, some of the men are wearing suits and ties, we are the only ones in robes and bathing suits. We order a huge lunch cheeseburgers and fries and ice cream and we eat and when we're finished we go back to our rooms. Leonard and Snapper say they have some business they will meet me later. I take a nap. I dream about drinking and drugs. I get fucked-up in the dream, fucking blitzed in the dream, I can't walk or talk, can't function in any way. When I wake I feel awful, as if the dream was reality. I lie in bed. The last ten days have been a lifetime. I feel awful.

I get up take a shower watch TV wait. I eat some chips and drink a cola and the chips are tasty and the cola is cold. Leonard comes back tells me to call all of my friends we're going out for dinner he wants all of them to come. I ask him where we're going and he gives me the name of a famous steakhouse, says we're eating at eight o'clock. He says get on the fucking horn, my son, call your fucking friends, we're going to have some fun. I laugh and he leaves.

I pick up the phone, start making calls. I ask my friends to dinner they can all come. Kevin says our friend Danny is in town I say bring him along. I put on my boots walk to Leonard's room knock on the door. He answers he is wearing a black suit it looks expensive. I laugh, look at my clothes. Worn khakis, a black wool sweater, scuffed black combat boots. I look back at Leonard.

They going to let me in like this?

Hah!

I laugh.

What's that mean?

That means Hah!

Yeah, what's Hah mean?

Hah means of course they're going to let you in. You're with me.

You sure?

Yeah, I'm fucking sure.

He steps out of the room, closes the door, starts walking toward the elevator.

Where's Snap?

He stops, turns around.

Snap's not coming.

Why?

He's just not.

Understood.

I start walking toward the elevator, know that there are things with Leonard that I should not question. He pushes the button and the elevator arrives and we go down walk through the lobby leave the hotel go outside. It's dark. It's cold. The wind. We start walking.

Five minutes later we're at the steakhouse. We walk through a set of large, unmarked oak doors. It's dark, the walls are wood, the carpet thick. It smells strongly of steak and cigars. I take a deep breath, we walk through a short hall to a reception stand. There is a man in a tuxedo behind the stand he steps around and greets Leonard calls him Sir and shakes his hand. Leonard introduces the man to me and we shake hands and the man says pleasure to meet you, Sir, which makes me laugh.

We are early, so the man leads us through the dining room to the bar. The dining room is large and open, candles on every table, white linens and silver, patrons in suit and tie, skirt and stocking. The bar is in a separate smaller room. It is large and oak runs the length of a wall. There are stools in front of it, there are small tables and low cushioned chairs spread through the rest of the room. Leonard shakes the man's hand and says thank you, the man bows and says my pleasure, Sir. We sit down at a table, the man leaves. Leonard reaches into the inside pocket of his suitcoat and removes two cigars. He offers one to me.

Cigar?

No thanks.

They're Cuban.

I don't like cigars.

I reach into my pocket, take out my cigarettes. Leonard stares at me.

How can you not like cigars?

Just don't.

Why?

Just don't.

Do you know how to smoke one properly?

No.

That's why you don't like them. You've never learned to enjoy them.

He hands me one of the cigars.

Time for you to go to cigar school, my son. Time for you to learn one of life's great pleasures.

I take the cigar, look at it. I don't want it, but know Leonard wants to teach me how to smoke it. He shows me how to cut it: find the tapered end, called the cap, cut leaving at least ⅛ inch of the cap remaining. He shows me how to light it: use a match, wait for the sulfur to burn away, do not touch fire to cigar, bring it close, use the heat. He shows me how to smoke it: do not inhale, draw in with your cheeks, hold it, enjoy the taste, exhale. I accidentally inhale a few times, and the smoke is strong and burning and it makes me cough. I don't like the taste, it is of smoke and dirt and sweat. Leonard tells me it is supposed to be a rich creamy taste with a medium body. I have no idea what he's talking about.

As my friends show up they are led to our table in the bar. Leonard greets them all the same way. He stands and he says hello, hello my name is Leonard, it is wonderful to meet you. He shakes hands with Kevin and Danny and gives them cigars. He bows to the women and pulls out their chairs. Everyone is surprised by Leonard. I did not tell them much about him, just that he was my friend from rehab. I don't think they were expecting a cheery, friendly ridiculous man in his fifties who says things like drink it up, boy drink that cocktail the fuck up, or my oh my dear lady, your perfume is so delicious I feel like I'm going to faint.

When everyone has arrived Leonard stands and says it's time to eat like pigs my friends, time for a fucking feast. We stand as a group and walk into the dining room and sit at a table in the center of the restaurant. There are immediately three waiters setting bottles of wine and water on the table, one of them sets a large crystal decanter filled with cola next to me. When they leave, Leonard stands again and raises his glass.

It is always a pleasure to meet strong young men and beautiful young women. I am honored by your presence at my table, honored that you have chosen to spend the evening with me. Let us all raise a toast to fine food, strong drink, delicious dessert and new friends.

Glasses are raised and the toast is made, hear hear, hear hear. As soon the glasses are back on the table, food starts arriving. There are jumbo shrimp cocktails, small bowls with lumps of crabmeat, scallops wrapped in bacon, oysters, clams and mussels. There are salads, Cobb and Caesar and iceberg drenched in Roquefort. There are bowls of lobster bisque and French onion soup. There is food everywhere, hands reaching for food everywhere, smiles and laughs around the table, other patrons are staring at our table, we don't care.

The appetizers are taken away. We are given a moment or two of rest. I hear two of the girls talking to Leonard they ask him where he lives he says Las Vegas for part of the year, southern California for part of the year. They ask him what he does he says I'm a businessman. They ask him what type he says the type that doesn't like to talk about work away from the office. He asks them what they do, they both work at a clothing store. He says he loves clothing, has closets full of clothing, buys clothing everywhere he goes, loves loves loves clothes. They laugh. He stands and asks them what they think of his suit, he turns in a circle to give them a complete view. They tell him they think it's beautiful and he thanks them and he compliments them on their fine taste.

More food arrives. Family style platters of steak, lamb, chicken and lobster. Bowls of creamed spinach, sautéed mushrooms, asparagus. Plates of baked potatoes, mashed potatoes and hash browns. We eat, laugh, Leonard and I drink water and cola, my friends, now Leonard's friends, drink wine and cocktails. If a platter bowl or plate is ever empty, it is immediately replaced. When everyone is finished, dessert is delivered: ice cream and pie, chocolate cake and fruit. Leonard lights a cigar, the restaurant is now empty but for us. He motions for the concierge to bring more cigars, the man brings a small humidor to the table, it contains cigars of different sizes and shapes, cigars from different countries. Leonard walks around with the humidor and selects a cigar for each individual. When he is finished, he walks them through the same steps he taught me earlier. They listen to Leonard, follow his instructions, start tentatively. They are not tentative for long.

As we smoke, Leonard stands, motions for me to stand with him. We walk into the kitchen. He takes out a large roll of cash from his pocket and starts handing out tips to everyone, to the chef, to the sous chef, to the pastry chef, to the busboys, to the dishwashers. We leave the kitchen go to the bar. Each of the bartenders receives a handshake filled with money. We walk to the reception desk Leonard thanks the man slides him cash tells him that I am his son and that if I ever show up here he expects that I will be treated accordingly. The man thanks Leonard and says of course, Sir, of course.

We walk back to the table. The cigars are out, the glasses empty, the dishes are being cleared. Leonard helps the women put on their coats. He tells each of them it was an honor meeting you, he kisses each of their hands. We walk out of the restaurant and there are cars waiting for us. My friends all thank Leonard, tell him how amazing the meal was, tell him they hope to see him again soon. He is gracious to them, says it was my pleasure, you are wonderful young people it was my pleasure. He opens car doors, pays drivers, sends the cars away. The windows in the cars come down and everyone waves goodbye to him. When the cars are out of sight it is me and my friend Leonard. He speaks.

Thought we'd walk back. It'll help settle the food a bit.

Sounds good.

We start walking. It is colder, darker, the wind stronger.

You have nice friends, my son.

Yeah, I'm lucky.

Very polite, very interesting. The girls were all beautiful.

I'll tell them you said so.

You have fun?

It was the best night I've had in years, Thank you for doing it.

We'll do it again next time I'm in town.

We turn a corner. The hotel is in sight. I see Leonard's white Mercedes sitting in front of the hotel. Snap is in the driver's seat, the engine is running. I speak.

Why's the car out there?

I need to go out for a while.

A little late, isn't it?

Sometimes I need it to be late.

I don't respond. We walk to the car. I nod at Snapper, he nods at me. I turn to Leonard.

Thanks again, Leonard.

No problem.

I'll see you tomorrow.

I'll come to your room when I wake up.

Cool.

You've got your key?

Yeah.

Goodnight, my son.

Thank you, Leonard.

Leonard turns, opens the car door, gets inside, closes the door. The car pulls away I watch it go.

Thank you, Leonard.

Thank you, Leonard.

Thank you.

For the next two days, we eat, sit around the pool, watch TV, sleep. I am rarely alone. When I am alone, and I'm not sleeping, I cry. I lie face-down on the bed and I cry. I stand in the shower and I cry. I stare out the window and I cry. It doesn't matter what I'm doing, or not doing, the littlest things set me off, everything sets me off. I cry when I'm alone. Whenever I'm alone. My bottle is always with me. An antidote to pain should I choose to use it. I keep it in plain view, on one of the nightstands next to the bed. I cradle it when I sleep. I have opened it twice, smelled, let it taunt me, let it enrage me. I do it because the test of it, the test of resisting it, makes me feel strong. Most of the time I feel like I want to die. The feeling of strength keeps me going.

On the morning of our fourth day in the hotel, Leonard shows up late for breakfast. When he arrives, he's wearing a suit.

My son.

What's up?

He sits.

Me and Snap are leaving in a little while.

Back to Nevada?

New York, then Nevada.

Why New York?

You remember the story I told you about my father? How he worked as a golf course maintenance man at a ritzy country club in Connecticut, just outside of New York, how he told me on his deathbed he wanted me to be successful enough to play that course someday, play it just like one of the members?

Yeah, I remember.

The older I get, the more anxious I am to do it. I got a line on somebody who might be able to help. I'm going to see him.

Good luck.

You gonna be okay without me?

Yeah.

You sure?

I'm a big boy, Leonard.

You need anything, you call me.

I will. Thank you.

You get close to picking up that bottle, you call me.

I will.

You know she'd want you clean.

I don't want to talk about it, Leonard.

She would.

I look away. He stands.

I gotta go.

Okay.

I stand.

Don't be mad at me, Kid. I'm just trying to help.

You are helping. It's just hard right now.

He nods. We hug each other, separate.

See you soon.

Thank you, Leonard. Thanks for everything.

He turns, leaves. I sit down, eat a huge breakfast, go back to the room, cry, take a nap, cry, leave.

I stop at Kevin's apartment. There are two messages for me. One from a bar, one from a gas station. I would rather work at the gas station. I call the gas station, the manager tells me to stop by so that I can meet him. I leave Kevin's, walk over, meet the manager. He's young, slightly older than I am. His hair is short, shoes shined, uniform clean and pressed. He asks me if I know anything about car repair and I tell him no. He asks me if I'm interested in a long-term position or short-term position, I tell him I need a job, have no idea how long or short a term. He nods, thanks me for coming, shakes my hand, I leave.

I call the bar. They give me an address, tell me to show up at four A.M. the next morning if I'm interested in the job.

I go home, sit on the floor, close my eyes, try to be still. It's harder than it was in jail. Harder because the same thoughts run through my head whenever I try to do it. I think about Lilly, about the last minutes of her life. I think about what was going through her head the moment she decided to die, as she tied the knots of her noose, as she put the noose around her neck, as she hung and started to fade. I wonder if there were regrets, if there was peace. I wonder if she thought about me as she hung. I try to avoid the images, change the course of my thought, empty my mind of all thought. It doesn't work. I do not possess the necessary discipline. I sit, I think about Lilly and her death, I hurt. My body hurts, everything hurts.

After an hour I stand, shake, smoke a cigarette, leave. I go to Kevin's. We meet our friends at a bar, we shoot pool, they drink, I watch them. There is temptation every second of every minute of every five ten twenty thirty minutes every single second. Temptation to drink, to annihilate myself, to make the pain go away, to hurt myself more than I already hurt. It ebbs and flows, this temptation sometimes easy to resist sometimes difficult, sometimes so overwhelming that I know if I move I'm done. The only way to deal with it is to not move, to sit and wait, to hold on until it goes away.

My friends get drunk. I sit with them. They all have jobs so we leave the bar, they need a few hours' sleep before they go to work. I have three hours to burn. I keep walking up and down cold, empty, black streets, block after block, block after block. Occasionally I see another person, usually drunk, stumbling along the sidewalk. Occasionally I pass an open bar or convenience store. The only vehicles out are either cabs or cops, I can't afford a ride with either of them.

As I walk, I start to shake. My clothes are worn and thin, I don't have a hat or gloves. The cold settles over me in layers, on my coat and pants, on my skin, beneath my skin, in my bones, in my jaw and teeth. I keep walking, hoping the longer I walk the warmer I'll become, but my theory is wrong. The cold hurts me and shakes me, makes me numb. The more numb, the better, the more numb the more comfortable. The numbness functions for me the same way the alcohol and drugs functioned for me. I am overwhelmed. Everything hurts. It hurts so much that I stop feeling. Everything is wiped away and the numb remains. I can deal with the numb. It is as it was before and it is the best I can do for myself. I walk and I walk and I walk.

I show up at the bar fifteen minutes early. Two doormen stand at the entrance. They're both in black, they both look cold, they're both scowling. They stop me as I start to walk in, one of them tells me they're closed. I tell them I'm here for the job. One of them laughs, the other says go around back, wait at the service door.

To get to the back, I have to walk around the block. There are two other men waiting, one white, one black, both young, neither looks happy. The black man paces, swears, hops up and down to try to stay warm. The white man stares at his feet, doesn't move, doesn't speak.

At four fifteen, the door opens. The doormen from the front lead us into a huge open room. Along one wall of the room, there are leveled risers with tables. The highest group of tables is surrounded by a red velvet rope. Along another wall, there is a stage. Above and at the edges of the stage are racks of lights and stacks of speakers, and at the back of the stage there is a DJ booth. Along a third wall is a long black bar. There are no stools in front of it. A group of bartenders and waitresses stand at one end of the bar talking drinking smoking laughing. A group of men with garbage bags are picking up trash.

We walk behind the bar, open a door at one end, walk into a bright hall. There are five doors in the hall. One labeled Men one labeled Women one labeled Office two with nothing. One of doormen tells us to wait, knocks on the office door, the doormen leave.

We wait for a few minutes. We stand and stare at the floor, occasionally look at each other. The door opens. A middle-age man steps out. He's short and fat, has dark, thinning hair, bad skin. He's wearing a black and yellow sweatsuit, black leather loafers. He looks us up and down.

Here for the job?

White man nods, black man and I say yeah.

Any of you ever been janitors or done any clean-up work?

White man nods, black man and I say no.

I need people to clean my places. There's this one and two others. You pick up trash, mop the floors, wipe down tables, shit like that. Hours are from four to eight every morning. Pay is seven bucks an hour. If you do well, you might become a doorman or a barback. If you're no good, I'll fire you. If you're interested, get out there and start working. We'll process you when you're done.

I turn, walk back to the room, ask one of the men with garbage bags what to do, he tells me to do what he's doing. I get a bag, pick up trash, take it to a dumpster. I get a broom, sweep the floor, get a mop, mop the floor, get a bottle of cleaner, wipe down tables, chairs, countertops. The white man and the black man have also joined the crew, there are seven of us. It takes an hour to clean the club. When we're done, we walk down the street to another one. It's larger, flashier, there are cages hanging from the ceiling, four bars, two separate sections with tables, three separate levels. Process is the same: pick up trash, sweep, mop, wipe. Takes two hours. When we're done, we walk to a nearby bar. Bar is in the basement of a large residential building. Has pinball machine, pool table, two televisions which hang in corners, free popcorn, free food every night from seven to

ten. Takes thirty minutes to clean. When we're done, most of the men leave. The white man, black man and I walk back to the office, fill out some paperwork, are assigned days. I get Thursday, Friday, Saturday, Sunday, Monday. From four to finish. Seven dollars an hour.
I leave, walk until I'm numb. I stop to talk to Lilly, tell her I miss her, tell her I love her. I leave, walk until I'm numb. Go home. Sleep.

My life becomes routine.

I work.

Sleep is still difficult I sleep for three or four hours a day. Usually sometime in the afternoon.

I walk in the cold, keep myself numb.

I cry less, cry less.

I go out with my friends every night. Go to bars, shoot pool, smoke cigarettes, watch them drink. Sometimes I talk, sometimes I laugh, both feel good. When I'm thirsty, I order a caffeinated cola drink, with ice and without a lemon. I start to feel more comfortable around people. The temptation is still there, always there, the urge to drink drug and destroy never leaves, but I'm getting used to it. It's like a rash, a nasty fucking rash, constant, annoying and painful. I'd like to scratch it till kingdom fucking come but if I do I die and I don't want to die.

When my friends go home I walk again, walk in the cold, keep myself numb, always numb.

I work.

Sometimes I read the Tao.

Sometimes I sit, stare at the wall, the wall is white.

Sometimes I feel too much, feel like I'm going to explode. All of me, all of what is inside of me, anger sadness confusion pain insecurity fear loneliness, heart soul consciousness, whatever words for some of what is inside me there are no words to describe, it swirls, it races, it taunts, it moves to the surface and pushes pushes, all of it pushes. I feel like I'm going to explode. I scream. At the top of my lungs. Long and hard, scream so that my lungs hurt, my throat hurts, my face hurts. I scream into pillows. I walk to the lake scream at the water. Stand in a park and scream into a tree. Doesn't matter where I am I just need to fucking scream. It makes me feel better.

My life is a simple routine.

Boss calls me into his office. I sit across from him. He speaks.

I need a doorman. Nobody else wants to do it. You interested?

Why won't anyone do it?

It's the late shift, nine to four. You gotta stand outside the whole time. The bar is on Chicago Ave., which is really fucking cold and windy, and you're gonna freeze your ass off. I'd need you Sunday, Monday and Tuesday nights. Those are the slow nights. The bartender and waitress are supposed to give you ten percent of their tips, but they don't make shit those nights, so you probably won't get shit. I'll give you a twenty-five cent raise, but it probably won't make up for it.

Sounds great.

I don't got time for fucking jokes.

I'm not joking. I'll do it.

He looks at me for a moment.

You start Sunday. Get there at eight, ask for Ted. He's the bartender, he'll tell you what to do.

I have a question.

What?

Is this a promotion?

What kind of question is that?

I've never gotten a promotion before. I'm wondering if I could consider this one.

Consider it whatever the fuck you want. Just show up at eight.

Thank you.

I stand, leave, start walking home. I smile for most of the walk, occasionally skip a few steps, occasionally snap my fingers. I have been fired from every job I've had in my life. There was usually yelling and screaming involved in my firings, always bad feelings on my employer's side, not one

would give me a positive reference. Boss told me to consider my change of
position whatever the fuck I want, I'm going to consider it a promotion,
the first one of my life. I might not feel like it most of the time, I may be
carrying around unbearable urges to drink and do drugs, I may be depressed and sometimes suicidal, I may be feeling a sense of sorrow and
loss greater and more profound than any other I've felt in a life filled with
sorrow and loss, but I'm getting better. I got a motherfucking promotion,
goddamnit. It's time to celebrate.

I take a long, nonsensical route home. I weave through the wealthy neighborhoods of the North Side of Chicago. I walk past fancy stores, past
clothing stores furniture stores I could give a fuck about clothes or furniture, past bookstores and art galleries I walk through them looking at
beautiful things I can't afford, I look at the windows of real estate offices,
they have listings hanging in silver frames greystone brownstone turn of
the century rowhouse an excellent value. It's gonna go fast. I walk up and
down the aisles of a gourmet grocery. I look at fruit and vegetables crisp
and nearly ripe smells like a summer garden under fluorescent lights. I go
to the cheese department cheddar Swiss mozzarella provolone Gruyère
blue Brie feta cow milk goat milk semi-soft extra creamy crumbly mild
stinky. I look at fish, pasta, tea that costs forty dollars an ounce, fish, eggs
that cost two hundred, beef raised on beer at three hundred and twenty
dollars a pound, they have twelve types of whipped cream forty types of
coffee fifty different brands of chocolate, flowers that cost more than I
make in a week. The colors the smells they make me delirious make me
want to eat until I explode make me salivate drool my head spins my
sight blurs.

I walk to the bakery section. I look at pastries and cakes, tarts and pies. My
body craves sugar, always craves sugar Years of alcoholism and the high
level of sugar in alcohol created the craving, which I feed with candy and
soda. I check my pocket, I have twenty-two dollars on me. I have twenty
or so more dollars in my apartment. The cakes have the most sugar, sugar
in the cake itself and sugar in the frosting. They come in two sizes large
and small, they come in four types chocolate with chocolate frosting
chocolate with white frosting white cake with chocolate frosting white
cake with white frosting. I would like to buy one of each type in both the
large and small sizes. I would have them put in nice white cake boxes and

have the boxes closed with finely tied and looped string. It would be a struggle carrying so many boxes home, but I would persevere. At home I would open the boxes one at time and work my way through all eight cakes systematically, starting with the small ones and finishing with the large ones. I would forgo fork and knife and eat with my hands, licking my fingers and my lips along the way. Once I was done, I would most likely either vomit due to excess, which I have done many times in my life, or spend several hours in some sort of sugar-induced mania, maybe pacing in circles, maybe walking endlessly around my block, maybe babbling idiotically at random strangers on the street. Eventually I would shut down and sleep, happy and full, every cell of my body saturated with sugar, cake and frosting.

A woman in a white baker's outfit steps to the counter opposite me.

May I help you?

How much are the cakes?

Which ones?

I point to the cakes.

The birthday cakes.

The small ones are fourteen dollars, the large ones are twenty-one.

Large please. White cake with white frosting.

Do you want me to put an inscription on it?

Does it cost extra?

Nope.

Yeah, I would like an inscription.

What would you like it to say?

I think for a moment.

How about—Big Promotion, Jimbo!

She laughs.

Who's Jimbo?

Me.

What kind of promotion?

I work at a bar downtown. Got promoted from cleaning crew to doorman.

Congratulations.

In a couple years I'm going to be President of the United States.

She laughs, opens the cabinet, reaches for my cake.

I'll be right back, Mr. President.

I will be anxiously awaiting your return.

She laughs again, turns around, puts the cake in a box and ties the box with a finely tied loop, hands it to me. I thank her and I go to the checkout line and I pay for my cake my beautiful cake.

I walk home. No more skipping and no more finger snapping, I don't want to hurt my cake. I do, however, smile, and I also greet people on the sidewalks with heartfelt and sincere hellos, how are yous, it's a beautiful days. As I walk into the building I see Mickey, the building superintendent, walking out of it. His eyes are swollen and it looks like he's been crying.

Yo, Mickey. You want a piece of cake?

What?

I just bought a cake. You want a piece?

What kind is it?

White on white.

I need some cigarettes.

If you want cake, I'll be in my apartment.

Mickey skulks away. I go to my apartment. I open the door, go to my little kitchen, set the cake on the counter. I open it, my oh my it is a beautiful cake. I get two plastic plates and a knife. I cut two pieces away and set them on the plates. I take the rest of the cake and I sit on the floor next to my bed. I carefully pick it up and take a big bite out of it. I chew my bite slowly, savoring the light, moist, airy cake and the sweet, thick, creamy frosting. I take another bite, another another. It's a great cake. More than suitable for my promotion celebration.

About halfway through my eating of the cake, there is a knock at my door. I stand, walk over, open it. Mickey is standing at the door, a pack of cigarettes in his hand. He speaks.

You have cake and frosting on your face.

I smile.

Is there any left?

I saved some for you.

He steps inside my apartment. I walk to the kitchen, get one of the plates with cake on it, get a plastic fork, give them to him. We sit on the floor, and as we eat, he tells me about his day.

He is miserable. His boyfriend broke up with him at breakfast, told him he needed someone with more ambition than Mickey, someone who

wanted more out of life than a job as building superintendent. Mickey
told him it was temporary, that he was working to make it as a painter,
that he felt his dreams were going to come true. The boyfriend said I need
more than your dreams, Mickey, and he walked out.
Mickey starts to cry. I eat my cake. I make sure to get some extra frosting
on my face. When Mickey looks up, he sees me and he laughs. I speak.
If you don't eat yours . . .
He laughs, starts eating. As we eat, we talk, he asks me where I'm from I
tell him Cleveland, he asks why I moved here I say I moved for a girl, he
asks if we're still together I say yes we're still together. I ask him the same
things he's from a small town in Indiana and moved here so he could be
himself, could live as a gay man without being harassed, could try to make
it as a painter. I ask him what he paints he says he'd rather show me than
tell me. He finishes his cake and he stands and he leaves my apartment.
I keep eating, I'm almost done. Five minutes later Mickey comes back
with a painting and sets it carefully on the floor in front of me.
It is a small painting, maybe six inches by six inches. The canvas is black at
the edges. The rest of it is covered with tiny faces. Some are smiling, some
are laughing, some are screaming, some are crying. The faces are painted
in perfect miniature detail, they look like little photographs, and it's a
beautiful painting, beautiful and horrifying, full joy and misery, laughter
and sorrow. Mickey speaks.
What do you think?
It's great.
You want it?
Absolutely.
It's yours.
Thank you.
If you need a nail to hang it, I've got them.
Once I decide where to put it.
I'm gonna go. Thanks for the cake.
Thanks for the painting.
Sure.
And forget about the boyfriend, that shallow fucker.
He laughs.
Yeah.

He leaves. I finish my cake. When I'm done, I lick my lips and fingers and clean the excess from my chin and cheeks. I want to see Lilly. I usually walk to see her, but I'm tired, so I decide to take the train. I've never used the elevated train system of Chicago. I have been told it is simple and easy. I'm wary of it. Most of the time someone says something is simple and easy it turns out to be complicated and difficult.

I put on my warm clothes. Get my last twenty dollars from beneath my mattress, which is where I keep my money. I wrap the last piece of cake, carefully wrap it. I leave, walk to the nearest train station. I look at the map, colored lines weaving through and across each other. I find the station on the map, find Lilly's station on the map, buy a token, step to the platform, wait. The train comes, I make the transfer, arrive at Lilly's station. The trip is simple and easy. I now know how to use the elevated train. So much for my bullshit theory.

I walk, stop at a flower shop, spend eighteen dollars on red roses.

I give her the roses.

I give her the last piece of cake.

I tell her about my day. The best day I've had on my own in Chicago.

I got a promotion.

I went for a nice, long walk.

I spent my hard-earned money on something beautiful.

I ate that beautiful thing, and it was tasty.

I made a friend.

I was given a gift.

I learned something.

It was a great, great day.

I tell Lilly I love her, miss her. I spend my last dollar on a token home. Part of me expects Lilly to be waiting for me. I would give everything for her to be waiting for me. She's not. I'm alone. I lie down, can't sleep.

I wait for the darkness.

I start my new job. The bar is small, nondescript, in the lower level of a large building, beneath a clothing store. Eight steps lead from the street to the ten tables, two pinball machines, televisions in two corners continuously playing sports. There is a popcorn machine near the door, the popcorn is free. There are three employees working at any given time, a bartender, waitress, doorman. Bartender Ted and waitress Amy always work the same shift as me. They are boyfriend/girlfriend, and in between serving the dozen or so customers usually in the place, they stand at the corner of the bar smoking cigarettes, giggling, whispering and kissing. I stand outside. It's cold as hell and I'm always numb. I always have a roll of drink tickets in my pocket. I'm supposed to offer them to anyone and everyone who walks by the bar, they are redeemable for either a free shot of watermelon liqueur or a free kamikaze. No one in the first three days takes me up on the offer, so now I rarely bother. When I do bother I choose people who I'm sure will say no, such as children, the elderly, or the very very well-dressed, and I beg them to go inside, tell them my job is on the line, tell them I desperately need their help. Every single one of them says no. From midnight on, I only see a few people. I stand and shiver and smoke cigarettes. Sometimes I test myself to see how long I can go without moving, I can last about two hours. Sometimes I sing to myself, sing silly love songs with titles like Just Once, Secret Lovers, Lost in Love, Down on Bended Knee. I don't know how or why I know the words, I just do. Sometimes I flip a quarter over and over, keep track of how many times heads, how many times tails, for some reason there are usually more heads. Sometimes I talk to Lilly. Carry on long conversations with her. Talk about random things, the news, something I saw while I was walking, something I read. I talk to her about our plans the plans we made while I was in jail. Where we wanted to live, the jobs we wanted to get, maybe marriage, maybe kids, what the kids would be named, she wanted a little girl, I wanted a little boy. Sometimes I cry while I talk to her. Sometimes I get angry. Sometimes I feel stupid, but I keep talking anyway. Sometimes I just stop, I have her image in my mind, and I have to stop.

My shift ends at four. I punch out, leave. It's always dark, the streets empty. I walk south into steel and concrete canyons. I move up and down vacant blocks, stare up at fifty, eighty, hundred and ten story monoliths, watch streetlight shadows move across lower floors, kick deserted papers, cups and bags lying on curbs. I walk down the middle of wide boulevards, stand on the centers of iron bridges, sit alone in huge sprawling plazas, parks, long expanses of dead public grass. I am the only person awake, the city and its citizens are asleep, my footsteps my breath and the whistling screaming wind are all I hear. The city is reduced, ceases to be a city, becomes a museum. Objects aren't banks, law firms, hospitals, courthouses, shopping centers, apartment buildings, they are huge sprawling sculptures of marble limestone iron steel and glass, without purpose or use, just huge beautiful objects.

When I start to see other people, as the eyes of the city start to open, I leave, walk out to the lake, start heading north. It is always colder by the lake. The wind is always stronger. The cold shakes me and the wind stings my face. I walk until I find a bench and I sit the bench is always cold. I stare across the frozen expanse of ice and encased debris, sticks, logs, cans, there is a football opposite a beach, a lifejacket opposite a marina. I watch as thin girders of blue light start glowing, as the light turns yellow, pink, orange, as it spreads across the horizon. The sun appears, slowly rising, an edge, quarter, half circle. It becomes full and red, envelopes the sky, dominates it. It makes the monuments of this city, of any city every city, seem small and insignificant. It makes me feel small and insignificant. Makes me forget the past, dismiss the future. Makes my problems disappear, feel like nothing nothing nothing.

When I hear cars on the highway behind me I stand walk home. As the
normal day begins, my day ends.
I lie down in my apartment.
Sometimes I sleep.
Sometimes not.
I lie there.
Alone.

It is eight A.M. As I walk toward my building, I see a white Mercedes sitting at the curb. I enter the building, the door to my apartment is open. I step inside, see Leonard and Snapper standing in front of my refrigerator. The refrigerator door is open and there are brown paper bags on the floor.

Leonard.

They turn around.

My son, my son.

Leonard steps toward me.

How are you?

He hugs me.

I'm okay. What are you doing here?

Filling your fridge.

You came here to fill my fridge?

No, but when we arrived, we saw it was empty.

You gotta stop breaking in, Leonard.

Get a better lock and we'll stop breaking in. The lock you got is a fucking joke.

Snapper speaks.

I'm the one who actually does it, Kid, and it's real easy. You're lucky you ain't been robbed.

Leonard laughs.

Look at this place. Who would rob him? He's got nothing to steal.

I step toward the refrigerator.

What are you putting in there?

Snapper speaks.

We got shit from all five food groups.

Leonard speaks.

Fruits, vegetables, proteins, grains and dairys.

Snapper speaks.

We got them all.

I laugh.

It's dairy, not dairys.

I know, but it's funnier saying dairys. Say it.

Dairys.

I laugh.

Told ya. Dairys is funnier.

I laugh again.

Thank you. For all five food groups.

And that's not all.

Leonard opens the cabinets. They're filled with cans of soup, boxes of rice and boxes of pasta, jars of tomato sauce.

Snapper speaks.

I got something special for you in there.

He steps over, pulls down a box.

Rice-A-Roni. The motherfucking San Francisco treat.

I laugh.

Thanks.

Leonard speaks.

You're still too skinny, my son. If you're gonna be a doorman at a bar you're gonna need to gain some weight. We drove by last night and saw you standing out there and you do not look particularly menacing.

You drove by to see me?

We did.

Why?

That's why we're here.

To talk to me about my job?

Yup.

What about my job?

Let's go down to the hotel, get some breakfast. We'll talk down there.

I need some sleep.

Then get some sleep, come down for lunch.

What time?

One?

Okay.

Leonard turns to Snapper.

You finished?

Yeah.

Let's go. He needs some sleep.

Okay.

Leonard turns to me.

See you at one.

Snapper speaks.

See ya, Kid.

I speak.

Thanks for the food.

Leonard speaks.

Eat some of it. Right now. Get fat.

Snapper speaks.

Yeah, get fat.

I laugh.

Bye.

They walk out. I lie down, sleep, wake-up, take a shower. I am confident now I take the El train downtown, walk to the hotel from the train. I ride up the elevator, walk through the lobby, Leonard is waiting for me in the restaurant, I sit down with him.

Where's Snapper?

He's out working. You sleep well?

I never sleep well.

You will.

I guess.

You hungry?

Yeah.

Leonard motions for the waitress, orders steaks and French fries for each of us, turns back to me.

Now tell me, how the fuck you end up working at a bar?

I laugh.

Tell me how you know I work at a bar and I'll tell you how I ended up there.

I had someone looking out for you. They told me.

Who?

Doesn't matter.

You got some flunky following me around?

I'm just looking out for you.

I can look out for myself.

Why you working at a bar?

It was the only job I could get.

Come on, you're a smart kid. You can do better than that.

I applied for a few different jobs, nobody wanted to hire me. I don't ex-actly have a sparkling resume.

It's unacceptable.

It's fine, Leonard.

You're an alcoholic and you're a drug addict. You've only been clean a couple months. You can't work at a bar. It's crazy and stupid and dangerous.

I actually work in front of the bar. I stand there and pick my ass for hours on end. It might be stupid and it might be boring, but it's not crazy or dangerous.

Until you feel like you want a drink and you go inside.

I feel like I want a drink all the fucking time. And if I decide I want one, it won't be hard to get one, regardless of where I am.

It's unacceptable, my son.

You got a better idea?

I do.

What's that?

Come work for me.

I laugh.

Yeah, that's a great idea.

Why not?

Because I've got a record, because I'm trying to stay out of trouble, be-cause an arrest of any kind means I go away for three to five.

I got good lawyers, you won't go anywhere.

I laugh.

That makes me feel better.

It should. You'll have the power of an entire organization behind you.

I laugh again.

That's what I'm afraid of, Leonard.

I won't let you work at a bar.

It's not a matter of what you will or will not let me do.

I'll say it differently—I can offer you a much better opportunity than you have at the bar.

Gonna make me an offer I can't refuse?

Leonard laughs.

I can offer you a much better opportunity.

What would I do?

Pick things up and take them places.

I laugh again.

Pick things up and take them places?

Yes, indeed.

I wouldn't want to know what I might be picking up.

That would probably be best.

Our steaks come, we start eating. We do not talk about my new opportunity. We talk about basketball, we talk about the upcoming baseball season, we talk about the cold, he hates it. We talk about our steaks, they're good, we talk about our fries, they're hot and crispy. When we're finished, we order coffee and ice cream sundaes, he gets hot fudge, I get caramel. I finish my sundae, light a cigarette, speak.

Will I do anything legal?

Depends on your definition of legal.

How about according to your definition?

There are very few things illegal according to my definitions.

If I get caught, I'll be in big fucking trouble.

You won't get caught. And if you do, I'll take care of you.

I think, take a drag, take another.

My son.

I look up.

If you don't say yes, I'll buy the bar and fire you.

I laugh.

I'm nervous, Leonard. I'm trying to live a better life, trying to be a better person. I do not want to get locked up again.

I understand, and think that working for me will only help. You won't have any financial pressure, you won't have a boss screaming at you, you'll have as much time as you need to figure out your shit.

How long are you in town?

As long as it takes to get you to say yes.

What are you gonna do tonight?

I thought we'd take you to a firing range, make sure you're handy with a weapon.

You better be fucking kidding.

He laughs.

We're going out. Going to a basketball game, then having dinner. I'm gonna introduce you to some people that you should know.

Sounds cool.

What are you gonna do for the rest of the day?

I don't know. Go walk around.

You should give notice at the bar.

I'll think about it.

No thinking, my son. Just do.

What are you gonna do for the rest of the day?

Snapper's picking me up. We have to run some errands.

Errands?

He chuckles, nods.

Yes, errands.

What time should I meet you?

Seven.

Cool.

I stand.

Thanks for lunch.

Get fat.

I laugh.

See you at seven.

I leave. Down the elevator and outside. It's cold and gray, always cold and gray. I start walking. Think about where I want to go I have no idea. The temperature is below zero, I'm going to need to make stops every ten minutes or so, it's too cold too cold. I stop in a clothing store, they sell suits for thousands of dollars, a man in a security uniform follows me up and down the aisles. I stop in a coffee shop, I don't order anything just sit at a table in the corner and breathe. I walk into the lobby of a famous building built by a chewing gum company. The floor is marble, the walls are marble, the ceiling is marble. The walls and ceiling have been carved, covered with flowers, intricate patterns, saints, gods, little snarling gargoyles, big snarling gargoyles. I walk into a fast food restaurant, a comic book store, a jeweler I get followed by another guard. I keep walking, walk into an office building quickly walk out, walk into an art museum take off my coat. The museum is offering free admission, as it does one day a week, I start wandering through the galleries. I stand beneath angels and saints, beneath the son of god, beneath his mother, beneath beheaded martyrs, sobbing virgins, angry popes, beneath marching armies, generals astride their mounts, looted burning ravaged cities. I stare at dead game, fruits and vegetables in a market, Dutch fishing boats, Merrymakers in an inn, Rinaldo being enchanted by Armida. I stare at Cupid firing arrows, the Crystal Palace, at the Seine, at Bennecourt. I watch a woman at a piano she does not move just stares at the keys making music I can't hear. I meet Henri de Gas and his niece Lucie de Gas, I walk through Paris, rainy day, wait for the arrival of the Normandy train at the Gare Saint-Lazare. I confront the Portrait of Man. He stares at me. I stare back, waiting for answers. I get none.

I spend hours slowly moving from room to room. I try to get as close to the paintings as possible. I close one eye and look at the individual strokes made by the painters. I close both eyes and try to smell the oil. I stand as far away as I can, walk forward the image coming gradually closer. I want to rub my hands along the surface, but don't want to set off an alarm or get arrested. Sometimes I talk to the paintings, to the figures in the paintings. I ask a farmer how's the weather, I ask a singer what's the song, I ask a baby what's your name, I ask a young woman why are you crying? I stand in front of Vincent's self-portrait. Vincent who knew pain and failure, who knew self-doubt and insanity, who cut off his ear, who shot himself. I know Vincent well. I have nothing to say to him.

I leave the museum at closing time. I walk back to the hotel, stopping along the way to get warm. When I arrive I wait in the lobby. Five minutes later, Leonard and the Snapper step out of an elevator, start walking toward me. I stand meet them halfway. Leonard speaks.

My son.

What's up?

Snapper speaks.

How ya doing, kid?

Good.

Leonard speaks.

Ready for some basketball?

Yeah.

Good.

We leave, go downstairs, pick up the car, drive to the stadium. The stadium is old and decrepit. It was built in the 1920s and is scheduled to be destroyed this summer, replaced by a newer version being built across the street. When we arrive we pull through rusted gates to an area of guarded parking, the parking lot where the players and team owners park. We get out of the car, walk into the stadium through a guarded door. We enter a series of tunnels beneath the main seating area of the stadium. We walk past locker rooms, training areas, administrative offices. We walk past men and women in uniforms rushing around I have no idea what they do. We walk out of a tunnel and onto the court. It's near game-time and the stadium is almost full. The game, as all Chicago basketball games are, is sold out. Leonard pulls three tickets from the inside pocket of his jacket, hands one to me, one to Snapper. He walks along the edge of the court, we follow him. He stops at three seats near the center, motions for us to sit. Five minutes later the lights go out, loud music starts blaring through speakers hanging from the ceiling, the Chicago team is introduced and runs to their bench. The opposing team, which is from New York, enters without fanfare. Everyone stands while the national anthem is played, the game starts with the tipoff. Chicago's team is the reigning champion and their star player is considered the best basketball player in the world. New York can't keep up and they get obliterated. At half-time, Chicago leads by eighteen, they win the game by thirty. Leonard acts like a little kid throughout, cheering, laughing, jumping up and down, eating popcorn, hot dogs and ice cream bars, drinking large cola after large cola after large cola. I skip the popcorn and hot dogs, I eat eight ice cream bars and drink seven large colas. Snapper doesn't eat anything, says he's watching his figure and waiting for dinner.

After the game we go to a restaurant. It's a simple Italian restaurant on the west side of the city, not far from the stadium. We walk in and Leonard and Snapper greet the owner, who leads us into a room behind the main dining room. The room has a long, simple table covered with a white tablecloth, there are ten chairs around it. We sit and the owner asks what we would like to drink, colas for Leonard and me, a glass of red wine for Snapper. Leonard looks at me, speaks.

You give notice today?

I shake my head.

Nope.

Why not?

Spent the day in a museum.

Snapper speaks.

What'd you see?

All kinds of stuff.

Leonard speaks.

Get more specific, my son.

Do you know anything about art?

Leonard looks at Snapper.

Do we know anything about art?

Quite a bit, actually.

Leonard turns to me.

We know quite a bit.

I laugh.

How?

How? We read. We go to museums and galleries. We pay attention.

I would have never thought . . .

Snapper speaks.

Tell him how we got into it.

Leonard speaks.

I have a house on the beach outside of LA. Every summer the town puts on this thing called the Pageant of the Masters.

Snapper speaks.

I love the Pageant of the Masters.

Leonard nods.

What they do is make stage sets that look actually like famous paintings. So let's say they were doing The Last Supper by Leonardo da Vinci. They'd get a bunch of men, dress them up so they look exactly like the Apostles in the painting. They'd get another fella and make him look like

the Jesus in the painting. They'd put everyone at a table that looked
like the table in the painting in a room that looked exactly like the room
in the painting. Then they pose in painting poses and they sit there.
Snapper speaks.
It's beautiful.
Leonard speaks.
And tons of people come see the paintings, which have now been brought
to life.
Snapper speaks.
They look so real it's crazy.
Leonard speaks.
We've been going every summer for years.
Snapper speaks.
And every summer it gets better and better.
Leonard speaks.
We're knowledgeable about everything from Pre-Renaissance work to
the Post-Impressionists.
Snapper speaks.
They don't do modern art very well. Too hard to break a real person down
into some form of cubism, pure abstraction or minimalism.
Leonard speaks.
They do Matisse and Modigliani. Don't forget about them.
Snapper speaks.
I shouldn't have forgotten Matisse, but Modigliani is boring.
Leonard speaks.
His work is not as dynamic as some.
Snapper speaks.
It's boring. Fucking boring.
Leonard turns to me.
What do you think, my son?
About Modigliani or this conversation?
Both.
I like Modigliani. I think those women are weird and gorgeous. I'm sort of
shocked by the conversation.
Everybody thinks we're barbarians, but we've got soft, sensitive, sophisti-
cated sides to us.

Snapper speaks.

I'm very soft, sensitive and sophisticated.

I laugh. The door opens, waiters start bringing in food, Platters of antipasti, mozzarella and tomato, fried calamari, fried zucchini, zuppa di clams, Caesar salad, crostini with chopped liver. There is more food than the three of us could eat, I ask Leonard if he's expecting anyone else. He tells me that there may be a few people stopping by to say hello.

We start eating. The smell of the food on the table and the smells drifting into the room from the nearby kitchen, garlic oregano olive oil peppers Parmesan pesto, roasting chicken beef and veal, sautéed spinach and scampi, strong espresso and chocolate, ignite my hunger I start eating. I eat slowly, one thing at a time, though the addict in me and the alcoholic in me say go go go more more more. As we eat, we talk, talk about the game we just saw, Leonard and Snapper debate the merits of this restaurant against Italian restaurants in Manhattan and the Bronx. As we finish the first course, the door opens and two men step into the room. Both are large, thick, menacing men, with short hair, simple dark suits. Leonard and Snapper rise, greet them, introduce them to me. Both slip me cards when we shake hands, which I slip into my pocket. I'm curious to know what the cards are, what they say, who these men are, but I know I should wait, look at them later, if they wanted me to look at them now, they would have handed them to me, not slipped them to me.

As more food arrives, large platters of food, spaghetti with meatballs, linguini with clam sauce, penne rigatoni pappardelle, chicken scarpariello, chicken contadino, chicken cacciatore, veal cutlets chops, veal saltimbocca, osso bucco, lobster oreganato, scampi fra diavolo, more people arrive. The table is filled, there are people standing around the table, in every corner of the room. I meet men some obviously Italian some not all wearing dark suits and wedding rings, I get slipped card after card. I meet women all beautiful some with the men, none wear wedding rings, I get slipped a couple of phone numbers. There are handshakes, kisses on cheeks, backslaps, laughter laughter laughter. There are cigars, cigarettes, red wine, white wine, beer, cocktails, colas for me I love an ice-cold cola. Leonard and Snapper are having a great time, laughing and happy, when I'm not talking to someone I'm watching them. Leonard commands the room everyone is aware of his presence when he talks to them, they listen, as he

moves from person to person, group to group, the attention is always focused on him.

Hours pass quickly pass. It's late, the room is still crowded. I'm full, tired,
wired on caffeine and nicotine. My clothes smell like deep, strong cigars.
My shirt has stains on it grease and tomato sauce. My pocket is full of
cards. I tell Leonard I'm going home I feel like I can sleep, he walks me
outside. I speak.

You have a lot of friends, Leonard.

Most of those people were there to meet you.

Why?

You ask them what they do for a living?

No.

You look at those cards they gave you?

No.

Look at them when you get home.

Why?

Every card you got tonight is more or less a get out of jail free card. You
come work for me and nothing is going to happen to you. Every person in
there will guarantee it.

I laugh.

You're not gonna stop are you.

Not until you stop working at the bar.

I'll give notice tomorrow.

Leonard smiles.

Ha-ha! That's great news.

I laugh.

We don't use contracts, but I'm gonna give you a signing bonus.

I laugh again. He reaches into a pocket, pulls out a wad of rolled cash held
together by a rubber band. He hands it to me.

I can't take this, Leonard.

Sure you can, and you're gonna.

No way. This is a ton of dough, I haven't done shit to earn it.

So what. Take it. It's your starting-up money.

No.

I hold the cash toward him. He shakes his head.

We've been through this before, my son.

What?

When someone wants to do something nice for you, don't argue, don't re-sist, don't say no, don't try to change their mind. Just smile and say thank you and think about how fortunate you are to have generous people in your life.

That's a lot of fucking money, Leonard.

Just smile and say thank you.

I put the cash in my pocket.

Thank you, Leonard.

It's good to have you, great to have you!

I laugh.

I need to go home.

Hold on.

He walks to a black town car sitting at the curb, knocks on the window. The window rolls down, he speaks to the driver, shakes his hand, turns to me.

You have a ride.

I walk to the car.

Thanks for the game, dinner, the cash.

That's your signing bonus. You're gonna earn it.

I laugh.

Yeah.

Since I got you to quit, and take a real job, I'll be leaving in the morning.

Safe travels.

Thank you.

When do I start?

Not sure. Somebody will come see you.

And they'll also tell me what I'm supposed to do?

Yeah.

Cool.

See you soon, my son.

Thanks for everything, Leonard.

He nods. I get in the backseat of the car.

I go home.

My mother comes to visit me. My parents live in Tokyo and I don't see them very often. They are responsible for getting me into the treatment center. I haven't always liked them, and I have hurt them over and over and over through the course of my life, but they have always loved me. I am lucky to have them.

My mother sees my apartment, laughs. She asks me where I sleep, where I sit, I tell her the floor. She shakes her head and says not good, James, not good. She calls someone in Michigan, which is where they used to live, they still have a house it sits empty now. She asks the person about furniture in storage, how easy is it to access, she asks if they can send me a bed and a desk and a table. She hangs up, says I'll have a bed and a desk and a table in a few days.

We go downtown. We walk down Michigan Avenue. My mother and father are both from suburban Chicago, met here, were married here. They didn't have any money when they were married, they spent their honeymoon in a downtown hotel. As we walk, my mother points out restaurants they went to, parks where they sat, held hands, kissed, stores where they wandered, looking at things they couldn't afford, hoping someday, someday. It's nice to hear her memories, I like that she's sharing them with me. It feels like a door opening, a door to her, to my father, to their life. It's a door that I have never acknowledged before, a door that I'm happy to step through, a door I'm fortunate to have still be open.

We go to lunch. A fancy place, a place my mother knows and loves, she tries to eat there every time she's in town. We wait for a table, sit, napkins on lap, glasses of water. My Mom starts asking me questions. How are you doing, I'm okay. How are you feeling, depends, I go up and down, way up and way down, mostly I'm down. Is it hard staying sober, yeah it is, every second of every day is a struggle, I know I'll die if I do it, sometimes I feel like I want to die. Do you need help, no, I'll get through it, I gotta believe I'll get through it. She asks about Lilly, I just shake my head. She asks what happened, I just shake my head, say it didn't work out, I don't want to talk about it, can't talk about it. She says that's too bad, I had hoped that would work out for you. I cannot respond.

As we finish our meal, someone approaches our table. I vaguely recognize the person, but can't place him.

James?

Yeah?

David. From school.

I still can't place him, pretend.

Yeah, how you doing?

Good. What are you doing here?

This is my Mom. We're eating lunch.

He looks at my mom.

Nice to meet you.

Mom speaks.

You too.

He looks back at me.

I'm surprised to see you because I heard you were in prison. For popping some cop.

My mom cringes.

Where'd you hear that?

I'm not sure.

As you can see, I'm not.

I guess. You living here now?

Yeah.

You wanna get together sometime?

Sure.

He reaches into his pocket, draws out his wallet.

You still partying?

I shake my head.

No.

He takes a card from his wallet, hands it to me.

If you ever get the urge, call me.

Will do.

See you later.

Yeah.

He walks away. I look at my mom. She speaks.

I hope you never call him.

I won't.

He seemed like an asshole.

I laugh. My mom has never spoken like that around me.

I have no idea who he is. I know I went to school with him, but other than that, nothing.

Good. He's an asshole.

I laugh again. We finish, leave, walk some more. My mom shares more of her memories, I listen, walk further through the door. We see the hotel where they spent their wedding night, a pizza place that my grandfather loved, a department store where my grandmother liked to buy presents. We see a jersey from the Chicago hockey team. My parents went to one of the team's games the night after they were married. They couldn't afford to do anything else, it was a big evening for them.

It starts to get dark, close to the time my mom will leave. Before she leaves, she wants to buy me some plates, forks, spoons, knives. Right now I use paper and plastic that I get from take-out restaurants. She thinks having normal possessions like plates, forks, spoons, knives will help normalize my existence, help me adjust more easily. We go to a store, look around, everything I like is black. My mom laughs, thinks it's strange that I like black plates and black utensils. I tell her that as much as she wants me to normalize, there are some parts of me that will always be a bit off. She laughs. We get all of the beautiful, semi-normal, black items.

We go back to my apartment. Put everything in the cabinets above my sink. My Mom has a car coming to pick her up, take her to the airport, she says she needs to go. I thank her for the day, a great day, probably the best day I have ever had with her. She smiles, starts to cry, she's happy, happy I'm alive, happy I'm becoming human, happy we can spend a day together without screaming. I give her a hug, walk her out, open the car door for her. The car pulls away.

I meet a man underneath the train tracks he calls himself a ragamuffin, the Ragamuffin King. He says he wanders the world looking for rags, beautiful rags, magnificent rags. I bow to him, the Ragamuffin King.

I go to coffee with Mickey. I am the only straight man in the coffee shop. Mickey introduces me to his friends as his hetero buddy James. Mickey has a new boyfriend. An attorney who says he loves him, loves his paintings, wants him to do whatever he wants, just be happy. And he is, Mickey is happy.

I meet a man at a bar while I'm waiting for my friends. He says he's forty-five, he looks like he's twenty-five I ask him if he has a secret he says never get angry and be as immature as you can for as long as you can get away with it. A man sitting next to him laughs and says that's bullshit, the great secret is eat food and drink beer till you drop.

I see an old friend. He and I used to drink together, do drugs together, deal drugs together. He cleaned up for a girl, a girl he lives with now, a girl he loves, a girl he wants to marry. We laugh about old times, good times, bad times, he got out before they got really bad. We go to a punk show at an old abandoned bowling alley. The band plays on one of the neglected lanes, they're young and loud and they can't play their instruments and the songs are awful and they look like they're having a great time. We move into the pit, the fray, the moving circle of young angry men in black jackets and combat boots throwing elbows, high-stepping and slamming into each other. We get hit, we fall, get knocked around a bit. It's fun every now and then, getting knocked around a bit.

I meet a third man he's an old man he trips in the street he falls and I help him up, walk him to the curb. He shakes my hand says keep the faith, young man. I ask him what that means, he says keep running and don't let them catch you.

I sleep during the day. I still dream about drinking and drugs. Sometimes I wake to a hang-over, sometimes I wake to a trickle of blood from my nose, sometimes I wake scared and shaking.

I read, go to museums and visit Lilly in the afternoon. Sometimes I read to her, sometimes I talk to her, sometimes I just sit and remember the times, remember the times, remember the times.

I go out at night. Go to bars with my friends. I drink cola, smoke cigarettes, shoot pool, talk, sometimes don't talk, just sit and watch. I start to laugh more and more easily, start to feel more comfortable.

When the bars close, I walk, walk randomly through the empty city, walk among the buildings, through parks, along the lake. I sit on benches, the wind and cold hurt me, numb me, I stop feeling. There is peace in pain so overwhelming that it shuts down all feeling. It is the only peace I know.

I go back to my apartment.

Sleep.

Dream.

It's morning the phone rings. A man a voice I don't know tells me to meet him at a local diner.

I walk to the diner, sit in a booth, drink coffee, wait. A man walks into the diner he's in his late-twenties, clean-shaven, dark hair, well-dressed, but not flashy, a gold watch. He stops in front of my booth, speaks.

Your name James?

Yeah.

He sits down across from me.

You got a good memory?

Yeah.

You better.

Why?

This is how it's gonna work.

He reaches into his pocket, pulls out a small pager, pushes it across the table.

Keep the pager on you at all times. You'll get a page, call the number. Always use a payphone, don't use the same one more than twice. When you call, you'll speak to someone who will give you instructions. Never write those instructions down, keep absolutely no record of them. If you fuck them up, it'll be your problem, so make sure you've got them before you hang up. When you do hang up, memorize the number on the pager, delete the number, follow the instructions. If you're driving, drive three miles over the speed limit, never faster, never slower. Always check the car to make sure all of the lights are working. If you get pulled over, don't say a fucking word. Ask for a lawyer and wait, tell the lawyer to get in touch with your friend Leonard. If the job goes well, and if you don't fuck up, when the job is done, call the original number to confirm. If you ever get a page that says 911, immediately stop whatever you're doing. Take whatever you're moving and put it in a safe place that is not your home. If it's a car, put it in a secure lot. If you get a page that says 411, stop whatever you're doing and wait for further instructions. Any questions?

No.

Do you want me to repeat what I just told you?

No.

Have a nice day.

The man stands and leaves. I order more coffee, some eggs, bacon and toast. I smoke a cigarette, read the paper, wait for the food. It arrives, I start eating, the pager goes off, two loud piercing beeps, two more, two more. I stand pick up the pager, walk to a payphone in the back of the diner. I drop in my coins, dial the number, there's a male voice after one ring.

Hello.

I got paged.

First timer.

Yeah.

You got a pen?

No, no pen.

Good. Good memory?

Yeah.

You better.

Voice gives me an address in a nearby suburb. Tells me to knock on the door, I will be handed a suitcase. Put the suitcase in the trunk of a white car sitting in the driveway, the keys are under the driver's side floormat. I am given a second address, which is in Milwaukee. Drive the car to the Milwaukee address, remove the suitcase from the trunk. Knock on the door, ask for a man named Paul, give him the suitcase, don't give it to anyone else, Paul is waiting for it. Drive the car back to the suburban Chicago address, leave it in the driveway, keys under the mat. Call to confirm.

I have the voice repeat both addresses. He asks me if I need them again, I tell him no, I got it. He says good, hangs up on me. I hang up, return to my booth, finish my breakfast, leave.

I take a commuter train north into the moneyed suburbs of Chicago. It's late morning, the train is almost empty. I'm nervous. My heart is racing, hands slightly shaking. I stare out the window, try to take deep breaths, try to stay calm. The few other passengers I see all look like FBI agents, middle-aged men in dark suits, and they all appear to be glancing at me, watching me. I tell myself that's bullshit, that I'm being paranoid, that nobody here gives a shit why I'm on this train, but I don't feel any better. Arrest scenarios roll through my mind I can see the cuffs, feel them on my skin, hear the cop reciting Miranda, smell the back of the car, feel a slight breeze as the door slams shut. I can imagine sitting with a lawyer, discussing my case, debating the merits of a plea agreement, trying to figure out ways to bring my sentence down. I can remember being processed, putting my few meager belongings into an envelope, changing into a jumpsuit, donning shackles, rambling down concrete and steel halls. My cell awaits me. I'm fucking nervous.

The train arrives at my stop, I get off, there are a couple of cabs waiting, I get inside one of them, give the cabbie the street name, he drives. We move through quiet neighborhoods full of large houses with wide lawns, manicured bushes, alarm system signs, foreign cars in the driveway.

I have him drop me on a corner. I start looking at the tastefully mounted numbers on porches and doors. I find my way to a large stone house with a white car in the driveway. I walk to the door, knock, wait, my heart is pounding. The door opens it's a middle-age man wearing silk pajamas. He does have a suitcase. He speaks.

Can I help you?

I'm here to pick something up.

What?

I wasn't told what.

You sure you got the right address?

My hands start shaking.

Yeah I'm sure.

I start to panic.

I don't think you do.

Panic.

This is the address I was given.

Panic.

By who?

I'm not at liberty to say.

This sounds awfully strange. You come to my door to pick something up, but you don't know what it is, and you won't tell me who sent you?

I'm just following directions.

Do you want me to call the police?

No sir.

They come quick in this town.

There's no need to call the police, sir. I must have made a mistake. I'll leave.

I turn, start walking away, can't run too obvious, I've got to get out of here now, how the fuck did I fuck this up, I've got to get out of here now now now.

Kid.

I stop turn around.

I'm just fucking with you. I heard you were new and thought I'd have some fun.

I smile, not because I think it's funny, if I could I'd hit this motherfucker, but because I'm relieved, and the smile is a nervous reaction. I walk back to the door. The man reaches behind and sets a battered brown suitcase in front of me.

You scared the shit out of me.

I couldn't tell.

You did.

You handled yourself well, stayed cool, no panic. If this ever happens for real, do exactly the same thing.

I hope it never happens.

Don't fuck up and it won't.

I pick up the suitcase.

Have a nice day.

You too.

I turn, walk toward the car. The suitcase is heavy, heavier than I expected, fifty pounds, maybe sixty. I hear the man shut the door behind me, I open the driver's door of the car, reach under the mat for the keys, find them. I put the suitcase in the trunk, get behind the wheel. As I pull out of the driveway I see the man is standing at one of his windows. He's smiling, waving at me.

my friend leonard

I know the highway is to the west I start driving west. I take the map out of the glove compartment, look at it. Interstate 94 takes me straight up, if I keep going where I'm going I'll run into it. I set down the map, light a cigarette, settle in for the ride.

The ride is easy, boring. I smoke cigarettes, listen to the radio, occasionally sing along to a cheesy love song or a heavy metal power ballad or one of the many classic rock anthems. I try to find a station that plays punk, so I can yell and scream and shout obscenities, but I can't find one. Every fifteen minutes or so, I shout obscenities anyway.

I see Milwaukee in the distance. It's a small city, an old city, one that hasn't experienced any form of renewal. When I was a kid I used to watch a TV show about two women who worked in a beer factory in Milwaukee, aside from that I don't know shit about it.

I pull off the highway, look for a gas station. I pull in, ask for directions get them, start driving again, find the address, it is another beautiful neighborhood huge houses sitting along the coast of Lake Michigan. I pull into a long driveway. A row of hedges runs along one side of it, a yard the size of a football field runs along the other side. A massive stone house sits at the end, it looks like it belongs in England, Ireland or Scotland, not Milwaukee. I stop in front of it, get out of the car, get the suitcase, carry it to the front door. I knock and wait. I hear someone behind the door, the door cracks open, I hear a voice.

I'm Paul.

I cannot see a person.

Leave the case and get out of here.

I set the suitcase on the step. Paul tosses an envelope out, it lands at my feet. I pick it up, look inside it's filled with cash, I leave. The drive back to Chicago is simple, just smoke and listen to tunes and swear. I put the car back in the driveway, take the train back to the city. On the way back to my apartment, I stop at a payphone, call the original number on the pager, confirm delivery.

I'm shooting pool for money. Playing against a guy named Tony I've played him before I lose to him every single time. I'm in good shape this time, shooting at the eight ball, he's got three to go.

I'm in a bar called The Local Option. There's a front room, a back room. A bar runs along one wall of the front room, the pool table is in the back room. My friends are here. They're getting drunk.

As I wait for my shot, I hear my pager go off. I tell Tony I have to make a call, ask him if he'll wait for me, he laughs, takes the money off the rail, where it's supposed to sit until someone wins. I speak.

I'm getting that back next game.

He laughs.

We'll see.

I leave the bar. Walk down the street, look for a phone. I find one outside a dry cleaner, it's quiet I can hear. I look at the pager dial the number it's not a number I recognize. I wait, Leonard answers.

Ha-ha!

What's up Leonard?

What's up? What's up? My son successfully completed his first mission. That's what the fuck is up.

I laugh.

How'd it go? Tell me how it went.

It was easy. I picked up the case, drove it to Milwaukee and dropped it off, went home.

That's it?

That's it.

I heard they were gonna have some fun with you. Shake you up a bit.

Yeah, that happened. The guy who gave me the case fucked with me, pretended I was in the wrong place.

Leonard laughs.

I bet you shit.

Sort of.

You meet Paul?

No.

Good. You're never supposed to actually meet anyone. That way if something happens, you can't testify against them.

I thought you said nothing would ever happen.

It won't, it won't. I'm just saying if. If, my son, never happens.

I hope so.

And forget you ever met that old fucker in his pajamas.

How'd you know he was in his pajamas?

He never leaves his house, and he always wears pajamas. That's how I know. He's been forgotten.

Any idea what was in the case?

Nope. And I don't want to know.

Take a guess.

No.

Come on.

No.

What do you think it weighed?

I don't know.

Guess.

Fifty, sixty pounds.

Fifty.

Okay.

You know a million dollars in cash in twenty-dollar bills weighs twenty-one pounds?

I did not know that.

And a common suitcase weighs about six.

I didn't know that either.

You learn something new every day.

Thank you for that bit of knowledge, Leonard.

You get your money?

Paul threw me the envelope. I wasn't sure it was mine because there was so much.

Helluva lot better than seven fucking bucks an hour.

I laugh. The envelope had five thousand dollars in it.

Yeah, much better.

You did good, my son. You did good. I'm proud of you.

Thank you, Leonard.

You're doing okay otherwise?

Yeah. I was shooting pool in a bar when you paged.

Well go back, have fun. Say hello to your friends if you're with them.

They'll be happy to hear it.

I'll come visit again soon, my son.

I'll look forward to it.

Keep up the good work.

I laugh.

Thanks.

I hang up, head back to the bar, lose three more times to Tony. I wander for a few hours, spend a few hours with Lilly. I tell her about my new job. I know she wouldn't approve, she'd say you're moving too close to your old life, you gotta leave that shit behind. I tell her I know there are dangers, but I feel strong, each day I feel stronger, each day I don't drink or use I am stronger. I tell her it would be different if she was around. I tell her she made her decisions, and now I'm on my own, and I will make my decisions.

I take a car to St. Louis. I don't know what's in the car, if there's anything in the car. Nobody tells me and I don't ask. I drive three miles over the speed limit. I leave the car in a shopping mall parking lot.

I move briefcases from the north side of Chicago to the south side of Chicago. I move briefcases from the south side to the north side. I ride the El train back and forth. I buy a set of nice clothing khakis black leather shoes a white oxford a blue sport coat, so that I look like a young ambitious commuter, so that people think I'm a law student or an apprentice currency trader or a young executive at a large multinational corporation, all of which, in a certain ridiculous way, I am.

I go back to Milwaukee.

Detroit.

Rockford, Illinois.

Sometimes I receive envelopes, sometimes I don't. When I do, the amounts vary, as high as five thousand, as low as five hundred, usually somewhere around three thousand. I don't have a bank account, so I keep the cash hidden around my apartment. I put the bulk of it under my mattress. I put more in a plastic Ziploc bag and place the bag in the tank of my toilet. I put more in a Captain Crunch cereal box, I bury the bills beneath the crunchy nuggets. I put the rest in an empty box of dishwasher detergent that sits beneath my sink. I never carry much cash with me because I don't want to draw attention to myself.

My friends ask me what I'm doing, ask me why I left my bar job. I tell them I left because it was too much to work in a bar too much temptation and torture. They ask how being in bars with them is any different I tell them when I was working I had to stand there I was bored out of my skull the boredom made me want to drink. When I'm in a bar with them I can occupy myself, talk, laugh, shoot pool, drink cola after cola after cola, that it is easier to be distracted. I tell them in a certain way it is easier when I'm with them because I see how they act when they're drunk and it reminds me of who I don't want to be and how I don't want to behave. They ask me how I'm making money I tell them I don't have much and what I do have is borrowed. They ask what I'm doing with my time, I tell them I'm trying to make it pass. And that at least is true. Sometimes all I want is for my time to pass.

My phone rings. It is morning. I'm smoking cigarettes, staring at the fucking ceiling. I pick it up.

Hello?

My son, I'm coming to town. Good times are on their way.

What's up, Leonard?

I'm up, you're up, that's what the fuck is up.

When are you coming?

This afternoon.

You want me to meet you at the airport?

Remember that steakhouse we went to with your friends?

Yeah.

Meet me there. Six o'clock.

Okay.

And call some of your friends. See if we can meet them out after we eat.

Okay.

You want anything from Vegas?

Can you bring me a showgirl who'll make all my troubles go away?

I actually can.

I laugh.

That's okay.

You sure?

Yeah.

If you change your mind, I'll be here for another hour.

Okay.

See you at six.

Yeah.

I hang up, smoke, stare at the fucking ceiling. The ceiling doesn't have much to say to me this morning, can't tell me why I can't get off my bed, can't tell me why my sorrow is starting to feel like rage, can't tell me how I'm supposed to deal with it, can't tell me shit. I smoke, stare, wait, wait, wait, nothing.

Sometime in the afternoon I get up, take a shower, pull some cash from beneath my mattress, put on my nice clothes. I call my friends see what they're doing tonight they're going to a pool hall/bowling alley, I tell them I'll meet them around nine. I leave, start walking it's not as cold, spring is slowly asserting itself. It's harder to become numb, I have to walk longer, wear less, it still doesn't always work, my body has adjusted to the cold. It takes an hour to get to the restaurant. When I walk in the host greets me, says nice to see you again, sir. I ask if Leonard is here he says yes, let me show you to his table.

We walk into the restaurant it's early so it is almost empty. Leonard is sitting in the corner, facing out, he sees me stands.

My son! **My son!** MY SON!

I laugh.

Hello, Leonard.

Come sit, come sit.

The host guides me to the table, pulls out my chair. I sit down, I am also facing out. Host walks away. I speak.

So it's true.

What's true?

Men like you never sit with your back to the door.

He laughs.

No way.

No way what?

Back to the door. That's bullshit.

Doesn't look like bullshit to me.

I'm a people person, a motherfucking people person. I sit this way so I can see the people.

The people?

Yeah, the people. I love them. That's me.

I laugh again.

Where's Snapper?

I left him at home.

Why?

This isn't a business trip. I just came to see you.

Thanks.

Thought it would be good to spend time together just us.

That sounds cool.

How's life?

I laugh.

Which part of it?

Which part do you want to talk about?

I like my new job.

I knew you would. What are you doing with all the money?

Hiding it.

Under your mattress?

Yeah.

In a cereal box?

Yeah.

In the toilet tank?

Yeah.

You probably thought you were being real sneaky.

I did.

Not good, my son. Everybody knows those spots.

I also got some in a dishwasher detergent box. Keep it under the sink. You know that one?

No, never heard that one before.

If I get robbed, at least I'll have that.

You're not gonna get robbed. I'm gonna teach you how to deal with the cash.

Okay.

He reaches into his pocket, draws out a black leather wallet, passes it to me.

There's an Illinois driver's license in there. It's a valid license, and it will register on the State's computers. I got a picture of you that I took at the treatment center and doctored it a bit, it looks real. I also invented a name for you.

I take the license out of the wallet, look at it. It looks real.

James Testardo?

Yeah. Testardo means stubborn in Italian. I thought it would be funny if you could call yourself Jimmy Testardo.

I laugh.

Okay.

The address on the license is an empty house owned by a shell company I am very very loosely associated with, though there is no record of the association. Go to a bank, the bigger and more anonymous the bank the better, and get a safe deposit box. Whenever you go there, wear a hat or sunglasses or something that slightly alters your appearance. Put your money in the account, and put it in slowly and in manageable amounts, three, four, five thousand at a time. Never approach ten thousand, because at ten thousand the bank is required to notify the IRS of the deposit. Once it's in there, take it out in cash as need be. Don't pay your bills with checks, always use money orders purchased with cash. If you start to accumulate too much, go buy something expensive, something in the three, four, five thousand range. Buy it with a credit card. If you don't have one, I can get one for you, in the Testardo name if you want it that way. Pay the credit card off in several installments using money orders purchased with cash. When you do buy something, I would advise buying small things, like watches or art or silver, jewelry, rare books, and don't go showing it off to people. Buy things you can sell for cash if you're ever in a jam, that can be moved quickly and easily. Use common sense and don't draw attention to yourself and you'll be fine.

I think I can handle that.

I know you can. You got any questions?

No.

You wanna order?

Sure.

Leonard motions for the waiter. We order lobsters and filets, creamed spinach and baked potatoes. We drink water, I drink cola, Leonard drinks diet cola. We talk about the upcoming baseball season, talk about our friends from the treatment center. One was a fugitive, he was caught and sentenced to life in prison, no parole. Another was beaten to death outside of a bar. A third is missing. A fourth committed suicide by shotgun. A few are still okay, still holding on, still struggling. I tell Leonard I spoke with our friend Miles, who is a Federal judge in New Orleans. He's still clean, feeling strong, taking care of himself. He's happy to be home, reunited with his wife and children, who he feared he might lose because of his alcoholism. Leonard smiles, asks me to tell Miles hello. He says he likes Miles, wishes he could stay in touch with him, but their respective positions prevent any sort of significant relationship.

Our food arrives, we eat. I ask Leonard about his ongoing quest to play golf on the Connecticut course where his father worked. He laughs, it's a bitter laugh, a laugh that masks anger and pain, he says no luck. I say sorry, he shrugs, says that's the way the world works, that people with privilege guard their privilege, that people take care of their own kind, that there are certain institutions that are exclusive whether it is right or not. He says it works the same way with his own organization, that only Italians can be full members, that there are no exceptions. I ask him what he's going to do he laughs again, the laugh different now anger mixed with menace, he says country club members do not take blood oaths, that there are certainly some that misbehave cheat on their wives sleep with whores run up gambling debts he is going to find one of them and have a conversation with that person and he will get in and play the course, just as his dying father made him promise he would.

We finish, our food is taken away. Leonard suggests we go to the bar for coffee and cigars. We stand as we walk away from the table he motions to the host we walk into the bar settle into two large plush comfortable chairs the host follows speaks to the bartender who walks into the bar's humidor. The bartender returns, hands the host a small box, the host walks toward us opens the box speaks.

Would you like a Cuban cigar?

Leonard smiles.

Matter of fact I would. Thank you.

Leonard reaches into the box chooses two cigars the host walks away. Leonard takes a cutter from his jacket, carefully cuts the cigars, hands one to me, lights them.

You remember how to smoke?

Yeah.

I take a drag, swallow. The tobacco is sweet, strong, my mouth is immediately overwhelmed by it. I prefer cigarette tobacco. Leonard speaks.

These are good.

If you say so.

If you ever smoke a shitty one you'll be able to tell the difference.

I only smoke them with you.

Then you'll never smoke a shitty one.

Without having ordered it, coffee arrives. I take a sip, it's hot, strong, I feel it immediately, my heart starts racing.

Time for the serious talk, my son.

What's the serious talk?

I want to know how you're doing.

I'm doing fine.

What's that mean?

I don't know.

So you're not fine.

No, all things considered, I think I'm better than fine, much better than fine.

Explain.

I'm holding on, getting through the days, feeling stronger, feeling more comfortable with myself. I don't know how I'm doing it really, but I am, and each day is a step toward some form of normalcy and security, a step toward having a real life. If I was in hell before, I'm in purgatory now, and I feel like I can get to whatever's next. I still can't sleep right, I still have cravings all day every fucking day, I'm still nervous around and uncomfortable around people, and I still feel scared sometimes, but I'm okay with all of it. I've accepted that all this shit is just part of the price for my former life.

What are you scared of?

I don't know.

Yes you do.

When you've spent your whole life drinking and doing drugs, you learn how to do everything in a fucked-up way. I'm having to learn how to do everything over, and sometimes it's scary, and most of the time I feel scared.

If it makes you feel any better, I'm scared all the time too.

I laugh.

A big old tough guy like you? I don't believe it.

I used to think I was tough, but I've realized I wasn't. I was fragile, and I wore thick fucking armor, and I hurt people so they couldn't hurt me, and I thought that was what being tough was, but it isn't. What we're doing now is tough. Rebuilding, changing, having to deal with the damage, having to face the fear. If I make it through, then you can call me fucking tough.

You'll make it through.

We both will.

We'll see.

How you doing with your loss?

I miss her.

Did you think you wouldn't?

No, but I didn't think I would either, because I didn't think this was gonna happen. I was prepared for something else.

But it did.

Yeah, it did, and it fucking sucks and I miss her.

What do you miss?

I miss everything. I miss talking to her, hearing about her day. I miss her voice all gravelly and smoky, I miss hearing her laugh, I miss getting her letters, writing her letters. I miss her eyes, and the smell of her hair, and the way her breath tasted. I fucking miss everything. I miss knowing she was around, because it helped me to know that she was around, that someone like her existed. I guess most of all, I miss knowing I would see her again. I always thought I'd see her again.

You gotta respect what she did and that'll help you.

I don't know why the fuck you keep saying that.

It's true.

That's fucking crazy.

No it's not.

She killed herself, Leonard, threw in the fucking towel, and I feel sadness and confusion and a lot of hate, hate for myself for not being able to prevent it, and hate for her for actually doing it, but I don't feel respect.

You remember how she used to say that a second of freedom is worth more than a lifetime of bondage.

Yeah.

She chose freedom, and you should respect her decision and admire her for being brave enough to follow through with it. It wasn't your kind of freedom, or my kind of freedom, but it was hers.

Suicide isn't freedom.

If all you feel is pain, and there's nothing but drugs to make it go away, and your choice is either living as addict or going out on your own terms, there's only one choice, and that's going out.

How about the third choice, which is dealing with the pain?

Not everybody can do it.

I look away, shake my head, clench my jaw. Leonard speaks.

You ever heard of the five stages of grief?

I look back.

No. What are they?

I don't know, I've just heard of them. Saw something about them on some ladies' show. I'm figuring you're going through them, and at some point you'll agree with me.

Fuck you, Leonard, and fuck your five stages of grief.

He laughs.

You want to get out of here?

Yeah.

He motions for the check. When it arrives, I reach for it. He speaks.

What are you doing?

I'm getting it tonight.

I reach into my pocket, get my cash.

No, you're not.

Yes, I am.

Unacceptable.

Not open to debate.

I pay for dinner. It's part of what I do.

Not tonight.

I have more money than you.

I look at the check, start counting the money.

You remember when you told me that when someone wants to do some-thing nice for you, that you should smile and say thank you.

That only applies when I'm doing something nice for you.

Smile and say thank you, Leonard.

I put the cash in the check, close it. Leonard smiles.

Thank you, my son.

I stand.

Let's go.

Leonard stands, we leave. We take a cab north to meet my friends. We get out of the cab, walk into an old time bowling alley/pool hall. There are three rooms. One has a long oak bar lined with stools, the bar is probably a hundred years old. Another has the bowling alley, five lanes, all of them manual. Two men crouch at the end of the lanes and replace the pins when they fall and roll the balls back to the bowlers. The third room is large, open, has twelve-foot ceilings. There are ten pool tables in two lines of five that run the length of the room. Overhead lamps hang above each of the tables. Stools and bar tables line the edges of the room.

Leonard and I walk into the pool room, look for my friends. They're standing around a table in the corner, we walk over to them.

Though most of them have met him already, I introduce Leonard to everyone. He kisses each of the girls' hands, tells them they look beautiful. He shakes hands with the guys, says nice to meet you, nice to see you again. When the introductions are over, he motions to the waitress tells her bring more of everything, bring a pitcher of cola and two glasses, and keep it coming all night, just keep it coming.

We shoot pool, my friends drink, we smoke cigarettes, Leonard smokes a cigar, we laugh, laugh, laugh. We start shooting pool for money, five, ten bucks a game. Leonard is a disaster, loses three games. The rest of us are more or less equal, split the games, split the money. When Leonard's not playing, he's dancing with the girls, twirling them around, teaching them fancy steps, lathering them with compliments. The night moves on, my friends get more drunk. My friend Kevin suggests we raise the stakes, we agree raise them to twenty a game. Leonard starts playing again, destroys every single one of us, giggles to himself as he does it. I ask him what the fuck happened, he laughs, says he used to hustle pool and wanted to see if he could still do it. I laugh, say yeah, you can still do it, now stop, my friends aren't made of money.

Leonard stops playing, gives everyone their money back, tells them he used to hustle pool for cash, offers each of us a couple of tips. He starts dancing with the girls again. My friend Scott, who is bombed, walks over to me. He looks pissed. He speaks.

You better tell your buddy to stop dancing with my girlfriend.

He's harmless.

I don't like the way he's fucking dancing with her.

I can promise you he doesn't mean anything.

I don't care. Tell him to fucking stop.

Scott is a big man, six foot three well over two hundred pounds, and he has a bad temper. I know Leonard's not interested in his girlfriend, but I don't want any problems. I walk over to where Leonard and Scott's girlfriend, whose name is Jessica, are dancing. Scott follows me.

Leonard.

Leonard spins Jessica.

Leonard.

Pulls her in, gives her a dip.

Leonard.

He looks over at me.

Just a second.

Scott steps around me. I try to stop him, he pushes me off.

Stop dancing with my girlfriend, motherfucker.

He pulls Jessica away. Jessica looks shocked, Leonard looks shocked.

No offense here, friend. No offense.

I'll kick your fucking ass if you touch her again.

You're misunderstanding this situation. I mean no disrespect.

Scott has no idea who Leonard is or what he does, has no idea the problem he's about to create for himself. I step toward him.

You gotta calm down, Scott.

He turns to me.

Fuck you.

Turns to Leonard.

And fuck you. I will kick your ass if you so much as look at her again.

People around have stopped playing, are watching.

You should watch yourself, kid. That temper is going to get you into trouble.

It's going to get you into trouble, old man.

Something in Leonard, who until now has been calm, changes. His face goes still, his eyes narrow, his body tenses. I have seen him like this before, once when I first met him in rehab, the other time when we got in a fight with two of the other patients there, one of whom was later killed.

You are making a big mistake, friend. You should turn now and leave.

Jessica starts pulling on Scott's arm and saying come on, come on, let's go. Scott stares at Leonard.

I'll fuck you up.

Leonard does not respond, just stares. Jessica pulls Scott away, they start walking toward the door, she's obviously upset, looks like she's going to cry.

I step toward Leonard.

Sorry about that.

Your friend shouldn't drink so much.

He can get a bit out of control.

Think I'm allowed to dance with the other girls?

I laugh.

Yeah, I think you are.

Good. Let's get back to the good times. That's why I came, for the moth-erfucking good times.

I laugh. Leonard walks over to Adrienne, asks her to dance.

She says yes.

I meet Leonard for breakfast, a late breakfast, we stayed out until four, Leonard dancing with the girls, me shooting pool with the guys, good times, good times.

Leonard asks me if I've spoken to Scott, I say no, I think it's best to leave it alone, he doesn't need to know about the potential consequences of his actions. Telling him would mean he would have to know what Leonard does for a living. Leonard agrees with me.

We leave the hotel. The sun is out. It's bright, warm, the streets are crowded with happy people, happy because winter is disappearing, happy because it's the first nice day in months. We walk down Michigan Avenue, occasionally stopping to look into the windows of expensive stores.

Leonard loves clothing, loves expensive clothing, loves tailored wool suits, handmade shoes, shirts made from Egyptian cotton, silk ties. He says that most people don't like wearing suits, and are uncomfortable in them, because they buy shitty, cheap, ill-fitting suits made from poor materials. He says a properly cut suit, made from quality materials, is the most comfortable thing one can wear. I tell him I prefer jeans and t-shirts, wool socks and combat boots, he laughs, says if you were my genetic son, you would think otherwise.

We end up at the art museum, the Art Institute of Chicago. We walk through the galleries of European paintings, we move through them in chronological order. We see six Giovanni di Paolo altarpiece panels depicting St. John the Baptist, who looks like he's starving, wandering through a wasteland his golden halo shining. We see a bright silvery El Greco of the Virgin ascending on a crescent moon. We see eight gloomy Rembrandts, stern men in capes and feathered hats staring into a black distance, we see desperate Rinaldo being enchanted by the sorceress Armida in her billowing shawl as painted by Tiepolo. We see Turner, Manet, Corot, Monet,

Renoir, Caillebotte. We see a dancing Degas, a strolling Seurat, a brooding van Gogh, once with his ear, once without. We see a Tahitian Gauguin and Leonard starts to cry, he just stands in front of it and he cries no words just heavy tears running down his cheeks. I stand with him, stare at the painting, which is of a young Tahitian woman, supposedly Gauguin's mistress, wearing a simple cotton dress, white flowers in her black hair, a fan in her hand. I don't speak, just let Leonard cry, he starts speaking. Gauguin was a stockbroker in Paris, married, had five kids. One day he came home from work and told his wife he was leaving, that he was through supporting the family, that he had had enough. Just like that he fucking took off. He said he had always felt that he was a painter, so he moved into a rat-infested shithole and he started painting. His wife begged him to come back, his bosses told him he was insane, he didn't care, he was following his heart. He left Paris, moved to Rouen, went from Rouen to Arles, from Arles to Tahiti. He was searching for peace, contentment, trying to fill that fucking hole he felt inside, and he believed he could fill it. He died in Tahiti, blind and crazy from syphilis, but he did it. He filled his fucking hole, made beautiful work, made beautiful, beautiful work.

Leonard wipes his tears away.

It takes a brave man to walk away, to care so much that he doesn't care about anything else, to be willing to obey what he feels inside, to be willing to suffer the consequences of living for himself. Every time I stand before his work it makes me cry, and I cry because I'm proud of him, and happy for him, and because I admire him.

Leonard takes a deep breath, wipes away the last of his tears, turns and walks out of the room, out of the museum.

Leonard leaves, goes back to Las Vegas. My life goes back to normal, or what I consider normal, which is as normal as life has ever been for me. I go to Kansas City.
Back to Detroit.
Indianapolis.
Milwaukee, three times to Milwaukee.
Northside. Southside.
Minneapolis.
Sometimes I drive, sometimes I ride the El, sometimes I take a bus. My friends start to wonder why I occasionally disappear I tell them that I need to be alone.
I spend my days walking endlessly walking. Spring arrives I don't have to wear a jacket the streets are crowded outdoor cafes full hot dog stands open on corners. I eat a lot of hot dogs. Extra mustard, hold the relish. When I'm not walking, I'm reading, for a few hours a day I sit and read. At home on benches on the grass in parks on the stairs of the museum I sit and read. I read the classics, or what are called the classics, try to catch up on what I missed in school.
I start to sleep more. I have fewer dreams. When the dreams come they aren't as bad, I don't wake up shaking, bleeding or vomiting, I don't wake up screaming, moaning or crying.
I gain weight. I look less like a drug addict and more like a poorly dressed young man.

I go to a punk club to see a band called The Vandals. I go with my friend Chris, who used to deal coke with me. We want to see them perform some of their hits, which include the classics *Anarchy Burger, A Gun for Christmas* and *Tastes Like Chicken*. They do not disappoint us. The guitars are loud and fast, the drums booming, the singer is on, his vocals moving effortlessly between yelling and very loud yelling. We march in the circle, high-stepping, throwing elbows, occasionally jumping into the middle and getting slammed.

At one of the breaks, Danny and Kevin show up with a group of girls. Danny grew up outside of Chicago, in one of the wealthiest suburbs along the North Shore. He has known the girls, who are all well-dressed and have nice hairdos and wear diamonds and pearls in their ears, since childhood. They look horribly out of place and uncomfortable.

Chris and I walk over to them, say hello, their names are Molly, Rory, Mila and Brooke. I've met three of them before, though my memories of the meetings are faint. I ask them if they want a drink one of them asks me what kind of beer is available I tell her cheap beer. She laughs, says okay, one cheap beer please. I look at the other girls they agree, they'd each like one cheap beer.

I walk to the bar, Kevin comes with me. I speak.

What's up?

Nothing.

What are they doing here?

Danny wanted to bring them.

And they agreed?

I don't think they knew where they were going.

How long do you think they'll last?

They'll take one sip of the beer and leave.

I laugh. I order the beers, wait for them get them turn around. Three of the four girls are still there, talking with Danny and Chris, looking at the club's other patrons, young men with tattoos, shaved heads and Mohawks, like they're zoo animals. I walk back, hand out the cans, I ask if the fourth girl left. I hear a voice behind me.

My name isn't fourth girl, it's Brooke.

Okay.

I went to use the restroom.

I chuckle.

How was it?

It was disgusting, and it was also out of order.

There's a urinal in the men's room.

No thanks.

She takes the last can out of my hand, steps around me, moves toward Danny, starts talking to him. I turn back to the other three start talking to them. One of them, her name is Molly, asks me how I've been and I laugh, tell her it's been a rough couple of years. She says she heard, was surprised when Danny told her they were meeting me tonight. I ask her how she's been, she says good, she's working for an interior design company and going to school for architecture. As I talk to her, I keep glancing at Brooke. Her hair is blond almost white, her eyes are ice-blue. She's tan, looks like she's been in the sun somewhere other than Chicago, she has pouty lips perfect teeth wears little makeup. I glance, I catch her glancing at me. I step away from Molly and toward Danny and Brooke steps away from Danny, goes to talk to Molly. I smile, know the little game that is being played here, a game that amuses me, that I haven't played for a long time. I step back and forth, she steps away every time I'm near her. She knows what I'm doing, doesn't acknowledge it, just steps away, steps away. The music starts again, Chris and I move back into the circle. We throw more elbows, get slammed, sing-along to all the hits. I know Brooke is watching me, I don't look toward her, know that not looking will frustrate her.

The music ends. Danny suggests we go to another bar, everyone but Chris and me are anxious to get out of this dump. We agree to leave pile into a couple of cabs I purposefully sit next to Brooke light a cigarette and ignore her.

We go to the Local Option. Our other friends are there, some other people we went to school with. Everyone is in the back room shooting pool I lay quarters down on the edge of the felt next game is mine. I shoot pool and drink cola and smoke cigarettes for the rest of the night and Brooke and I both work very hard to ignore each other.

When the bar closes I leave start walking home. I walk alone my friends take cabs. For the first time in several hours I think about Lilly, I have never gone so long without thinking of her. I feel guilty, as if I've done something wrong, as if I have somehow betrayed her. I turn away from home and I walk to her and I tell her I'm sorry and I cry.

I hate myself for losing her.

I hate her for leaving me.

I don't have any answers.

Two nights later I see Brooke again she's with Danny I don't acknowledge her don't say a single word to her. I'm not playing a game, I am trying to be loyal, to be faithful, to honor Lilly's memory.

The next night I'm at the bar I see her again. She's with one of her
friends, someone I don't know. She walks over to me, speaks.

Hi.

I nod.

You can't say hi to me?

I can.

I'm waiting.

Hi.

How are you?

Fine.

I turn, walk away, walk into the bathroom it's empty. I open a stall door
close the toilet sit down on the lid. I hold up my hands, they're shaking. I
light a cigarette, it doesn't calm me. My heart is hammering, I'm nauseous,
dizzy. I put my head in my hands, close my eyes, take deep breaths. This
shouldn't be happening, I'm not ready for this to happen and I don't want
it to happen. I want to be with Lilly. I want to be alone. I'm safe alone and
I can't be hurt alone. My heart is hammering. She could hurt me.

I stand walk out look through the bar she's gone. Part of me is relieved,
part of me disappointed. I'm still rattled, my hands are in my pockets still
shaking. I leave start walking. I want to talk to Lilly, need to talk to her,
I'm scared to talk to her. I walk for an hour two three think. I buy flowers
red roses at a 24-hour grocery store. I lay them down, sit beneath them.

I speak.

Hi.

I miss you.

I'm trying not to, but I do. I miss you.

I want to talk to you about something. I'm scared to do it, but it's going to come up sooner or later.

I met a girl.

I don't know her really, I've hardly spoken to her, and I don't know if anything will happen with her, but she's the first person to make me feel anything since you left me.

I'm sorry, I'm sorry.

I don't know what to do.

If you were here this wouldn't be happening.

I wish you were here.

I wish you hadn't left me.

I hate you for it.

But I'll forgive you, if you forgive me.

I love you, and will always love you, but I want to see her.

Forgive me.

As I dial my heart pounds hands tremble. First ring, second ring I think about hanging up. She answers.

Hello?

Hi.

Who's this?

You know who it is.

No, I don't.

Yes, you do.

It's eight in the morning.

So what.

Why are you calling so early?

Were you sleeping?

No, I wasn't. Is there something I can do for you?

You like baseball?

I don't really think about it much.

You ever been to a game?

No.

You want to go to one?

When?

Tomorrow.

What time?

One.

Cubs or White Sox?

Cubs.

Let me check my schedule.

I laugh.

Why are you laughing?

Why don't you give me your address.

There's a pause. My heart is still pounding, my fingers still trembling.

65 East Scott.

What's the apartment number?

There's a doorman. He'll call me when you get here.

I'll be there at noon.

I hang up. I smile. My heart pounds my hands tremble not because I'm nervous not anymore. I stand walk in a circle smile walk in a circle. I feel something other than sorrow and loss, confusion and uncertainty. I feel urges that I don't have to fight, that are not part of the horror of my former life, that are not going to kill me if I indulge them. I feel, something more, feel. I walk in a circle.

I take a shower smile in the shower. I spend the day walking around smiling, sitting in a park along the lake smiling, I eat a huge banana split in the afternoon I'm not full I eat another one smiling. I don't do anything, but when afternoon arrives, I want to sleep. Being lazy is very hard work and can be very tiring. I decide to try and take a nap. I can't remember the last time I took a nap. If I can actually do it, my body may be finally starting to recover, normalize.

I walk into my apartment lie down sleep. Sleep comes easily, deep sound dreamless afternoon nap sleep. When I wake it's dark I brush my teeth leave go to the bar to see if my friends are around they're in the back room shooting pool and drinking. I see Danny he walks over to me.

You call her?

Yeah.

You gonna see her?

I'm taking her to a Cubs game tomorrow.

He laughs.

No fucking way.

Yeah fucking way.

How was the conversation?

I called her and asked her if she wanted to go to the game. The entire thing lasted about two minutes. I was distant because I know girls like her get hit on all the time, and if you're not distant, they're not interested.

Do you know anything about her?

I know her name's Brooke. I know you grew up with her. I know she lives
in a nice part of town, and she doesn't seem to have to work. I know some
other things, but I'm not sure they're any of your business.
Like what?
I said I'm not sure they're any of your business.
He laughs again.
Come on.
I know that she's beautiful. I know that I get nervous around her. I know
that she feels whatever it is that I feel.
Those are good things to know.
Yeah.
You want to know some more?
Like what?
She's from one of, if not the wealthiest family in Chicago.
I could give a shit about that.
She's also kind of tough, and won't tolerate any bullshit.
I don't intend to give her any bullshit.
She's also really picky.
No problem there, Danny. I'm the catch of the motherfucking century.
He laughs again.
If you ever meet her parents, I hope I'm there.
Why?
They're cool, but they're very conservative, old-money people. They'd
probably freak out if you told them anything about your past.
I laugh, spend the next couple of hours smoking cigarettes, drinking cola,
sitting in the corner watching the pool table, occasionally talking to one of
my friends. I get tired, leave, think about going to see Lilly, walk home, decide to try and sleep, I need my motherfucking beauty sleep. It comes easily I close my eyes and I'm gone.
I wake up early. Shower with soap, put on clean clothes, get coffee, walk. I
walk into the Gold Coast, which is the wealthiest neighborhood in
Chicago. It sits on the near north side, along the lake and just above
Michigan Avenue and the shopping district. The streets are lined with ivy-
covered brick, brown and greystone mansions built at the turn of the
twentieth century by rich industrialists. European sedans sit at the curb,
some of them have drivers in them. Women with children have nannies,

men wear dark conservative suits and carry rolled newspapers. I walk up and down the blocks looking at the houses looking at the street names looking for East Scott. I find it, it runs parallel to the lake, a block off Lakeshore Drive. Compared to everything else in the neighborhood, Brooke's building is new, built in the sixties or seventies, twenty-five or thirty stories, simple white stone with large windows.

I walk into the lobby. A middle-aged man in a coat and tie sits behind a reception desk. He looks up, speaks.

Service entrance is around back.

I'm not here to perform any sort of service.

Can I help you with something?

I give him Brooke's name, he asks me my name, picks up a phone and dials. He speaks into the phone, hangs up, tells me she'll be down in a minute. I thank him, step outside, light a cigarette. I'm nervous, scared. I have never been on a date sober. Except for Lilly, I've never been with a woman sober. My time with her was spent in an institution where we were safe, where we were shielded from the temptations and the self-created nightmares of the outside world, where we could pretend we were normal, where we could dream we had a future. It's different now, different because Lilly is gone, because I'm alone, because Brooke and I don't know each other, because I'm vulnerable, because I can be hurt. The nicotine doesn't make me less nervous or less scared. It doesn't make me invincible. It gives me something to do while I wait for Brooke to come downstairs.

I hear the door open behind me. I turn around. She's walking toward me she's wearing jeans, tennis shoes, a sweater, she's smiling she speaks.

Hi.

Hi.

I drop my cigarette, stomp it out. Nervous.

You ready to go?

Yes.

You want to walk or take the El.

Do we have time to walk?

Probably.

Let's walk.

We start walking, as we walk we talk, the small talk bullshit of first dates.

As we get closer to the stadium, the streets become more crowded. We don't have tickets, so I start looking for scalpers. I see three men on a corner pretending to be busy. I walk over ask them if they have tickets one of them asks me if I'm a cop I say no he gives me a price. I hand him some cash he gives me the tickets.

Brooke and I walk into the stadium. I offer to buy her souvenirs, a hat, shirt, perhaps you'd like a miniature bat, she laughs at me. We find our seats, they're in the upper deck along the third base line. We settle in I ask her if she knows the rules she smiles says I've never been to a game, but I'm not a fucking idiot.

They play the National Anthem, the game starts. A minute later, a beer vendor walks up our aisle.

You want a beer?

Didn't you just get out of rehab?

Not just, but not too long ago.

Won't it make you uncomfortable?

I'm not gonna have one, but if you want one, you should have it. Beer is part of the great American baseball tradition.

Okay, I'll have one.

I motion to the vendor, pay him, hand the beer to Brooke, she takes a sip.

How is it?

Good. Thank you.

Good.

Do you mind if I ask you a question?

Ask me whatever you want.

Why were you there?

Alcohol and cocaine.

Are you an alcoholic?

Yeah, I'm an alcoholic and I'm a coke fiend. I also have a record.

What kind of record?

Sold drugs, a couple DUI's, vandalism, a couple of assault charges, all kinds of stupid shit.

I'm sorry.

No reason to be sorry. Wasn't your fault, wasn't anybody's fault but my own.

How long were you there?

Rehab?

Were you somewhere else?

I went to jail when I was done.

How long were you in rehab?

Few months.

How long were you in jail?

Few months.

Which was worse?

Rehab was worse and it was also better. My body was fucked from too much liquor and too many drugs so I was sick for a long time and the sickness was a fucking nightmare. Once I started to feel better, I had to decide whether I wanted to live or die, and that was a hard decision because it meant coming to terms with a lot of pretty awful shit. After I made the decision I met a bunch of cool people and I started to get a bit more healthy and it was kind of amazing. Jail was boring and occasionally scary and a waste of fucking time.

How are you now?

At this moment I'm good, and I'm generally okay, but those are relative terms. Compared to normal people I'm a wreck, extremely troubled, extremely fucked-up.

She laughs.

At least you're honest about it.

If we become friends, you'd have found out sooner or later.

She smiles.

If?

I smile.

If.

As soon as the game starts the weather starts to turn. Heavy black clouds roll over our heads, we hear the quiet rumble of distant thunder. The temperature drops five degrees, ten degrees. The sun is gone, the wind back. I look at Brooke.

Think it'll pass?

The weather here is crazy. It could be sunny in fifteen minutes, or it could start snowing.

You want to risk it, or you want to take off?

The game just started. Let's risk it.

We stay, but don't pay much attention to the game. I ask her about her family, she has an older sister, a younger sister, she gets along with both of them, her parents are happily married. I ask her where she went to school she went to a small, private liberal arts college. I ask what she studied she says psychology, I ask her what she wants to do she says she doesn't know, she's trying to figure it out.

It starts to rain. Within fifteen minutes the rain turns to sleet. We're beneath the canopy of the upper deck, so we stay dry, but it's cold and I can see goose bumps on Brooke's arms. I ask her if she wants to leave she says let's stick it out, ten minutes later I ask her again, I don't want her to be uncomfortable, she says let's stick it out. I ask her again when the game is delayed and a tarp rolled across the field and she smiles and says, yes, I think we can leave now.

We walk out of the stadium, start walking back toward the city, we're both getting wet I try to hold the program over Brooke's head, it doesn't do much good. I lead her away from the stadium away from the bars away from the people she asks where we're going I say to a place I know.

We run a few blocks. We try to stay under trees or awnings so that we stay dry. We go to a small bar. I have been to the bar before, it's a dive with a pool table. I know it will be quiet. I know we'll be alone.

We walk in there are two people at the bar and the tables are all empty. I ask Brooke if she wants a drink she says sure I get her a beer, I get myself a cola. We walk to the back room which has the pool table and a few stools. I look at Brooke, speak.

You wanna play?

Sure.

Do you know how?

Sort of.

Do you want me to teach you?

You can give me pointers.

I put the balls in the rack, hand Brooke a cue.

You wanna break?

Okay.

I take off the rack, hand her the cue ball, step back. She leans over, lines it up, cracks it, the cue ball blows the rest of the balls all over the table.

Doesn't look like you're gonna need many pointers.

She smiles.

We play for an hour. She slowly sips her beer, I drink five colas. We both smoke. She wins two games, I win three. We talk easily, no uncomfortable silences, no awkward pauses. She asks me how often I want to drink and use I tell her always. She asks me if being in a bar is hard I tell her I can get alcohol whenever I want, wherever I am, there are liquor stores on every block, being in a bar is no different than being anywhere else. She asks me if it's hard not drinking, I tell her it's miserable, that I spend a lot of my time crying, that sometimes I feel like I want to die. She asks me how I deal with it, I tell her I always know that at some point I will feel better and if I'm patient and hold on, that point will come. She asks me what I want to do with my life I tell her I have trouble getting through the day most of the time and I'm not really worried about it yet. She asks me how I make my money, I tell her I don't have much I scrape by doing bullshit jobs. I'm open with her, more open with her than just about any-one else, but there are some things she doesn't need to know, and there are some things I'm not going to tell her.

We leave around five. We get a cab I ride home with her. I spend the en-tire trip trying to decide if I'm going to kiss her. Though we talk to each other, I don't hear a word, don't have any idea what I'm saying. I just stare at her and think will she let me should I try will she let me should I try will she let me.

We get to her building, get out of the cab.

Can I walk you to your door?

Don't expect to be invited inside.

Who says I want to be invited inside?

She smiles.

Yeah, you can walk me to my door.

We enter the building, should I, get into the elevator, will she let me. She pushes the button for her floor, looks over at me.

Thanks for taking me to the game.

Thanks for going.

She smiles, we don't speak anymore, just awkwardly look at each other. The elevator stops, doors open. We step out, start walking toward her door. My heart starts pounding my feet are heavy I'm nervous scared I want to kiss her don't want to get rejected I think she'll respond but you never know nervous scared. We stop at her door. She speaks.

This is it.

You have a nice looking door.

She looks at the door. It's a plain gray door with a number on it. She looks back.

I never noticed.

It's nice. I like it.

She laughs.

Thanks for a cool day.

Nervous.

My pleasure.

Scared.

See you soon?

Heart pounding.

Yeah.

She reaches out her hand, I take it, pull her toward me, kiss her. It is a simple kiss. Lips slightly open, a few seconds long. I pull away slowly, open my eyes. Brooke looks surprised. Sort of shocked. Sort of scared. I smile.

Bye.

I turn, walk to the elevator, push the button the door opens, I step inside, wait for the door to close. I don't turn around, look back or look up, I leave her with the kiss. The door closes, I immediately smile, take a deep breath, let it out. I push the button the elevator starts moving down. A rush runs through my body, something similar to the rush of speedy drugs, a rush of pleasure, security, joy, a rush of hope fulfilled, a rush of love or something that could be love.

I step out of the elevator still smiling leave the building still smiling. I start to walk down the street I think of Lilly my smile fades. Something inside hurts something between the happiness of moving forward and the sorrow of letting go. I go to a florist spend every cent I have on roses red roses.

I get down on my knees. Lay the flowers before me.

Hi.

I saw the girl I told you about.

It went well with her.

I haven't felt good about anything since you left, but today I did, I felt good, I finally felt good.

I want to see her again.

I need to see what happens.

I'm not going to come around so much anymore.

I miss you, and I wish you were here, and if you were this wouldn't be happening.

I start to cry.

You left me.

I cry.

You left me.

Cry.

I'm not going to come around so much.

Cry.

I see Brooke the next day.

Again the next day.

Again the next.

We go for walks, go to the movies, go for cheeseburgers at a cheap diner. We go to a bar, shoot pool, smoke cigarettes.

After a week she lets me into her apartment. It's a two bedroom with views of Lake Michigan. Nice, but nothing extraordinary.

After ten days she lets me into her room. She has a soft white bed, she has clean beautiful sheets, she has more pillows than she needs. We lie on her bed and kiss, kiss, kiss long and deep we lie facing each other our legs entwined we kiss. We don't move beyond kissing I'm not secure enough to move beyond. I tell her I'm scared that she scares me that my emotions scare me that opening myself scares me. She asks about my past I tell her stories about dealing drugs about being arrested about being addicted about falling apart. I feel no pride in telling the stories, I feel no shame. It was my life, and now it isn't.

I meet her roommate Heather. Heather is nice to me, but I can tell that she thinks I'm a hoodlum, and I can tell that she thinks Brooke could do better than me. I agree with Heather, Brooke could definitely do better than me.

I meet her friend Ned. Ned is openly hostile toward me. He tells Brooke that I'm going to hurt her, that I'm dangerous, unstable, insane. We have dinner with him in an attempt to calm him down, he doesn't speak to me except to occasionally correct my table manners. I ask Brooke if I can kick Ned's ass. She says no.

I stay with her for the first time I feel safe in her arms I sleep easily no dreams.

We rent movies.

Order pizza.

Hold hands as we walk.

Stay up late watch the sun rise.

Sleep through the afternoon.

See Danny, Kevin. They are both amused by what is happening between us. Kevin says it's just like the movies I say what movie he laughs, says Beauty and the Beast.

I don't work. I don't know why I'm not being called, don't know why I haven't had to go anywhere.

I make Heather laugh, once, twice, three or four times my sparkling wit starts to win her over. We both know Brooke could do better than me, but Heather starts to believe that maybe I'm not so bad.

We have another dinner with Ned. I know he likes sports I try to engage him. We talk about baseball, basketball, football. He loves the Chicago teams I know enough to carry on the conversation. At the end of the night, while I'm in the bathroom, he tells Brooke that maybe he was wrong about me. Later, when Brooke tells me, I say that I am happy he said it, because if he hadn't, despite your objections, I was going to kick his ass. She laughs at me.

I start to stay with her every night.

I go home in the mornings. I shower, pick up my mail, replenish my supply of cash. I am home one morning the phone rings I pick it up.

Hello.

Leonard speaks.

Harry motherfucking Houdini.

I smile.

What's up, Leonard?

Where you been, my son?

Been around.

Doing what?

Not much.

Hah! HAH!

I laugh.

What the fuck is that?

I say **HAH!** You've been running around with a little lady.

Maybe.

Maybe my ass. One of my reporters said you've been cavorting with a
pretty young blonde.

One of your reporters?

I have people who report things to me. I call them my reporters.

And they watch me?

They check on you occasionally.

That's gotta stop, Leonard.

It's for your own good.

Stop having people watch me, Leonard.

Okay, okay, I'll stop.

Thank you.

Have you been enjoying yourself?

I laugh.

Yes.

Bet you don't miss working

Is this why I haven't gotten any calls?

I thought you deserved some time off to concentrate on more
important matters.

Thank you.

You seem to have done well.

Yeah.

I'm impressed.

What do you know about her?

I know she's very attractive, I know she's very rich. I know she's from an
old blue-blood family. I know you sound better than you have sounded in
a long time.

You have someone watching her?

No, just did some checking.

No more of that.

I understand.

No more.

You're protective of her.

Yeah.

I'm happy for you.

Why?

If you're protective of her, it means you care for her. It's a good thing, a beautiful thing, if you're able to care for someone again.

You should come meet her.

Won't be anytime soon.

Why?

I'm doing some deals right now, significant deals, and I have to pay close attention to them. I'll come meet her when they're finished.

Okay.

Anything you need?

Nope.

You've got cash?

Enough for a year.

He laughs.

I doubt that.

I don't spend much.

You've got a girlfriend. You'll start spending.

I laugh.

She's not that way.

We'll see.

Anything you need?

No.

Stay in touch?

Of course.

Good luck with your deals.

Goodbye, my son.

I hang up, leave, walk back downtown. Brooke is waiting for me.

We are having dinner with Brooke's older sister Courtney and Courtney's husband. It's a test run for a potential meeting with her parents. We go to a fancy restaurant. I wear nice clothing, khakis and a blue shirt and a sport coat, the same clothing I wear when I am carrying something on the El and pretend to be a commuter. We sit down, we're early, I'm nervous. I feel like an impostor in my outfit, like an actor in costume, like I'm pretending to be something I'm not. Brooke and I talked about what I should admit and what I shouldn't admit, Brooke told me to be completely honest. She's right, I should be honest, but I want the sister to like me and I know she probably won't if she knows about my past. I know in many ways I shouldn't give a shit, I am what I am, but I do give a shit. I don't want to embarrass her.

We sit at our table, wait for her sister to arrive she's late. Brooke takes my hand, speaks.

You okay?

Nervous. You?

A little nervous.

No need for you to be nervous, I'm going to behave.

I know you are, and for whatever it's worth, Courtney's probably more nervous than either of us.

Why?

I've told her about you, she's nervous and excited to meet you.

What'd you tell her?

Just nice things. You have nothing to worry about.

Brooke motions toward the door. I turn, see a man and woman walking toward us. The man has dark curly hair, olive skin, is in his late twenties. The woman is a taller version of Brooke. Same blond hair, same blue eyes, same skin, same lips. Same air of reserve, same air of wealth. She's slightly taller than her husband, who walks a step behind her.

I stand say hello she smiles says hi, I'm Courtney, and this is my husband Jay, I shake each of their hands say I'm James we sit down.

The dinner is easy, comfortable. Courtney does most of the talking, she talks about her children, about her house on the North Shore, about how busy she is, about how much she loves her husband. Just before our food arrives, she asks if I mind if she orders wine I say no she asks how I'm doing with everything I know Brooke has told her about rehab I say well she orders a glass of chardonnay. She talks all the way through dinner, doesn't touch her food. I eat a steak it's great but I'm still hungry she doesn't touch her salmon if I could I'd reach over the table and take it and eat it.

We finish dinner her husband picks up the bill. We walk out together she gives me a hug gives Brooke a hug we say goodbye they leave. Brooke and I start walking back to her apartment. She speaks.

That went well.

You think?

Yeah, she liked you.

How do you know that?

If she didn't like you, she would have scowled at you and complained about everything and tortured Jay.

I laugh.

Poor fella.

Poor fella my ass, he knew what he was getting into when he married her.

I laugh again.

I'm glad it went well, glad you think she liked me.

She'll report back to my parents and tell them that you're completely acceptable.

Which is good.

Very good.

I motion toward my sport coat.

Now that I've done well, can I take this thing off?

No.

No? Why not?

I've never seen you dressed up before. I think you look handsome. Humor me and wear it until we get back to my place.

I smile, take her hand. A warmth and a chill roll through my body they settle softly they linger they scare me. I feel very close to Brooke, strong with her hand in mine, invincible to the rest of the world, but fragile to her, vulnerable to her, she could hurt me, she could hurt me, nothing else but she could hurt me.

We walk back to her place. We go to Brooke's room. Brooke shuts the door, lights a candle. I sit down on the bed she sits next to me. We stare at each other for a moment, silently stare at each other. We both start moving forward we close our eyes, reach, meet, hands breath lips bodies meet. There is something more this time, walls are down, armor discarded, defenses breached. There is something deeper faster more urgent in our hands in our breath in our lips in our bodies. We stand her hands run beneath my shirt my hands beneath her shirt around her back we briefly separate my shirt comes off we lie down. I can smell her hair, soap on her skin, perfume beneath her wrist. Her lips are soft against me, her hands firm. I take her shirt off. My chest against her chest I can feel her heart beating. I'm close to her in body and elsewhere I'm close to her.

I feel weak fragile vulnerable. She could hurt me. I'm close to her. I'm scared. She could hurt me. I can feel her heart beat, I can feel my heart beat, she could hurt me. I can't go through with this she could hurt me. I can't handle any more, any more she could hurt me.

I want to kiss her keep kissing her I haven't felt this good since Lilly since Lilly. I want to keep kissing her I start to panic I'm fucking terrified. I pull away.

Why are you stopping?

I can't.

What's wrong?

I just can't.

What'd I do?

Nothing.

Did I do something wrong?

I'm sorry.

For what?

I'm just freaking out.

Why?

I'm just freaking out. I'm sorry.

She stares at me. I look away. I'm embarrassed, ashamed, confused. My hands are shaking, my body is shaking. Her arms are around me she can feel me shaking I hate myself she could hurt me like Lilly hurt me I'm fucking terrified.

What's wrong?

I can't look at her.

What's wrong, James?

I shake my head, bite my lip. I don't want to cry in front of her I don't want to cry. She pulls me toward her, pulls my head into her shoulder holds me there.

I want to love her. I want to give myself to her. I want to take her in every way I want to be normal with someone to have a normal life with some-one. I don't want to be scared to love to give it and receive it. I'm tired of being fucking alone. I can't do it and I'm ashamed of myself. I speak softly speak.

It doesn't have anything to do with you.

Something before?

Yeah.

Do you want to talk about it?

No.

We can just lie here. You don't have to talk.

I'm sorry.

Just lie here.

We lie on her bed our legs entwined she holds my head against her shoul-der. My heart slows, I stop shaking. Walls are up, armor on, defenses manned. She holds me I feel secure I'm safe again. She leans kisses my forehead.

You want a cigarette?

Yeah.

She pulls herself away from me. She stands walks to her dresser opens a drawer takes out a t-shirt. She puts it on and leaves the room. I sit up, lean against the headboard. I take a deep breath, stare at the sheets. I hate my weakness, hate my fear, hate myself. Brooke comes back into the room. She's carrying a pack of cigarettes, an ashtray, a bottle of water. She sits in front of me, hands me a cigarette, I take it she lights it.

Thank you.

You want some water?

I take the bottle, take a sip.

Thank you.

You okay?

I shake my head.

No, not at all. I'm totally fucked-up.

Is there anything I can do?

I wish there was.

I'm sorry.

Don't be sorry. You've got nothing to be sorry about.

She leans forward, kisses my forehead. She moves so that she is sitting next to me. We smoke our cigarettes, take alternating sips from the bottle of water. I stare at the sheets, occasionally look over at her. She stares at the sheets, occasionally looks over at me. We finish our cigarettes, put them out. She takes the ashtray, sets it on the nightstand next to the bed. She looks over at me, speaks.

You want to go to sleep?

Yeah.

We lie down next to each other. She leans forward again gently kisses my lips, puts her arms around me, lays her head on my chest. I watch her fall asleep. After about an hour, I get out of her bed. I walk into the living room, light a cigarette, stare out of her windows stare at the lake, smoke and stare at the lake it is quiet, black, still. I wish I could let her help me. I wish she could do something for me. I smoke and stare at the lake I'm scared, she could hurt me, she could hurt me.

I don't sleep well. I leave early the next morning. I kiss Brooke goodbye start walking try to walk off my fear it doesn't work. I walk all day walk until my legs hurt my feet hurt it doesn't work. I go back to my apartment read the Tao it doesn't work. I tell myself I have nothing to be scared of it doesn't work. I tell myself that she's not going to hurt me it doesn't matter. I tell myself I can deal with whatever comes I have been through worse endured worse it doesn't go away.

Brooke calls asks me how I'm doing I tell her okay. She asks if I want to meet her at a bar she's going out with Heather I say yes. Maybe I'll see her and feel differently, maybe, maybe.

I take a shower, change clothes, walk to the Local Option. I get there I see Brooke and Heather sitting at a table. I walk over to them as I walk I see Brooke looks upset. I arrive I speak.

Hi.

Hi.

Hi, Heather.

Hi, James.

I look at Brooke.

How you doing?

Brooke glances at Heather, looks back at me.

I'm fine.

I pull up a chair, sit across from her.

What's wrong?

Nothing.

Something's wrong.

It doesn't matter.

Yes it does.

She shakes her head.

Just tell me.

She glances at Heather again, looks back at me.

We were standing at the bar and some guy came up next to me and grabbed my ass. I asked him what he was doing and he said grabbing your sweet ass and he did it again.

Is he here?

It doesn't matter.

Is he here?

Heather points to three guys standing against the bar, speaks.

He's the one in the middle.

I stand up.

I'll be right back.

Brooke speaks.

What are you going to do?

Don't worry about it.

I start walking toward the three against the bar. A gate inside of me opens. I am flooded with rage, fear, aggression, an urge to protect and an urge to inflict, an overwhelming urge to destroy destroy destroy. I know this feeling lived with it for years the Fury is back. I don't like it, it almost killed me before, it is back. My heart starts pounding. I clench my fists, clench my jaw. Every cell in my body tenses, prepares, tightens up, coils. My mind slows down my eyes focus on three men leaning against the bar. They are all about the same size as me, they are facing the bar, facing away from me. They wear pressed khakis, leather shoes, stiff-starched shirts, expensive watches. They have clean-shaven faces and short, conservative haircuts. They may wipe me out, I may wipe them out, maybe nothing happens. I'm trying to control myself, trying to prepare.

I stop a couple of feet behind them, speak.

Excuse me.

No response. I raise my voice.

Excuse me.

One of the others not the one in the middle turns around.

Yeah?

I want to talk to your friend.

He taps his friend on the shoulder, motions toward me. The one in the middle turns around.

Yeah?

My heart is pounding. I motion to Brooke and Heather, who are watching us.

Don't touch her again. Don't touch her friend.

His friends turn toward me.

What?

She doesn't want you touching her again. It was inappropriate the first time, there shouldn't be a second time.

Who are you?

Doesn't matter.

Did she ask you to talk to me?

Doesn't matter.

I stare at him. He looks back at me. I'm nervous tense scared ready to go not sure what I'm going to do about his friends. He looks at each of them, looks back at me.

There are three of us and one of you.

I stare at him. Three of them, one of me. I don't know what I'm going to do.

I don't care how many of you there are. Don't touch her again.

We stare at each other. I see Derek reach beneath the bar for a short, thick, wooden club he walks toward us, speaks.

James?

I look up at him.

There a problem?

I look back at the one in the middle, he looks toward Derek, sees the club. He speaks.

No problem.

He turns back to me.

Tell your friend I'm sorry.

Thank you.

I walk back to the table sit down with Brooke and Heather. Brooke speaks.

What happened?

He told me to tell you he's sorry.

What'd you say to him?

It doesn't matter. He's not going to touch you again.

She takes my hand.

157

Thank you.

Don't worry about it.

She can feel me shaking.

Are you okay?

I'll calm down in a few minutes.

She smiles.

Thank you for doing it.

I nod.

Sure.

I sit with them, drink a cola or two, smoke, wait to calm down. My hands stop shaking but the calm never comes. The Fury stays with me, taunts me, says drink motherfucker drink motherfucker, says destroy destroy, says I'm going to hurt you. I haven't felt like this felt the Fury like this since rehab I already feel fragile and vulnerable. I don't want to be in a bar right now. I want to make the Fury go away and alcohol destroys it. I want to drink. With each moment the need grows, grows, each moment is more of a struggle to resist. I need to leave. I want to drink. I need to leave.

I wait for the three at the bar to leave first, I don't want Brooke alone with the one in the middle. They leave after an hour I watch them go I wait five minutes stand, look at Brooke, speak.

I gotta go.

What's wrong?

I just can't be here right now.

I'll come with you.

Stay here, have a good night. I need to be alone.

I lean over, kiss her goodbye, walk out of the bar. I start walking down the street. I want to calm down. I want this Fury to leave me. I want to feel safe, I want the urges to go away. This shouldn't be so difficult this shouldn't be bothering me. I know my problems are nothing. I know I have been through worse, seen worse, felt worse. I know my problems are minuscule and pathetic compared to other problems in the World. I know I should get the fuck over them and deal. Knowing, however, doesn't make a difference. If anything, knowing just makes me feel stupid, feel weak, feel worse.

I walk for hours, for the rest of the night. I walk and I look and I don't find anything no answers nothing. I'm the same person feel the same as

when I walked out of the bar. I don't want to admit it but I know I can't
go on I'm not ready to be with anyone but myself. She could hurt me. I
am protective of her, feelings that strong are dangerous for me. I'm scared.
I go to her apartment I say hello to the doorman he knows me now I go
upstairs knock on her door. It's nine in the morning she should be up she
answers the door in her pajamas. She smiles, speaks.
You don't look so good.
I'm not.
She invites me inside I walk into her apartment. I walk into her living
room sit down on her couch, she walks into the kitchen.
You want a cup of coffee?
Sure.
She pours two cups, puts some milk in her cup, walks in the living room.
She hands me one of the cups, sits down next to me. She kisses me on the
cheek, pulls back.
You look sad.
I shrug.
What's wrong?
I look down, shake my head. I hate myself, hate my weakness, hate that I
can't go on. She puts her hand on my hand.
What's wrong?
I look up, shake my head, bite my lip. She watches me for a moment,
reaches for her cigarettes.
You want a smoke?
I nod. She hands me a cigarette, lights it, lights one for herself, looks
at me.
You can't go on, can you?
No.
Why?
I just can't.
Did I do something?
I shake my head, bite my lip. I don't want to cry.
Then what's wrong?
I'm just fucked-up. Confused and scared and fucked-up.
A tear starts rolling down one of my cheeks.
It doesn't have anything to do with you.

Both cheeks.

And I wish it wasn't this way.

Tears down both cheeks she nods, leans forward, puts her arms around me, speaks.

I thought this might happen. I could see you hurting all the time and wanted to do something for you. I don't know what happened to you before, but I'm sorry, and I hope you can get over it, and if you need a friend, you know where I am.

I let her hold me and I cry. I'm sick of fucking crying there has been too much in the last year too much. I'm sick of crying. Brooke holds me and lets me and even though nothing is right and I hate myself for leaving her I feel okay because she's holding me.

I cry.

I'm so fucking sick of it.

I cry.

I find Leonard's card five names five numbers I start at the top pick up my phone dial the first number it rings rings rings a voice.

Yeah?

Mr. Sinatra available?

No.

Voice hangs up the phone I dial the next number. Ring ring a voice.

Hello?

Mr. Kennedy available?

No.

Next number.

Mr. Bob Hope please?

He's not here.

Next number.

Joe DiMaggio around?

Nope.

Final number.

May I speak to Leonard?

Who's this?

James.

He's not here. You want to leave a message?

Tell him I called.

Will do.

Thanks.

I hang up. Five minutes later my phone rings. I pick it up.

Hello?

My son, you called.

Yeah.

What's wrong?

Nothing. I want to go back to work.

Why?

I just do.

You left her, didn't you?

Why do you think that?

I can hear it.

Yeah, I left her.

I'm sorry.

Shit happens.

Don't try to be cool with me. You're upset. I can hear it in your voice.

You're right, I am upset. Nothing to do but move on, try to keep myself occupied. That's why I want to work.

I'll see what we got, maybe try to come visit later this week. Cheer your ass up.

That would be cool.

You need anything?

What I need I can't have.

That's the fucking truth. Keep away.

Call me if you're coming.

I will.

Thanks, Leonard.

Goodbye, my son.

I hang up.

What I need I can't have. I drink coffee smoke cigarettes read the Tao go for long walks wander the galleries of the art museum talk to Lilly don't sleep. Time moves slowly. What I need I can't have. I want to stay occupied. I wait for the phone to ring.

Knock on my door. It's around noon I'm lying in bed staring at the ceiling I get up knock again I stand in front of the door.

Who is it?

I hear Leonard's voice.

Mr. Happy and his Cheer Squad.

I laugh, open the door. Leonard and the Snapper walk into my apartment. I speak.

This is a surprise.

Leonard speaks.

We got some business in New York. We set up our travel schedule so we have an eight-hour lay-over.

I look at Snapper.

How you doing, Snap?

I'm the fucking Cheer Squad. Nothing better than that.

I laugh again. Leonard speaks.

Throw on some nice clothes and grab your credit card, we have an appointment.

Where?

Surprise.

What are we doing?

Bringing some beauty to your life.

What's that mean?

It means throw on some nice clothes and grab your credit card, we have an appointment.

I need to take a shower.

Fine. We'll wait.

I go into the bathroom, take a quick shower, go to my room, put on my nice clothes, Leonard and the Snapper and I leave. We walk to the curb get into a large white Benz start driving downtown. Leonard asks me if I'm hungry I say no, he says he's hungry we stop at a small restaurant he eats a green salad. He finishes the salad we get back into the car drive into the gallery district of Chicago park the car on the street get out of the car start walking down the street. Leonard speaks.

Do you know what happened to this neighborhood a couple years ago?

I have no idea.

The art market crashed and it, like every gallery district in the country, got fucking crushed. Do you know what that means for us?

I have no idea.

It means most of these galleries are on the verge of bankruptcy and they're desperate to sell their inventories and they're willing to make very, very, very good fucking deals. Do you know why we're here?

To buy art?

More specifically.

I don't know.

We're here to find you a Picasso.

You're kidding me.

Leonard looks at Snapper.

Am I kidding him?

Snapper looks at me.

He ain't fucking kidding you.

I look at Leonard.

I can't afford a Picasso.

You can't afford a painting. You can't afford a large drawing or an important drawing, but you can most likely afford something small.

Snapper speaks.

Picasso's work is surprisingly affordable.

Leonard speaks.

Snap has a couple of his own.

Snapper speaks.

I have a nice crayon drawing of a woman's head and a pencil drawing of a dove.

Leonard speaks.

And he got 'em cheap because dealers need to sell.

We stop in front of a building. Leonard speaks.

I did some research before we arrived. There's a place in here. High-end, but not super high-end. They have nice pieces in stock and they're in a deep, deep financial hole.

He opens the door and we step into the building. The gallery is on the second floor, we walk up a flight of stairs. Snapper opens a polished steel door we step into a large open room with white walls a gray wood floor and a lofted ceiling. Art hangs on the walls, some pieces are large abstract colorful some are small simple drawings, some are minimal monotone panels. In the back corner of the room there is a reception desk, behind it a door that leads into an office. Leonard looks at me, speaks.

Let's go back there.

We walk toward the office. As we approach it, an attractive woman in her late thirties steps out. She has short black hair, wears deep red lipstick, a black suit. She smiles.

May I help you?

Leonard speaks.

We're looking for Picasso drawings.

I have a few.

We'd like to see them.

Come with me.

We walk through the door into a small room. There is a large cabinet against one wall, the drawers are labeled with artists' names, a couple of small framed drawings sit on top of it. There are two chairs against another wall, a door against a third. The woman speaks.

Have a seat, I'll be right back.

Snapper offers us the chairs we sit. The woman walks through the door, quietly closes it behind her. I look at Leonard, speak.

This is fucking weird.

He laughs.

Why do you think it's weird?

The idea that I might be going home with a Picasso is just weird.

Get over it.

I laugh.

What do I do with it when I get home?

You put it on your fucking wall, what do you think you do?

What if someone steals it?

Leonard looks at Snapper.

Snapper?

Snapper looks at me.

You find 'em and you fucking shoot 'em.

I laugh. The woman opens the door. She steps into the room with one small drawing, probably eight by ten, and a slightly larger one, probably ten by twelve. She moves the drawings currently on the cabinet and replaces them with the new ones. We stand and look at them.

Leonard speaks.

If what you see doesn't move you, make you smile, make you happy, make you feel something, then fuck it, don't buy it.

I laugh. The woman laughs. I look back at the drawings. The woman speaks.

You feel anything?

I shake my head.

No.

I have more.

She picks up the drawings, leaves, comes back a few moments later with two more. I look at them feel nothing she leaves brings back two more nothing two more. I like one of them. It's two pieces of paper set on top of each other, a smiling male face is simply drawn in blue crayon across both of them. The word *papiers* is scrawled in gray pencil across the top of the lower piece of paper, the word *colles* is scrawled along the bottom of the top piece of paper. A large star, also in gray pencil, is haphazardly drawn over both pieces and the blue face, Picasso signed his name in large letters along the bottom. The work is about fourteen inches wide and twenty-eight inches tall, and it is housed in an old, ornate, black, carved-wood frame. I look at it and it makes me smile. I imagine Picasso sitting in a messy studio somewhere in France, I imagine him making it while he was bored, I imagine him sticking it in a drawer and forgetting about it. Maybe he gave it away, maybe he sold it when he needed some money, maybe someone found it after he died, I don't know how it ended up here, in this gallery in Chicago, but I look at it and it makes me smile and I know it's going home with me.

I ask the woman how much she tells me, Leonard says no way, that's above-market and he gives her a number. She responds they go back and forth back and forth until they arrive at an agreeable price. They look at me I smile and say okay.

I give the woman my credit card she says she prefers checks. I say I prefer credit cards she says okay she rings it up. I sign the slip. She asks me if I'd like it delivered, I say no I'll take it with me

I pick it up, take it off the cabinet. Leonard and Snapper and I thank the woman and we walk out of the gallery. I carry the Picasso under my arm. I smile as I walk I have a Picasso under my arm I think it's completely ridiculous. Leonard looks at me, smiles, speaks.

You look good with that thing.

I laugh. He looks at Snapper, speaks.

He looks good with it, doesn't he?

Snapper speaks.

It really fits him.

Maybe he should come back tomorrow and buy another one.

Why not? You only live once.

That is certainly the truth. You only live once, buy Picassos whenever possible.

We laugh, walk down the street back to the Mercedes, get inside, pull away. We drive back to my apartment. Leonard says they have to get to the airport, they have a flight in a few hours. I say thank you for stopping it has been a great day. Leonard says no problem, we'll be back soon.

I get out of the car, they pull away. I walk into my apartment. I don't have a hammer or a nail so I lean my Picasso against the wall near my bed. I laugh every time I see it.

Spring becomes Summer.

I talk to Lilly. Sometimes I read to her, sometimes I just sit with her.

I go to St. Louis.

Milwaukee.

North side, South side. Northside. Southside.

I go out every night. I go to bars with my friends. I smoke play pool watch my friends get drunk. I stay out late I still can't sleep when the bars close I walk through dark, silent, empty streets. I walk until it starts to become light. I sit by the lake and I watch the sun rise.

I sleep during the day, a few hours a day.

I read, look at art.

I go to Detroit.

Rockford.

Gary, Indiana.

I decide I want to write something. I have no idea what, I don't really care, I just want to try. I buy a computer. I sit down in front of it and stare at the screen. I open a word-processing document and with two fingers I type—What are you staring at dumbass?—over and over and over again.

A woman stops me on the street and she says you won't always feel this way. I ask her what she means and she says I can smell your pain, I can smell it. I'm not sure if she's a genius or a lunatic. I turn and quickly walk away.

I see someone I used to know, someone I haven't seen for a few years. He sees me smiles walks over and says how's your fucking drinking problem, Frey? I say it's good, how's your drinking problem? He says he's broke and unemployed and it sucks, but it allows him to go out every night. I give him ten bucks, say have one on me, old friend, have one on me.

I go to Milwaukee again.

Rockford twice.

Minneapolis/St. Paul.

I'm still too thin, I go on a special diet. I eat all of my meals at either The Weiner Circle, Taco/Burrito Palace #2, or The Olympic Gyro House. I only order items with red meat, I always order extra red meat, with most things I also order extra cheese.

A man offers to sell me a six pack of whoop-ass and a bottle of I know you can. I ask him how much? He says you ain't got enough, mother-fucker, but I bet you can afford some of that lonely shit.

I visit Lilly. Sometimes I read to her, sometimes I speak to her, sometimes I just sit with her.

Summer becomes Fall.

I had my last drink one year ago, exactly one year ago. I took my last hit from a pipe one year and two days ago.

I am on the train going to the Northern suburbs. I have been to the house before. It is the house where I did my first pick-up, where the strange man in silk pajamas played a joke on me. I've been here three or four other times, each time someone different came to the door. I am supposed to get a briefcase and take it to the South side of the city.

It is late morning. The train is almost empty. I sit alone reading, occasionally glancing out the window, the sky is gray, the leaves have turned, they are starting to fall. It is starting to get cold.

I get off the train take a cab. I remember how to get there. I see the house large gray stone. I walk to the front door, knock, no one comes, I knock again, hear shuffling feet heavy breathing. I wait. The feet stop shuffling I still hear breathing. I knock again the door opens it's the pajama man again. He's wearing a pair of dirty white underwear briefs and a dirty white t-shirt, there are deep dark circles beneath his eyes. His nose is running and he's shaking and he looks like he hasn't slept in a long time. He is holding a nine millimeter pistol in one of his hands and he is pointing it at my face.

What do you want?

I am shocked terrified can't speak.

Who sent you here?

I don't want to die I immediately start shaking.

WHO SENT YOU HERE?

The black hole of the barrel is an inch from my face I can smell the metal. I don't want to die I can't breathe move speak I don't want to die I'm frozen.

MOTHERFUCKER.

The man cocks the gun.

WHO THE FUCK SENT YOU HERE?

I don't want to die I piss myself. Urine runs down my leg, into my shoes, it
keeps coming my bladder is done.
WHO?
He shakes the pistol fuck fuck fuck.
SENT YOU?
I don't want to die he shakes the pistol fuck me.
MOTHERFUCKER?
I've got to get away move move move if I don't get away I'm going to die.
I take a small step back. The man stares at me, the pistol is still aimed at
my face. I take another small step I am so scared I don't want to die please
please please. I take another step the man stares at me his finger is on the
trigger please.
LEONARD SEND YOU?
Please another step please don't shoot me please.
LEONARD SEND YOU?
Another step don't shoot me please.
LEONARD SEND YOU?
I don't want to die. I don't want to die.
YOU TELL LEONARD.
Another step.
THAT I'LL SHOVE THIS GUN UP HIS ASS.
Another step.
AND BLOW HIS MOTHERFUCKING HEAD OFF.
Another step back. Another step, another step. The man watches me
please don't shoot me please another step another step. Please please
please let me get away. The man watches me, I'm almost gone. He lowers
his gun, wipes his nose, shuts the door. I keep moving back until I reach
the sidewalk. I turn and quickly walk away. My heart is exploding my legs
are jelly. I'm shaking there is urine all over my legs and feet, my pants and
my socks and my shoes. When I reach the end of the block I turn the corner I'm away holy fuck I'm away. I fall to my knees on a small patch of
brown grass between the sidewalk and the street. I start vomiting.

I take the train home my pants are covered in piss. I buy a newspaper to keep over my lap so that the other passengers don't see my pants it's not a comfortable ride.

I call Leonard tell him what happened he is not happy. He tells me he's coming to Chicago to handle this personally he wants me to meet him at his usual hotel in the morning.

I spend the rest of the day chain-smoking cigarettes. I can still see the black hole of the barrel. I can still smell the metal. I can still hear the bullet entering the chamber. I can still feel the urine running down my leg. Night comes I can't sleep. I can still see his eyes, hear his voice. He had his finger on the trigger and he could have killed me.

I go to the bank. Fill a bag with cash. I walk to the hotel it's a long walk. I want to burn away the fear I still feel it, it doesn't work I still feel it. I take the elevator up, go to the restaurant. Leonard and Snapper are sitting at a table waiting for me. They do not look happy. They stand as I approach them. Leonard speaks.

My son.

What's up, Leonard?

How you doing?

I'm good.

I look at Snapper.

What's up, Snapper?

You tell me.

Had a weird day yesterday.

So I fucking hear.

Leonard sits, we follow. Leonard speaks.

Have you eaten?

No.

Let's order, and then I want you to tell Snapper what happened.
We order, and unlike most of our meals together, the order is not exces-
sive. After we order I recount yesterday's events. Midway through, our
food comes and I continue to speak as we eat. Neither Leonard or
Snapper interrupt. They just sit and quietly listen to me. When I finish,
Snapper takes a deep breath, pushes his plate away, looks at Leonard
and speaks.
You know what this means?
I do.
He's finally gone completely crazy.
I thought he was getting better.
Am I authorized?
Yes.
Snapper turns to me.
You're coming with me, kid.
I speak.
No way.
You owe him.
I don't care.
He stuck a fucking gun in your face.
I don't care, I'm not going.
I lean over and pick up the bag of cash, which has been sitting at my feet.
I set it in front of Leonard.
I also don't want to do this anymore. I brought you the money I owe you.
Leonard looks surprised.
You're gonna quit because some crazy fuck pulled a gun on you?
That's part of the reason.
What's the other part?
I feel good about staying clean. I feel like I can do it long term. Knowing
that, I've got to figure out what I'm going to do with my life. No offense,
but I don't want to be a deliveryman anymore, no matter how much I get
paid. I don't want guns in my face. I want to try to have a normal life, or
at least something that resembles one.
Holy shit. This is crazy. You should hear yourself.
I laugh.

What if I promoted you?

You know I can't really be part of what you do, and I don't want to be any more a part of it than I already am. I gotta do something on my own.

What?

I don't know, but I have enough money to take some time and figure it out.

Leonard motions to the bag of cash.

I don't want the money.

I owe it to you.

I want to know what you spent it on.

Just take it.

Why won't you tell me where you spent it?

I just don't want to.

Tell me what you spent it on, and you can keep it, and you can leave your job, and you can let Snapper deal with your friend in the suburbs. I agree with your intentions, and think it will be good for you to start dealing with the future, I just want to know where the money went.

I'd rather show you than tell you.

Fine. Show me.

You have a car downstairs?

Of course.

Let's go.

Leonard motions for the bill gets it signs it. We stand, I pick up my bag, we leave. Snapper gets the car he picks us up in front of the hotel. We start driving north and west it isn't far. I give Snapper directions we stop at the florist where I always stop, as soon as I walk through the door they know what I'm going to buy. I buy red roses beautiful red roses. Lilly loved them when she was alive, I hope she still loves them.

We pull through the gates. We are still in the city but on its edges, we can see the towering skyline in the distance. Land spreads out before us, around us, there are thousands and thousands of stones. We drive slowly along a thin, winding road. It is quiet, still, empty. We turn off the main road onto a smaller road, drive for a moment, I motion for Snapper to pull over.

I step out of the car, Leonard and Snapper step out of the car. I lead them through the aisles. We do not speak. The only sounds are our steps and the chatter of small birds. Thirty yards in from the road I stop in front of two simple white stones. The stones are identical to each other. Words in simple print read—

Katherine Anne Sanders	Lillian Grace Sanders
1932–1994	1970–1994
You were Loved	You were Loved

There are dead roses in front of Lilly's stone. I pick them up and put the fresh roses in their place. I lean toward the point where the stone meets the grass, where I imagine she lies, her head resting on a pillow. I whisper hello, I love you, I brought some friends with me, you probably remember Leonard, he always asks about you, I hope you're well, I love you, I love you.

I step back, stand with Leonard and Snapper, who are staring at the stones, and I speak.

They didn't have any family except each other, so I took care of them. I had them moved from the county morgue to a funeral home. I bought them dresses for burial, had them placed in silk lined coffins and I got these plots and the stones. They were Catholic, which I didn't know until after, so I had a Priest perform the services. Lilly had a shitty life, a shitty fucking life, and I thought I could change that, but I couldn't, so I wanted this, at least, to be nice for her.

I look at Leonard, tears are streaming down his face. He speaks.

They're beautiful.

Yeah.

I've never seen anything so beautiful.

I nod, start to tear up.

I'm gonna have roses sent here once a week forever.

You don't have to do that Leonard.

And these graves will always be tended.

You don't have to do that Leonard.

I know I don't have to, but I'm going to.

Thank you, Leonard.

He looks at Snapper, speaks.

Let's pay our respects, let them know we're thinking about them.

Snapper speaks.

I got a feeling they know.

I'm sure they do.

They step forward and they cross themselves, get down on one knee, start to pray. I don't believe in god, but I like to think that Lilly is in a better place, so I get down on one knee and I close my eyes and I pray.

I hope she knows.

That for her and only her, for her and only her.

I pray.

Fall becomes winter.

I sit in front of my computer for hours I write what are you scared of dumbass, why are you scared?

A man at a bar tells me I look like a fly. I ask him why he thinks I look like a fly and he tells me that flies are born in shit and live in shit and he tells me that I look like shit and look like I've lived in, with and through shit, thus I look like a fly. I don't know what to say so I say thank you, my friend, thank you.

I meet a girl named Julianne she's Danny's friend she wants a roommate. We get along, she's from the South and her accent makes me laugh, I decide that I will be her roommate. We start looking for an apartment. We find a big apartment with two bedrooms, high ceilings, a living room dining room and kitchen, it should be expensive but isn't. We're trying to figure out why there is a loud rumble, and the building shakes and the windows shake and the floor shakes everything fucking shakes. Julianne wonders if we're having an earthquake, I laugh, walk to the back of the apartment, look out the window. The El tracks are ten feet away. I like the El tracks, like the shaking and the rumbling, like the apartment. I tell Julianne that I think we should move in, she agrees with me, we sign a lease. We move in and every fifteen minutes we rumble and shake, rumble and shake.

I meet another man at another bar he looks me in the eyes and he says I am mentally ill and unstable. I tell him I am mentally ill and unstable as well. He tells me that his doctors have advised him to never drink again, that it could kill him. I tell him my doctors have given me the same advice. He tells me that he goes to bars because he doesn't know what else to do with his life. I tell him I know the feeling and I buy him a cola, an ice cold glass of cola.

I sit in front of my computer.

Every fifteen minutes I rumble and shake.

Winter in Chicago is cold as hell.

Leonard's visits stop he hates the cold he avoids it. I talk to him once a week or so he calls me from strange places Venezuela and Costa Rica and Barbados, Guadeloupe and the Dominican Republic. I ask him what he's doing why he's traveling so much he says I'm TCB my son, T, C motherfucking B. I ask him what that means, he says it means taking care of business, taking care of motherfucking business.

Leonard calls tells me he's sending me a plane ticket he wants me to come to his beach house for the Super Bowl. I get the ticket, get on the plane, fly to LA, get off the plane. My friend Chris is picking me up. I went to college with him, lived with him for a year. He works at a golf course in Orange County. He wants to own his own golf course at some point, right now he works as an Assistant Greenskeeper. I ask him what that means, he says it means I mow fucking lawns all day.

I walk out of the terminal it's bright, warm, sunny. Chris is waiting for me at the curb I climb into his SUV he says what's up I say not much he asks where we going I say Orange County and I give him an address.

The drive takes just over an hour. We talk about friends laugh he asks me how I'm doing I say well, I ask him how he's doing he says fine all he does is work. I see a big sign for the Pageant of the Masters, it makes me laugh. We drive past an outdoor theater called the Irvine Bowl, which says it is the home of the Pageant of the Masters I laugh again. We get to Laguna Beach. We get lost. I call Leonard he gives us directions. We find his house at the end of a dead-end street. It's a large, white, contemporary house, all angles and glass, built into the side of a cliff overlooking the ocean. There are ten or so cars parked in the driveway and along the curb. All of them are expensive European cars: Porsches, Bentleys, Mercedescs, Jaguars, BMWs.

We park, walk to the door, there's a man at the door he asks for our names. I give him my name and he lets us in. We walk through the door into a large open living room. Everything is white, the floors, the walls, the furniture, there are white flowers in white vases, white lamps with white shades, long white linen curtains on the edges of the windows. There is a stairway leading down at the back edge of the room, we hear noise from below we walk to the stairway and descend. We walk into another large open room. The front wall of the room is made of glass, beyond the glass there is a deck and beyond the deck open views of the Pacific ocean. Along another wall there is a pool table with black felt. Along a third there is a bar a long white bar, a bartender in a white tuxedo stands behind it serving drinks. Along the back there is a huge television, the largest television I have ever seen, its image coming from a projector hanging on the ceiling. There are three large, soft couches in a U in front of the television. There are about thirty people spread through the room and on the deck, there are many more women than men. The men are diverse, black white and Asian, some in suits, some in shorts and t-shirts. The women are all white, all beautiful, most are blond. Most have surgically enhanced chests, and are all well-dressed, though some wear less than others. When we reach the bottom of the stairs Chris looks around and looks at me and smiles and says holy fuck, this is going to be fun.

I see Leonard on the deck he's smoking a cigar and talking to a man in his sixties with long white hair and a long white beard the man has a young blond girl with him. I walk toward Leonard he sees me raises his hand yells.

My son. My son has arrived.

The man and the blonde turn and look at me I laugh.

Hi, Leonard.

You just get here?

Yeah.

That your friend?

Yeah. Chris, Leonard. Leonard, Chris.

They shake hands. The man interrupts, tells Leonard they'll talk later. He walks away with the woman, who glances back at us. Leonard looks at Chris, speaks.

You live nearby, right?

Yeah.

You smoke weed?

Yeah.

You like fucking hot chicks?

Chris laughs.

Of course.

The guy who just walked away is the biggest pot dealer on the west coast and the woman is his wife, who's a porn star. She likes to fuck and he doesn't care who she fucks and I could tell by the look she gave you that she wants to fuck you, so if you want either weed or her, let me know. Chris laughs again.

Seriously?

Leonard nods.

Yeah, but you better be ready.

Ready for what?

She stars in S&M porn films, and she might want to beat you up before she fucks you.

Really?

Yeah, and she can kick some ass. I've seen the results. It isn't pretty.

Chris turns around, looks at the woman, who is standing with her husband near the pool table. He turns back to us.

You got any beer? I think I need to have a beer and think about it.

Of course I've got beer, I've got whatever you want. Go tell the bartender and give me a minute with my son.

Cool.

Chris walks to the bar. Leonard turns to me.

Thanks for coming.

Thanks for having me.

This may be the last of these parties. I thought you'd want to see it and I thought you'd enjoy it.

Why the last?

Making some changes.

Care to elaborate?

Not yet.

Okay.

I look around.

Who are all these people?

Gambling fools, a number of whom will lose enormous sums of money to me tonight.

All of them gamble with you?

All of the men, and a couple of the women. The other women are either with one of the men or were hired by me to keep the men happy.

Which ones are hired?

183

You like one of them?

Just curious.

See the one talking to your friend?

I look at Chris, who is standing by the bar. He is talking to a tall blond woman, she's taller than him, who is wearing a short skirt and a tube top, neither of which covers much of her body.

Yeah, I see her.

She's a pro, and at some point in the next couple minutes she's going to lean into his ear and offer to go upstairs with him.

He's gonna shit.

If he's smart, he's gonna go upstairs. It'll be the ride of his fucking life.

I laugh.

You do this often?

As I said, this may be the last time, but I usually do it for the Super Bowl, the NCAA basketball championship and the Kentucky Derby, which are the biggest betting days of the year.

Why here and not Vegas?

Same reason I've never brought you to Vegas.

Which is?

I get followed around in Vegas. My every move is monitored by people whose sole aim in life is to figure out some way to lock me up. You're already a blip on their radar, but if you were to show up in Vegas, you would become a much larger blip, which doesn't need to happen. I have parties here because I can control what happens in this house and what people see and hear in this house. It's no coincidence that it's at the end of a one-way street, and that it's built into the side of a cliff. Both things make surveillance of it much more difficult. I also found these former spies from England who opened a spy shop that sells high-tech spy shit and they sweep it once a month for listening devices.

They ever find anything?

Yeah, but not in a while, which means the government has either given up on this place or is using shit my guys can't find. Won't matter soon anyway, because, as I said, these parties are ending.

And you're not gonna tell me why?

Not yet.

He takes a drag of his cigar, speaks.
Everything good with you?
Yeah.
Keeping busy?
Yeah.
Doing what?
I wrote a movie script.
Leonard smiles.
Hah! That's fucking great. Why didn't you tell me you were doing that?
I didn't want to be embarrassed if I couldn't finish it.
You want to be a writer?
I thought I'd try it.
Can I read this script?
No.
Why?
It's awful.
Come on.
No way.
It can't be that bad.
It's fucking awful. I showed it to a couple of people and everyone agrees, even though some of them won't say it directly.
Why'd you write a script? I thought you were gonna write a book.
Scripts are easier and take less time and I thought I might be able to make some money at it.
Most movies are awful, so it's probably perfect.
This is awful even on the movie scale of awful, and it wasn't supposed to be awful. While I was doing it, I thought it was brilliant. Nobody in their right mind would give me a penny for it.
There are plenty of people in Hollywood who aren't in their right minds. Some of them are here, right now, in this fucking house.
Trust me, even they would think it was awful.
You gonna write another one?
Yeah.
Good. You should write the dumbest, most commercial thing you can think of and I bet you'll sell it.

Maybe.

How's your money holding up?

I still have too much of it.

Go spend it. Buy something beautiful.

I saw a Matisse drawing recently.

I'll expect to see it on your wall next time I'm in town.

You should come soon. My friends miss you and they're hungry.

He laughs, motions toward the house.

Game's about to start, I gotta go in and take action.

Where's Snap?

Dallas is playing, and for some reason Snap, despite the fact that he is from New York, has always been a Dallas fan, so I got a pair of tickets for him and his brother and sent them.

You're a good man, Leonard.

He laughs.

No I'm not.

Yeah you are.

Let's go inside. I gotta get to work.

I follow him inside. Chris is still talking to the girl. Leonard walks toward the couches, a platinum selling R&B star is singing the National Anthem on the television. Leonard starts mingling with his guests, telling them jokes, laughing with them, shaking hands with them. I go to the bar, get a cola, find a seat, wait for the game to start. Almost immediately, Chris sits next to me, speaks.

Dude.

What's up?

That chick, I think she's into me.

I laugh.

What's so funny?

Are you into her?

Look at her. She's gorgeous. Of course I'm into her.

And why do you think she's into you?

She asked me if I wanted to go upstairs, have a private conversation.

What'd you say?

I said hell yes. She's grabbing her purse and we're going up.

I laugh again.

What's so funny?

I shake my head.

Come on, Dude. What's so funny?

She's a hooker, Chris.

No way.

Yes, way.

How do you know?

Leonard told me.

She's a fucking hooker?

Yeah.

I thought she was into me.

She probably was, though she gets paid to be into everyone here, literally and figuratively.

Goddamnit.

Get a drink. Let's watch the game.

He goes to the bar, gets a drink, comes back. As the game starts, most of the people in the house gather in the area around the television. Leonard is sitting in the middle of the couch taking bets. From where we are sitting we can hear the amounts fifty, seventy-five, one hundred thousand, we hear one man say two hundred and twenty-five, we hear another say four hundred. During the game, we hear more ridiculous bets. One man bets one hundred thousand dollars that Dallas will get a first down, he loses the bet. Another bets fifty that the other team's kicker will miss a field goal, he wins the bet. Leonard takes every bet offered, though he often adjusts the odds. There are bets on first downs, fourth downs, on extra points, passing yards, rushing yards, points above and below, there are bets on fucking everything. At halftime everyone goes upstairs, where a huge buffet has been laid out. There is prime rib, there are crab claws, there is Caesar salad, baked potatoes, creamed spinach. There are salmon steaks, there's pasta salad. There is a separate buffet with dessert cakes and tarts and pies and cookies and chocolates and éclairs. We get plates of food, go back downstairs, watch the halftime show. Chris meets two other women one of them is a hooker, the other is married to a record producer, I meet the owner of a chain of car dealerships, an Israeli weapons dealer, a man who exports used American clothing to Japan, two professional gamblers, a man who says he is Iranian royalty and had to flee the Ayatollahs. Near the end of the show, Leonard sits down next to me. I speak.

How's it going?

Bad right now.

Why?

Down 1.2 million.

Fuck.

I'll get it back.

That's a lot of dough.

Just wait. People start getting stupid in the second half. You having fun?

Yeah, I am. This is ridiculous.

It is indeed.

You having fun?

It's work.

You should grab one of your girls, relieve some stress before the game starts again.

They're not here for me. If you want one, though, you can have my room.

No thanks.

Across the room, a man starts calling for Leonard.

I gotta run.

Cool.

He gets up, walks to the man. The game starts again. Chris shoots pool with two of the hookers, tries to decide if he wants to sleep with one of them or both of them or both of them at the same time. I try to convince him that he should have both of them at the same time, he decides against it, says it doesn't feel right to him. I tell him it would probably feel awfully fucking right while he was doing it and he laughs and says yeah, yeah, yeah.

As the game goes on Leonard's guests get more and more drunk, some of them start snorting coke off the coffee table, the bar, off compact disk covers, some of them start smoking weed. There are more bets, and the bets, fueled by liquor and drugs, are riskier and more ridiculous. Leonard starts winning more of them, makes his money back, starts racking up huge gains. By the time the game ends, which Dallas wins, Leonard is obviously happy, though it doesn't show because he keeps a straight face.

After the game the women turn on music, start dancing. The liquor is still flowing, the drugs are still out, some of the women start making out with the men, some of them start making out with each other, some of them stand on top of the bar, take off their shirts and dance. I have a red-eye and Chris has lawns to mow early in the morning, so we find Leonard he's on the deck smoking a cigar. I speak.

We're heading out.

You've had enough?

It was cool. I'm glad I came. Thank you for bringing me.

Of course. What are you going to do when you get home?

Write another dumb movie.

Make it really dumb.

I'll do my best.

And I'll come visit when I can or when I finish with my new business.

The secret business.

Leonard laughs.

You'll understand when I tell you.

Be careful.

I am being careful. That's why shit like this . . .

He motions toward the house.

Is ending.

I'm glad I got to see it.

He laughs.

If you stay a bit longer, you'll see a whole lot more.

I laugh. He puts his arm around me.

I'll walk you to the door.

Thanks.

We walk to the door. Leonard opens it we step outside. He speaks.

Safe travels.

You too.

He looks at Chris.

Good to meet you.

Thanks for having me.

You change your mind about those girls, let me know. It'll be on me.

Chris laughs.

Thanks.

Leonard looks back at me.

See you soon, my son.

Later, Leonard.

Chris and I walk to his truck get inside pull away. Leonard stands at the end of his drive, watches us go.

Later Leonard.

Winter becomes spring.

I write another movie script. I think it's great until I show it to my friends. They let me know that it is not great, not even close to great, that it should be thrown away.

I meet a girl named Tanya at the Local Option. She's small, blond, British. She has bright blue eyes and she likes to laugh. Fifteen minutes after we meet she asks me if I want to take her home. I know I'll never love her, so I say yeah. We have a lovely evening together.

I buy the Matisse. It looks nice on my wall.

I celebrate April Fools' Day. The one day a year when we are reminded what we are for the other three hundred and sixty-four. Happy Fools' Day, motherfucker, happy April Fools' Day.

I see Brooke on the street. She's shopping, I'm walking. We talk for three or four minutes and it hurts me for three or four days.

I go out every night with my friends. We go to bars shoot pool, we go to clubs listen to music, we go to parties they drink, we go to dinner eat.

I still don't sleep well after a year and a half I still can't fucking sleep. I read every night until four or five I read until my eyes fall until the rumbling and shaking lull me into black.

I bring Tanya home again and again I bring her home. She doesn't want anything from me or expect anything from me she's easy to be with and she likes to laugh and she makes me laugh. I bring her home again and again.

Spring becomes summer.

The phone rings I answer it. It's early in the morning I just fell asleep.
Hello?
My Son. MY SON. It's a beautiful, beautiful day!
It's not day yet, Leonard. It's still fucking morning. Early fucking morning.
Early to bed, early to rise, that is the man who wins the prize.
I laugh.
What the fuck happened to you?
Wonderful things.
Like what?
I'm coming to town. I'll tell you in person.
When are you coming?
Today. Meet me at the hotel for lunch.
Okay.
See you then, SEE YOU THEN!
I laugh.
Yeah, see you then.
I hang up the phone, go back to sleep. I wake up around noon, take a
shower, walk down to the hotel. Leonard and Snap are sitting in the
restaurant when I walk in they stand. Leonard speaks.
My son.
Leonard.
He hugs me, releases. I look at Snap.
Long time.
Been busy.
Good to see you.
You too, kid.
We sit. I speak.
What's the big news?

Leonard smiles, reaches into his pocket, pulls out a plastic card, sets it in front of me.

Phone cards.

I laugh.

Phone cards?

You got it. Phone cards.

So what.

So what? Think, my Son, think.

You want me to make a phone call?

No.

You want me to sell it?

No.

I have no idea. It's a phone card. I can buy one of those anywhere.

Leonard shakes his head.

Not one of these.

It's somehow different?

Leonard nods.

Where have I been traveling for the last several months?

All over the place.

All over the place where?

The Caribbean and Central America.

Why would I go there and what does that have to do with me and my business and phone cards?

No idea.

Think, my son, think.

Just tell me.

Leonard looks at Snapper.

He has no vision.

Snapper shrugs, speaks.

Some people don't.

It's obvious to me.

He ain't you.

Leonard looks back at me.

As you know, a large portion of my income is generated through the making and taking of bets. As you can imagine, the manner in which I take these bets, and the organization set up to handle and administrate them, is entirely illegal.

Right.

For a number of reasons, I don't want my businesses to be illegal anymore. The two primary reasons are that with the implementation of RICO laws, which are designed to put people like me away, my life has become increasingly more difficult. I'm tired of being followed, surveyed, I'm tired of fucking FBI agents harassing people who do business with me, I'm tired of having to monitor everyone I fucking know to make sure they're not ratting me out. I don't want to go to jail. I don't want to die in jail. I have some things I want to do before I'm gone and I will not be able to do them if I'm in jail. If I legalize my businesses, I can't be sent to jail.

Perfectly understandable.

The other reason is the pledge I made to my dying Father, which was to play the golf course where he labored as a lawn-mower and play it just like one of the fucking members. As you know, I have had a very difficult time doing this. One of the reasons it has been so difficult is because I am a known criminal. If I stop being a criminal, and I can prove I have stopped being a criminal, it may open certain doors for me.

Also perfectly understandable.

In 1982, the Federal government ordered the break-up of AT&T, which held a monopoly on local and long distance telephone services. The break-up was ordered so that competition would be spurred and consumers would no longer be forced to pay rates that were much higher than they should have been. More recently, the Telecommunications Act was passed because the net result of the '82 break-up wasn't as positive as was hoped. The new act opens long distance lines to dozens of new phone companies, most of which will go out of business. A few won't, and a few will carve out specific little niches, and one of those niches is the phone card business.

Leonard picks up the card.

You buy a card, you have a specific amount of money on the card, ten dollars, twenty dollars, fifty dollars, whatever, you make long distance calls through the card company's operators, you talk until the card runs out and then you buy another one. You with me?

I nod.

Yeah, I'm with you.

You understand where I'm going with this?

No I don't.

Leonard looks at Snapper, speaks.

He has no vision.

It ain't that, it's that you got a lot. That's why you're in charge.

He's my son, he should have it too.

Well he don't, and that's that.

Leonard looks back at me.

Do you happen to know what's legal in the Caribbean and certain parts of Central and South America that is illegal here?

I would imagine there are a few things.

You're right about that, but what that might be directly related to me?

Again, probably a few things, but I'm guessing from this conversation that you're referring to gambling.

Bingo! It's a fucking gambler's paradise down there. And what isn't legal becomes legal with a wad of hundreds slipped into the hands of the correct local official. I love it, I fucking love it.

I laugh.

So what does that have to do with phone cards?

Phone cards make it all legal, and let me make money off it regardless of the outcome of the bets.

How is that?

I recently relocated the bulk of the people who work for me in my gambling businesses to the Caribbean and certain parts of Central and South America, where what they do is entirely legal. I'm having everyone who places bets through my people buy phone cards from the phone card company that I now own, and I am charging very high rates for those calls. All of the money involved is moved through offshore banks, which are not beholden to the laws of this country, and the only person breaking the law in this equation is the individual placing the bet on American soil.

Really?

Let's say you were one of my clients. You go to a retail location that sells my phone cards. You buy a few of them. You call a number you've been given, that's been mailed to you from an offshore location. That number only receives calls through the operators who work for my phone company and who take calls using my phone cards. They put you through to someone sitting at a desk in a location where gambling is legal. That person takes your bet, and either takes a credit card number or provides you with wiring instructions for payment. You place your bet, you are given a confirmation number. The call costs you ten dollars per minute. You have broken the law by placing the bet, but no one on my end has broken the law because they are all working in places where their activities are legal. You're sure about all this?

There are a few gray areas, but they're gray enough so that if someone wants to arrest me or tries to prosecute me, I'll tie them up in court for fucking decades.

Very impressive, Leonard.

I'm going to send the Federal Prosecutor in Las Vegas a note inviting him to come over to my house and kindly kiss my ass.

I laugh, Snapper laughs. Leonard looks around.

I hope those fuckers have someone watching or listening to us right now. He lifts his middle finger, waves it around.

If so, this is for you, because you're not gonna get me, you fuckers.

I laugh again. When I stop, I speak.

Congratulations, Leonard.

Thank you.

I'm incredibly impressed.

Thank you.

We should celebrate.

Why do you think we're here?

Good. This time, though, I'm taking care of the check.

No, that's not how it works.

It is tonight.

No.

Leonard.

What?

I hold up a wad of cash.

This is the last of the money I made working for you. I've been keeping it so I could spend it on one of our dinners. You're going to shut the fuck up and let me take care of the check tonight.

He laughs.

Thank you, my son, thank you.

I cut up the fake driver's license throw it away Jimmy Testardo no longer exists.

I close the safe deposit box.

I get a job at a clothing store on Michigan Avenue. I work in the stockroom with a Filipino and two Mexicans. Most of my work is at night, after the store is closed. My co-workers and I are given a list by the manager with such tasks as replace flat front khakis, replenish and fold all fashion t-shirts, replace ribbon dispensers behind counter, sweep and mop entrance floor. It's a dumb job, and I don't get paid shit, but it feels good to work.

I write another script. I send it to my friends I know they're tired of reading my awful scripts. I tell them this will be the last one.

I start sleeping, every second or third night I sleep easily, well. The shaking and rumbling of the train is a song that lulls me into six, eight, ten glorious hours of peace, silence and blackness.

I walk in the heat in the rain in the day night morning afternoon sunrise sunset I walk for hours. I walk along the lake and I jump into the water. I see a bench and I sit and have a smoke. I see an ice cream truck and I order the largest cone they sell. I take naps on the lawns of public parks, I listen to music played in bandstands, I read in the shade of trees in the shade of towering trees. I go to the zoo look at the animals, yo gorilla, what the fuck's up!

My friends tell me the script isn't bad might actually be good. It's a romantic comedy a love triangle between friends with a happy ending. I decide to try to sell it to Hollywood I don't know anyone in Hollywood, but so what I'll try anyway.

I wander the halls of the art museum the pictures are still beautiful and the galleries are air-conditioned I wander the halls.

I visit Lilly. Her flowers wilt in the heat so I bring more of them. I don't talk much, don't feel the need to talk anymore, just sit with her, it's good to know she's there, just sit.

I get fired from the job at the clothing store. The manager decided she wanted every article of clothing in the store, and there are thousands of them, taken off the shelves and re-folded. I ask her why she says because I said so. I try to organize a strike with the other stockroom guys and I succeed and we buy a box of doughnuts and sit on the floor in the middle of the store and refuse to work. She tells the other stockroom guys they can keep their jobs if they end the strike and she fires me and tells me if I don't leave the store immediately she's calling the police. I take the doughnuts with me.

My friend has a cousin that works for a famous director in Hollywood. I call her and I ask her to read my script, she says send it and I'll read it when I have some time. I call her once a week to remind her. She doesn't read it, so I keep calling her.

Leonard calls me tells me he's coming to town, he says he's touring with
a rock band, they have a show in Chicago. I ask him what band he tells
me I laugh ask him what the fuck is he doing touring with a rock band he
tells me the singer is a friend and he felt like having a strange summer. I
ask him if he wants me to meet him at his hotel, he says no he's staying
somewhere else, he tells me where I start walking downtown.

The hotel is on Michigan Avenue, across the street from his regular hotel.
Its lobby is also several stories up, above a high-end shopping center. I take
an elevator to the lobby. The doors open to a vast room that takes up the
entire floor of the building. Along one wall are the reception and
concierge desks, along the other three are floor-to-ceiling windows. In the
middle of the room there are tables and chairs, long, luxurious sofas, waiters and waitresses carrying trays of appetizers and drinks. I look for
Leonard, see him sitting on a sofa with several women and one man. I recognize the man as the singer of the band. I walk toward them, Leonard
sees me coming, stands, yells.

MY SON, MY SON!

I wave, laugh. Everyone on the couch turns and looks at me.

MY SON HAS ARRIVED.

What's up, Leonard?

Living the rock 'n roll lifestyle, loving the rock 'n roll lifestyle.

I laugh again, sit down in a chair across from Leonard. He introduces me
to the singer and the women. The singer, who also plays the drums, is in
his early forties, has short graying hair, the slight accent of a Texas childhood, he wears jeans and t-shirt. None of the women are older than
twenty, and on a scale of one to ten, they all rank somewhere around fifty.
They each wear different versions of almost nothing, which is fine with
me. Although Leonard seems perfectly comfortable with them, he doesn't

really fit in. He is significantly older than all of them, and his clothes are more like those of an accountant. The singer and the girls are all drinking, Leonard has a pitcher of water. I order a cola and sit and listen to the singer tell stories about his life on the road as a rock star. He talks about trashing hotel rooms, orgies in the backs of buses, sets of twins, a set of triplets, about things in his contract that venues are required to provide, such as peanut butter cups stacked in perfect pyramids and cans of cola cooled to exactly thirty-six degrees. The girls hang on every word. Leonard seems to know the stories, adds certain details to them and says that's rock 'n roll, man, that's rock 'n roll at the end of each of them. I just sit and laugh, though I'm not sure if I'm laughing with the singer or at the singer. At the end of a story about a particularly randy mother and daughter team, which draws big laughs and several oohs and ahhs, the singer says he needs to go upstairs and meditate before he leaves for the show. One of the girls asks him what kind of meditation he practices and he invites her to come upstairs with him so that he can show her. She obliges and they leave together.

The rest of the girls, now sitting with Leonard and me leave fairly quickly, each inventing a different excuse. When the last of them is gone, Leonard looks at me and he speaks.

What'd you think?

About him or them?

Them.

I love them all.

He laughs.

And him?

He was fine.

Leonard laughs again.

He's a dick.

I laugh.

He is, he's a dick.

Why do you hang out with him?

Because this is fun. I rock, I roll, I live it, I love it. And even though he's a dick, he's a fun dick.

I laugh.

You're doing good?

Yeah.

Anything new?

I got that girl in Hollywood to read my script.

Leonard smiles.

You just kept bugging her and finally she caved in?

I nod, smile.

Yeah.

What'd she say?

She said it's really good, that I could probably sell it, that I should move out there and try to keep doing it.

Leonard smiles, claps his hands.

That's fucking great.

There's more.

More, what kind of more?

After we finished talking about the script, we just kept talking. First night we talked for five hours. Next night five more. For the last three nights we've been up until dawn just talking.

What do you talk about?

I don't know. Everything and nothing. We just talk.

Talk for hours and hours and hours?

Yeah.

What's her name?

Liza.

That's a good name, a strong name. Are you in love?

I've never met her.

Are you in love?

I don't know.

My oh my, this is fucking wonderful. You're in love and you're moving to LA.

I'm not moving.

Why?

I'm just not.

Are you fucking crazy?

No.

You just got a new job, right?

Yeah.

What are you doing?

I work at a frame store. I'm the cashier.

That's a bullshit job.

Yeah it is.

You'd rather do that than be a writer?

No.

Then move to LA where you can make silly movie money doing what you want and spend time with the girl you stay up all night talking to.

I don't want to leave here.

Why?

I just don't.

You gotta let her go.

What?

You heard me. You gotta let her go.

This isn't about that.

You don't want to admit it, but it is.

No it's not.

You leave here and you leave her and you leave your memories and leave all those dreams you had behind and you finally let go.

Fuck you, Leonard.

She left you, you gotta leave her.

Fuck you, Leonard.

She did what she thought was right for her, you gotta do what's right for you. You respect her decision, and you know she'd respect your decision.

Fuck you, Leonard.

And if you don't leave, ten years from now you're gonna look back and re-gret it, and you're gonna hate yourself for being a coward and you're gonna hate Lilly for keeping you here and you'd know you fucked-up and blew it.

FUCKING DROP IT, LEONARD.

I'll drop it, but you should think about it, and we're going to talk more about it.

I look away. Leonard doesn't speak, just lets it sit there. I turn back, speak.

What time's the concert?

The opening band is at seven, but they're no good. They don't rock like a

good band should rock, so fuck them. We should show up at around
eight thirty.

You want us to meet you here?

Who you bringing?

My friend Erin.

Good, I like Erin. She dresses well, speaks well, has a nice smile and a nice
laugh. I'll pick you up at seven thirty at your apartment.

I stand.

See you then.

Think about it, my son.

I walk home and I take a shower. I hang out with Julianne she has a beer
and I have a cola, I let her talk listen to her talk even though her accent
has become familiar I still love to listen to it. Erin shows up a little early.
She has a beer. We wait for Leonard who arrives at exactly seven thirty.
We walk out of the apartment. There's a large black limo waiting at the
curb, a uniformed driver standing near the open rear door. I look at
Leonard, speak.

Black?

He speaks.

Yeah, black.

I thought you only drove white cars?

There's an exception to every rule and the exception to that rule extends
to limousines, because white limousines are silly.

I laugh. We get into the limo and the driver closes the door behind us.
There's a fridge stocked with cola and champagne, a television, a stereo.
Leonard and I drink cola, Erin drinks champagne, and we listen to music
by the band we're going to see as we drive out to the venue. When we get
there we're waved into a reserved parking area and we're led to our seats,
front and center, by a representative of the band. The show starts and the
singer, who may be an asshole in his life, rocks the fucking house once he's
on stage. I rock with him, Erin rocks with him, Leonard rocks with him.
We rock and fucking roll all night.

Live it, love it.

I think about leaving. I think about Lilly. I think about my life and what I want from it, I think about these things as I walk, as I work, as I eat, as I shower, as I read, while I'm on the phone, when I'm with my friends. My last thoughts before I sleep, my first thoughts as I wake, I think about leaving here.

I sit before her. I sit and I stare at the stone, at her name, at the dates of her life, at the words, You were Loved, at the words You were Loved. I sit before her and I remember the first time we met she smiled and said hello we were standing in line at the clinic medical unit and she turned around and she smiled and she said hello. I remember our first cigarette she said want a smoke, tough guy and she laughed at me. I remember the first time we were alone she came upon me in the woods I was broken and she held me and said you'll be okay, you'll be okay, and as long as she held me I was okay. I remember our first kiss, the way she tasted, her breath, the smell of her skin, the way my heart beat, beat, beat. I remember every minute of our time, every minute spent hiding from people who told us we shouldn't be together, every conversation, every kiss. I remember her eyes those beautiful blue eyes like deep water, I remember staring into those eyes and knowing. I remember how her hand felt small and fragile and stronger than I thought it could be. I remember her hair long and black a beautiful mess she used to hide it from the world with a baseball cap. I remember her smooth cold pale skin like marble the way my hands felt as they moved around it. I remember the scars on her wrists I thought were behind her. I remember crying with her and for her and because of her. I remember laughing with her and for her and because of her. I remember the peace I knew with her, the security I knew with her, the strength I knew with her, the hope I knew with her, the love I knew with her. I knew love with her, love like nothing before it. We had dreams, plans, we were going to spend our lives together. We carried each other through blackness and I thought through death and I was wrong. She did what she did. I don't hate her for it anymore. I'm going to do what I'm going to do. I start to cry. Some of the tears are sadness and sorrow, some are pain and rage, some are for loss, some for forgiveness and some of them, the best of them, are because I am fortunate to have known her at all. I lean toward the stone where she lies and I cry and I whisper I love you, Lilly, and I'll be back to see you, I love you, I'll miss you and I'll be back.

I stand and I walk away.

It's time to go.

los angeles

My second friend with the name Kevin lives in Los Angeles. He's an actor who lives in a Hollywood apartment and takes acting classes and goes to auditions and waits tables and struggles. We went to college together. He's twenty-six, but looks eighteen, he has dark wavy hair and blue eyes and big rosy cheeks. He likes to talk and he's funny most of the time and he's easy to be with most of the time and he wants to drive with me from Chicago to Los Angeles. It'll be good to have him.

He comes to Chicago and we pack up my truck and plan our route. We're going to cut straight across the Midwest, head south into New Mexico, cross Arizona, Nevada and California.

We leave early the next morning. As we pull out I stop at a random corner in a rundown neighborhood. I take my bottle of rose, the bottle I bought when I arrived, the bottle I've had during my entire time here, the bottle I've always kept as an option, and I leave it unopened on the corner. I hope somebody finds it, and I hope they enjoy it.

We drive straight west through hours and hours of farmland, hundreds of miles blend together in a sea of gently waving green and yellow, every red barn white farmhouse gray silo looks the same. We stop in Kansas City for the night, get up early, keep going. In Colorado we cut south, head into New Mexico. Kevin gets a message about an important audition, he needs to be back in LA sooner than planned. We decide to keep going straight to California, we'll stop for gas and food, we'll drive in shifts one sleeps while one drives. Kevin starts checking the fluids every time we stop for gas, he checks the oil, coolant, wiper. I tell him not to worry about it, that the car was just tuned-up and is in good shape. He tells me he's just being careful. We cross the mountains of New Mexico, drop into Arizona, it's two in the morning, I pull into a truckstop. I go inside for coffee and cigarettes Kevin starts checking everything again. Ten minutes later we pull out.

It is the middle of the night. We're in the middle of the desert. Kevin isn't talking anymore we're both tired he tells me he's going to sleep. I turn on the radio. I listen to someone talking about stormtroopers who fly around in black helicopters and kidnap and brainwash people who speak out against the government. It's part of a conspiracy controlled by the Freemasons and the Jews. I start to hear a strange ticking coming from the engine. I start to smell burning plastic. I laugh, think maybe the Freemasons and the Jews are after me. The ticking becomes louder, the smell stronger. There is a large BOOM, the engine immediately loses power, smoke starts pouring from beneath the hood, the smell is over-whelming. Kevin wakes up and says what's happened, what's going on, I tell him something seems to be wrong with the engine and I think it has to do with Freemasons and Jews, and I guide the car to the shoulder of the highway. We get out of the car Kevin is still confused.

What happened?

I don't know.

We've got to get away. I think the car is going to explode.

I think we're okay.

What's wrong with it?

I look at the truck. It is smoking less, it still smells awful.

I have no idea. Something bad happened.

How?

Did you put all the caps and shit back on?

Of course I did, I'm not stupid.

Just checking.

We stand and stare at the truck. The smoke is almost gone. We stand and stare for a couple of minutes. It is the middle of the night. We're in the middle of the desert. I look at Kevin.

Looks like we're fucked.

Try to start it.

It's not gonna start.

Just try.

I get in the truck, try to start it. Loud clicking noises come from beneath the hood, it doesn't start. I get out.

Didn't start.

Maybe if we wait awhile.

We wait for ten minutes. Not a single car or truck passes us. I try to start the engine, same thing. Kevin speaks.

What do you want to do?

Sit here.

We sit there. A couple cars pass by, no one stops. Thirty minutes a state trooper pulls over. An officer gets out of the cruiser, for the first time in my life I'm thrilled to see a law enforcement officer walking toward me. He asks what we're doing we tell him the truck broke down. He asks where we're from and going and I tell him. He asks us if we know what's wrong with the truck I say no idea. He goes back to his cruiser, gets on the radio, speaks for a few minutes, comes back.

I called a mechanic I know who has a tow truck. He can come get you if you want, but it's not gonna be cheap. If you don't want to do that, you can wait till morning and the highway patrol will tow the car.

Can your guy get here faster?

It's the middle of the night and he's not close.

I don't want to wait till morning.

I'll call my guy. He can be here in an hour.

The trooper goes back to the cruiser gets on the radio, he comes back and tells us the mechanic is coming. He gets back in the cruiser and drives away.

We wait. I sit on the side of the road and smoke cigarettes. Kevin paces back and forth, he's worried we won't get back in time for his audition. An hour passes, two hours it is starting to get light when we see a tow truck approaching us. It pulls over behind us, a tall skinny man his arms covered with tattoos, a cigarette dangling from his lips, gets out of the truck starts ambling toward us he speaks.

Looks like you're having some trouble here.

Yeah.

What happened?

Funny noises and smoke.

Pop that hood the fuck up.

I reach in, pop the hood. He opens it, looks at the engine. Kevin and I stand behind him, watch him as he looks around the engine, he turns around.

You're fucked, man, fucking fucked.

What happened?

Your engine blew up.

How?

Was somebody messing around with it?

I motion toward Kevin. The man speaks.

He forgot to put the radiator cap back on and all your coolant evaporated and the thing, boom, blew the fuck up.

Kevin speaks.

Impossible.

Nah, that's what happened. I'm looking at it.

I put the cap on.

It ain't there, and as far as I know, they can't take themselves off.

Kevin gets angry, defensive.

You're not funny.

Ain't trying to be funny, just trying to tell you what happened, and what happened is there ain't no radiator cap on here and the motherfucking engine blew.

That's not what happened.

I look at the mechanic, speak.

How long will it take to fix it?

He thinks for a moment, speaks.

Probably a week, ten days. Ain't quick, this kind of job.

Kevin speaks.

A week?

At least, man. The engine is fucked, that shit is fucking fried.

Kevin turns to me.

I have to be back, I have to be back soon.

I look at the mechanic.

Any way to do it faster.

Nope.

Is there a truck rental place nearby?

In Flagstaff.

How far is that?

110 miles or so or something like that.

Can you tow us there?

I'll tow you to Japan if you fucking pay me, man. I'll tow you anywhere.

How much will it cost?

Well, it's four thirty in the morning and I fucking hate Flagstaff and my
wife don't like me right now and I need some money to make her happy,
so it's gonna be pricey.

How much?

Seven hundred fifty bucks.

No way.

Five hundred bucks.

Three fifty.

My wife's really fucking mad, man, I need five large.

Fine let's go.

The mechanic goes back to his truck, pulls it in front of my truck, starts
hitching my truck to the towing mechanism on the back of his truck.
Kevin is still angry, still doesn't believe this is happening, absolutely
doesn't believe he had anything to do with it. I get in next to the mechanic, Kevin is next to me, we start driving toward Flagstaff.

We watch the sun rise over desolate flats. The mechanic talks and smokes
he talks about his wife he says she hates him, about his two brothers he
says they hate him, about his girlfriend he says she hates him. He talks
about his truck he calls it Wayne it is his prized possession. He talks about
shooting guns in the desert he's hoping to find someone who will sell him
a bazooka so he can do some, he says, real true-to-life destruction-style
shit. I listen to the mechanic and laugh for most of the trip. Kevin stares
out the window, clenches his jaw and shakes his head.

We pull into Flagstaff. It is still early morning. Almost everything is closed
we find a gas station with coffee and cigarettes and beef jerky. The mechanic drops us, with my truck, in the parking lot of a truck rental company. I write him a check, he says thank you and advises me to leave
Flagstaff as soon as possible. I ask him why he says strange things happen
around here. I ask him what he shakes his head and says man, just trust
me, there is fucking ugly, scary, wack-ass shit in the air here. He gets in his
truck and leaves us.

Kevin and I sit and wait. We have two hours until the office opens Kevin
spends most of it cursing the mechanic and his faulty diagnosis. When the
office opens I rent a large truck and a trailer and I push my poor broken-
down truck onto the trailer. We start driving west. I haven't slept in

twenty-four hours. The desert plays tricks with my mind with my eyes I see mirages, I see silver flashes, blue lights. I drink coffee, smoke cigarettes, turn the volume on the radio all the way up, hallucinate.

Once we enter Los Angeles County it takes four hours to go sixty miles. When we pull into West Hollywood I can't think straight, see straight, walk straight. I leave the trucks my truck on the trailer and the big truck on the side of a street they take up half a block.

I call Leonard I told him I'd call as soon as I arrived. He wants to have lunch with me. He gives me the name of a restaurant, tells me he'll be there on Wednesday at one o'clock.

I get a ride to the restaurant. I arrive a few minutes early. I walk inside the Maitre d' is at a stand just inside the front door. I give him Leonard's name he tells me that Leonard has not arrived I should wait for him at the bar.

I walk to the bar, which is a few feet behind him. I sit down on a stool, look around me. It's crowded, noisy, I am the youngest person in the restaurant, and the worst-dressed. Most of the customers are middle-aged men in suits, the suits are all gray, black or navy blue they look like expensive suits. Most of the men are immaculately groomed perfect hair, smooth tans, manicured hands, those that aren't look deliberately ruffled, as if they spent the morning in front of the mirror making sure their hair was just the right kind of messy. The walls are covered with cartoon drawings of famous people almost all men who are regular customers, some are movie stars, some athletes, some famous directors and producers. I order a nice cold tasty cola and I wait for Leonard.

He arrives five minutes later he's wearing a suit, he's with the Snapper who is also wearing a suit. He sees me I stand we hug each other.

Welcome to California, my son.

Thanks, Leonard.

We separate, I shake hands with Snapper.

Welcome, kid.

Thanks, Snap.

The Maitre d' leads us to a table. We sit in a booth along a wall Leonard and Snap sit on one side, I sit on the other side. Leonard speaks.

Here you are, in the land of sunshine and dreams. You will either love it or hate it, and you will either flourish or fail.

I'm looking forward to finding out.
Love it, my son, and flourish. FLOURISH.
What are you doing in town?
I was seeing a nutritionist.
Why?
Because I want to live forever.
I laugh.
Seriously?
Yes, seriously. A proper diet may be the key to immortality. I would like to
be immortal.
I laugh again.
That's crazy, Leonard.
Snapper speaks.
That's what I told him.
Leonard speaks.
To each his own.
You really think a special diet will make you immortal?
No, I don't, but I do think it'll keep me here awhile longer.
Probably.
Definitely. So, now I'm going to see this nutritionist once a week, on
Wednesdays, for the foreseeable future.
I look at Snapper.
Do you go?
Snapper speaks.
Fuck no. I like cheeseburgers, pizza, fried chicken, ice cream, all the good
stuff. I don't care if it kills me, I'm eating it.
I'm with you.
I'll dance on your graves, spin and yelp and sing happy gravedancing songs.
I laugh, Snapper speaks.
If I die, it won't be cause my fucking diet.
We all laugh. A waiter comes to our table says hello to Leonard says nice
to see you again, sir he gives us menus we order. I get a ribeye and creamed
spinach, Snapper gets a porterhouse, French fries, onion rings, tomatoes
and onions and a blue cheese salad, Leonard orders a chopped salad. As we
wait for the food Leonard asks about Liza I tell him it's too early to tell.
He asks where I'm living I tell him I'm living at Liza's. He asks about my

job prospects I tell him I may work shitty production jobs while I try to sell the script. He tells me he has friends in Hollywood that will help if I want them to, I tell him I want to do this on my own. The waiter brings Snapper and me steak knives, refills our drinks. As he walks away another man walks toward us, Snapper sees him alerts Leonard to his presence. The man is probably in his fifties, but looks older. He has dark wavy hair it looks like it's been dyed, he's extremely thin and extremely tan his skin looks like leather. He's wearing a suit and a sparkling watch and a pinkie ring. Snapper looks at Leonard speaks.

He still owe you?

Leonard speaks.

Yeah he does.

How do you want to handle it?

I don't want to deal with him. This is not the time or the place.

The man arrives at our table looks nervous slightly shaky he's starting to sweat he speaks.

Hello, Leonard.

Leonard looks at him, speaks.

It isn't a good time.

I need to speak to you.

It isn't a good time.

I'm sorry about my payments, I really am, I won't miss . . .

Snapper interrupts.

We're having lunch. We would like you to leave.

The man continues. Leonard looks away.

I'm sorry, Leonard. If you could just give me . . .

Snapper interrupts again.

We would like you to leave.

People at tables near us turn, start watching, Leonard shakes his head, the man continues.

Please, Leonard, please . . .

I see Snapper reach for his steak knife the man doesn't see it he's looking at Leonard who's looking away. BOOM. Snapper slams the knife into the table and pulls his hand away. The knife is sticking straight into the table it's wobbling a bit the man looks shocked. Snapper stands, towers over him, stares at him, speaks.

It isn't a good time.

Everyone near us is silent, staring, the man's eyes are wide and filled with fear, he turns and walks out of the restaurant. Snapper sits back down, takes the knife out of the table, wipes it with his napkin. Leonard speaks.

That guy's a fuckhead.

Snapper speaks.

Just say the word.

Fuck him. Let's enjoy our lunch.

Snapper chuckles.

Someday you'll let me.

Our food comes we eat Leonard eyes my steak I offer him some he says no. After we finish eating we order dessert Snapper gets cheesecake I get a hot fudge sundae Leonard gets a fruit plate. After dessert Leonard says I'll see you next Wednesday?

I say I'll see you next Wednesday.

I stay with Liza we talk for hours I get along better with her than any woman I've ever met we laugh and laugh we sit and talk for hours. As easy as it is to be with each other and as much as we like each other there's still something missing. We both feel it we both know it there's something missing between us and we both mourn it.

I take my battered truck to get fixed it's going to take ten days.

I drive around with Liza start to get a feel for the city. It's a strange city, unlike traditional cities. There is no central downtown. What is called downtown is a ghost town, empty but for a few high-rise office towers filled during the day. The only residents of downtown Los Angeles are the people who live in a self-governing ten block area filled with cardboard box houses and tents. The rest of the city is broken into small neighborhoods, though there is no feeling of neighborhood in them. The sidewalks are empty, people don't interact with each other. There is a feeling that people are living where they are and waiting to move somewhere better, that the dream is almost fulfilled, and when it is, they'll move to one of the wealthy areas of the city and finally make friends with those that live around them.

I find a house. It's a three-bedroom Spanish-style house on a busy street. It stands out among the other houses on its block because the front yard is filled with garbage. I walk around the side of the house and the backyard is also filled with garbage. I look in the windows of the garage it's filled with garbage, I look in the windows of the house also filled with garbage. I ask one of the neighbors what's happening with this house she tells me no one has lived there for three years, occasionally a truck comes by and drops off more crap. I go downtown to the city tax office find out who owns the house call them. I ask them if they'd be interested in getting the house cleaned up and fixed-up, tell them I'll do it for free if they'll let me live there. The man tells me to meet him at the house later in the after-noon I meet him his name is Al he's a mechanic and inherited the house from his grandmother. He agrees to let me live there he also wants a small amount of rent fine with me.

I clean the entire house, the yard, the garage. I tear out carpets there are nice wood floors beneath them. I get a mattress, a desk and a table, some-where to sleep somewhere to work somewhere to eat. I get a roommate. His name is Jaylen. I know him from Chicago, where he was a wholesale weed dealer, never selling less than a pound at a time. He says he's through selling weed, that he wants to be a music video director.

I go out every night. Go out to bars with my friends, friends from the old days who have migrated here, all are working in some area of the enter-tainment industry. We go to the Three of Clubs, the Room, Smalls, DragonFly, the Snakepit, Jones, El Coyote. The bars are filled with beauti-ful young people it's as if the three best-looking people from every town in the country have come to Los Angeles. Everyone wants to be famous, everyone is well-connected. Everyone is just a step or two away they're waiting for that break it's almost there they can taste it fucking taste it.

I miss Chicago. I miss my friends, miss walking, miss seeing Lilly, miss liv-ing without ambition. Los Angeles is a lonely city. Everyone is focused on advancement success fame and money, it is hard to adjust to a culture based on always wanting more, on never being satisfied. I'm lonely, I miss my old life.

I see Leonard for lunch every Wednesday. He looks thinner and in better shape each time. Snapper and I both eat steaks and multiple side dishes and dessert, Leonard sticks with salad and fruit.

I decide I want a dog. I start paying attention to other people's dogs, to their temperaments, to their habits, to their needs, their cost. I meet a pit-bull named Grace 2000. Grace 2000 is short and heavily muscled, white with brown patches, she has deep brown sparkling eyes. She's very excitable, runs in circles around my friend's house, loves to play catch. Sometimes she bites the end of a spring attached to a thick branch of a tree and bounces from it. Sometimes she chases her tail. She never barks and she loves to give kisses. She's a fifty pound ball of energy and love.

I decide that I want a dog like Grace. I buy a paper, look in the classifieds, see ad after ad after ad, pitbull pitbull pitbull. One of the ads says Sons of Cholo. I didn't know what Cholo means or who Cholo is, but I like the sound of it, so I call the number and get an address. I start driving.

The address is in East Los Angeles, in a working-class Hispanic neighbor-hood. I park walk toward the house there are two men sitting on the front porch they're drinking beer and smoking cigarettes their arms are covered with tattoos. I stop in front of them, they stare at me, I say hello they nod. I ask if they're selling the dogs, they say no habla inglés. I don't speak Spanish so I hold up the paper, say Sons of Cholo, they smile, nod, one of them stands up and motions for me to follow him.

We walk around the house. In the backyard there is a small fenced area. Inside the fence is a small doghouse. The man whistles and a giant pit storms out of the doghouse and starts barking.

I've never seen a dog like him in my life. He's short and gigantic, has lay-ers and layers of rippling muscle, his coat is the color of milk chocolate and he has bright green eyes. His head is huge and thick, as if carved from a block of stone, and it's covered with scars. He stands at the fence and snarles at me, his teeth are huge and a perfect white. I stare at him. He barks and snarls, looks like he wants to eat me, I am scared to death of him. The man taps me on the shoulder and points and smiles and says *Cholo, undefeated campeón.* He motions for me to follow him.

We walk to a garage. He lifts the door and puppies begin streaming out, adorable little chocolate puppies, small versions of Cholo, minus the scars, minus the snarling. They yip and tumble over each other, jump on my feet, bite at the bottom of my pants. The man points to the puppies and says Sons of Cholo.

I smile, sit down on the concrete. The puppies run into my lap, start jumping on my chest, licking my face. A hierarchy has been established among them and the larger puppies start muscling the smaller puppies away. The smallest of them falls off my lap and immediately starts climbing back. He gets pushed off again, starts climbing again. All he wants is to get close enough to lick my face.

I stand up, the puppies start nipping at my feet again, I look at the man and point to the smallest puppy. The man nods and holds up three fingers. The price had been listed in the advertisement, I brought cash with me. I take it out of my pocket and hand it to him he picks up the puppy and hands him to me. We shake hands he says gracias I say gracias.

I walk toward my car. The puppy starts whining. The further we get from the garage, the louder the whining. When I open the driver's door, the puppy starts crying, looking toward the garage, where the other Sons of Cholo are still running around. I sit down in the driver's seat. I brought some puppy toys and puppy treats with me, I hold the little fellow in my lap and try to get him interested in them, he just looks toward the garage and cries. I give up trying to make him stop and I start the car and I drive away.

He sits in my lap on the ride back to my house. He cries and he shakes. He pees on me, pees on the seat, pees on the floor. Son of Cholo is scared to death, and he pees all over me.

I call the puppy Cassius. He's a smart pup he knows his name after a few days. I potty train him in a week. He can sit, shake, stay, lie down in two weeks. He goes everywhere with me, rides shotgun in my truck, sleeps in my bed.

I go to parties with my friends. We go to apartments to the courtyards of apartment buildings to houses in the Hollywood Hills. When I meet new people the first question they usually ask me is what do you do? I tell them I am an unemployed aspiring writer and they realize I can't help them in any way and they can't use me in any way and they usually walk away from me.

I send out my script everywhere to everyone I meet who might be interested in it I call them follow up with them no luck no luck. Hearing people say no doesn't bother me, doesn't discourage me. I'm confident in what I can do and I believe that, to a certain extent, I'm playing a numbers game. If I get myself and my work in front of enough people, sooner or later someone will like it.

I go back to trying to write a book I spend most of my time staring at a blank computer screen.

Jaylen and I decide to fill the third bedroom in our house, figure it will be good to have someone to share expenses. Jaylen brings an old friend from Chicago to the house, his name is Tommy. Tommy is Korean, grew up in a small farm town forty miles west of Chicago, his father and mother are both doctors. Tommy dresses like a thug and talks like a thug with a thick inner-city accent. He wants to be either a rap-star, a deejay or a rap video director. I ask him if he ever feels like a phony with his clothes and his accent and he says motherfucker, I grew up in the fields, but my heart's from the motherfucking streets. I ask him if he's ever been in a fight, been arrested, held a gun or dealt drugs, he says he keeps it real with a peaceful vibe.

I see Leonard on Wednesdays he is always thinner, always looks healthier.

Leonard calls says it's a big, big day, round up some friends I'm taking
you to dinner. I ask why it's a big day, he says I'll tell you when I see you. I
ask when and where he says he'll pick me up at my house, round up some
motherfucking friends. I call Liza, Mike, Jenny, Quinn, Mark, my friend
Andy who is visiting from New York. Everyone meets at my house,
Leonard arrives in his white Mercedes, Snapper is driving. There isn't
enough room in his car so my friends drive their cars and I ride with
Leonard. Leonard has a small briefcase at his feet. I look at it, speak.
That's not for me, is it?
Leonard speaks.
You're retired.
Good.
And I want to do this one myself.
Does that have to do with this being a big day?
Indeed it does.
I don't need to know anymore.
You can ask if you want.
I don't want to know.
You can ask.
That's okay.
Really, it's fine. Ask away.
No thanks.
Snapper turns around.
He wants you to fucking ask him, so ask him.
I look at Leonard, speak.
What does that briefcase have to do with the big day?
Leonard smiles.
My last truly illegal act.

I laugh.
Congratulations.
He nods.
It's a big fucking day.
Why are you bringing me and my friends with you?
For a celebration.
Are we at risk?
Of course not.
What's happening?
Russkies.
Russkies?
Yeah, the Russkies have come to town.
So what?
Leonard looks at Snapper.
You want to take this one?
Snapper nods.
Sure.
Leonard looks back at me.
He's taking this one.
I nod.
I got it.
Snapper speaks.
Russians are mean bastards, have always been mean bastards. They kicked
Napoleon's ass, kicked Hitler's ass, kicked every ass they ever encountered.
When people like us started coming over here, the Russkies were in
Russia and had no interest. Then the Soviet Union kept 'em locked up for
seventy years. Now those fuckers are free, and they see what we got, and
there's fucking hordes of 'em coming over here, and like I said, they're
mean fucking bastards. If I'm a six on the mean scale, they're twelves.
They're greedy and aggressive, and now that we're legal, I think we'd just
as soon step the fuck out of their way. We can't, however, just step away,
because then we look weak and scared and then we get popped. So we
work out a deal. We give them certain considerations that they want, they
give us a bag of Russian sparklies that we sell. Everybody wins, everybody's happy, nothing bad happens. We're through with all the illegal
rackets we had, and we can't get caught for nothing, except maybe tax

cheating, which might happen, because this is gonna be the first year I ever filed a tax return, and the IRS notices that shit.

You have a good accountant?

He laughs.

I do, at least I think I do, and I better, or he's in trouble.

He chuckles again.

Tax return. I'm actually excited about it.

I laugh, turn to Leonard.

So what's in your briefcase?

Nothing. It's empty.

And you're trading it for one that looks like it, but isn't empty?

You learned well, my son. You were a natural.

I laugh. We turn on Sunset start heading east, away from the glamour of the Sunset Strip and into the reality of Hollywood. The apartment blocks are lined with decrepit buildings. Because it is night, there are hookers, women who are women and men who are women and some unknown, walking up and down the street, standing in small groups on corners, they wave and shake their asses and flash their tits and yell at us as we drive past them. Every other shop is a pawnshop, the windows are filled with guitars and amps and drumsets filled with the dead dreams of rock superstardom. There is a Space Burger restaurant their burgers are out of this world, there is a diner filled with people sitting alone staring out the window. It's a common sight in Los Angeles, someone sitting alone staring out the window.

We pull off Sunset. We pull up to a valet in front of what looks like a Mosque. It's a large white building with a gold dome, it has spikes along the edges of the roof, iron doors with engraved Arabic words. We get out of the car. Snapper waves off the valet pulls down the street I look at Leonard, speak.

What the fuck is this?

Leonard smiles.

Belly dance!

Belly dance?

Yeah, belly dance!

My friends pull up get out of their cars. They seem to know the place I ask them if any of them have been here they say no. Leonard leads us inside. There is a large central room, it's a light room, an open room. There is a fountain in the center of the room, an ornate tile floor, mosaics cover the walls. There are smaller rooms off the central room, smaller rooms in every direction, they're dark rooms, thick dark oriental rugs cover the floors, they're lit by candles there are people sitting on cushions on the floor. Leonard greets the host who leads us to one of the smaller rooms. We sit on cushions around a low, circular table. A waiter brings us water and menus Leonard waves off the menus, orders for the table. Snapper joins us sets the briefcase near his feet.

Leonard introduces himself to my friends, introduces Snapper. He asks them where they're from, why they live in Los Angeles, how they know me. Snapper sits, doesn't speak, occasionally glances toward the entrance to our room, occasionally glances at his watch.

A first round of food is delivered. It comes on large round plates. The plates have sections for meats lamb and beef, thick flat bread, dark heavy sauces. None of us knows what it is or how to eat it Leonard tells us it's Persian we eat it with our hands just dip the bread and the meat into the sauces don't worry about the mess don't worry about manners. The food is rich, strong, spicy, my friends drink beer I drink water. As we finish the plates, I see Snapper nod to Leonard they both stand with the briefcase. Leonard excuses them they leave the room.

Our plates are taken away we wait.

Our drinks are refilled we wait.

Liza asks if I know where Leonard is I say I have no idea. Mark asks if we should order more food I say I'm pretty sure it's covered. More food arrives it never stops. We wait.

I think about going out to find them to make sure everything is okay, I laugh at myself know I'd last about five seconds against some mean fucking Russkie. I think about going to speak with the host I hear a bell, multiple bells, moving toward the entrance to our room. Above the bells I hear Leonard laughing, saying woohoo, woohoo, saying shake it shake it shake it. Everyone at the table turns toward the entrance. A belly dancer, in a traditional belly dancing outfit, her hips wiggling her stomach gesticulating cymbals on her fingers clashing clashing comes shaking into the room. She is followed by another dancer who is followed by Leonard hooting and laughing who is followed by a man with a guitar frantically strumming who is followed by two waiters with giant trays of food who are followed by a smiling Snapper carrying a briefcase identical to the one he was carrying when he left the room. The belly dancers start moving around the table. The waiters set the trays on the table, start unloading heaping bowls of rice and platters with stacks of kebabs beef, lamb and chicken. Leonard follows the dancers, pretending to be one of them, making a complete fool of himself, knowing he's doing it, laughing. Snapper sits back down, smiles. My friends eat, drink, watch the show, laugh. Leonard sits and picks at a chicken kebab he says I'm watching my weight has the dancers start dancing again. Whenever I look at Snapper he nods and smiles, two or three times he mouths the words tax return, oh yeah, tax return, oh yeah. We stay at the restaurant for hours eating more drinking more listening to music watching the dancers laughing laughing laughing.

It's all legal now.

Snapper is going to file a tax return.

The phone rings I pick it up Leonard speaks.
MY SON MY SON MY SON.
I laugh.
Hi, Leonard.
How you doing?
I'm good. You?
I'm very upset with myself.
Why?
I forgot to give you the secret.
What secret?
The secret to kicking ass in dumbshit Hollywood.
You know it?
Of course I fucking know it.
I laugh again.
What is it?
Be bold.
Be bold.
But not bold, be fucking **BOLD.**
Okay.
Every time you meet someone, make a fucking impression. Make them
think you're the hottest shit in the world. Make them think they're gonna
lose their job if they don't give you one. Look 'em in the eye, and never
look away. Be confident and calm, be fucking bold.
That sounds more like the secret to kicking ass in life.
It is, but I was gonna wait and tell you that some other time.

Liza and her friend Mitch find a play they want to make into a short film. They ask if I want to direct it I say yes. Liza convinces the famous director she works for to fund half of it, her friend Mitch convinces the famous producer he works for to fund the other half of it. I'm not sure I'm a director, I have no real experience with actors and don't really know how a camera works, but I pretend to be one, and pretending seems to be all that matters in Hollywood. Pretend to be something, be convincing, and people will treat you differently, as if you actually are what you are pretending to be. It's a game, embarrassing and fake, but it is a means to an end here, so I play the game, and I quickly learn that I play it pretty well.

Tommy and Jaylen decide they're going to be deejay partners. They pool all of their money and they buy two turntables, a sound system and several crates of records. They stop working, spend all of their time smoking weed and spinning records.

Cassius grows and grows and grows. At four months he weighs thirty pounds at five he weighs forty at six he weighs fifty. The weight is all muscle. His coordination lags behind his growth so he stumbles and trips and seems confused by his own size.

I start to sleep again. I get used to going to bed without the rumbling and shaking of the El train.

I go to meetings with development executives. I go to meetings with agents. Development executives are people who read scripts, hire writers to write or re-write scripts, agents are the people who arrange for the jobs and negotiate the deals. The meetings are general meetings, which means we say hello, nice to meet you, they tell me they've heard great things about me, I tell them the same thing, and we spend the next hour kissing each other's asses. I try to make an impression with everyone I meet follow Leonard's advice speak simply and directly and look everyone in the eye. Part of me hates going to the meetings they're fake and stupid and I feel insecure after each of them, part of me knows I need to and I have to if I want to work and make money. Part of me is happy that I'm doing something other than making deliveries, working a bullshit job or going for walks. It feels good to actually do something.

Tommy and Jaylen start throwing parties at our house. They set up the turntables in our living room and charge ten dollars to walk in the door. The parties start at midnight and end sometime near dawn. The parties keep me awake, I can't fucking sleep.

We finish the movie. Liza and Mitch want to have a screening and a party. The studio where they work has a theater they convince the man who runs it to let us use it.

I tell my parents, who I talk to once a week or so, they want to come to the screening. I tell Leonard he wants to come to the screening. Liza and Mitch send out invitations they say there's going to be a crowd of people at the screening, actors and directors and writers and agents and managers and producers. Most of them, Liza tells me, will be coming to see if they like my movie and want to work with me. I ask her how they know about me she tells me that she and Mitch have big mouths. I thank her, thank him. The days leading up to the screening drag I'm nervous. If it goes well I'll get work, if it goes poorly I'll be forgotten. I feel good about the movie but I also know that it's not going to change the world. If I fail, I fail. I've been through worse.

My parents arrive. They recently moved from Tokyo to Singapore, the trip to Los Angeles took twenty-six hours. I pick them up at the airport they're tired. I tell them I'll take them to their hotel they want to see where I live. I tell them I'll take them to their hotel. On our way we talk I ask them how the adjustment to Singapore has been, my Mom says it's a much easier place to live than Japan, everyone speaks English and they don't hate foreigners, my Dad says it's no different for him, an office is an office. They ask about Los Angeles I tell them it's fine I'm getting used to it, they ask about my friends here, they know them from before, I tell them they'll see my friends tonight. It's good to see my parents, it's easier than I expected it might be with them. Our relationship has been strained and difficult for most of my life, now it gets better and more healthy each time I see them. I know they love me they always have, I know they want the best for me they have always tried. It's good to have them here.

I drop them off at the hotel. I go home smoke cigarettes listen to Tommy and Jaylen practice, they sound worse than when they started, none of the beats match, the transitions from song to song are obvious and clunky. Time is slow as it always is when I want it to be fast I have nothing to do but wait. I sit in my room can't think or talk on the phone because of the noise, if I make some money because of this movie I'm going to buy a bomb and blow those motherfucking turntables to bits.

I take a shower put on some nice clothing, the same clothing I used to wear when I was working for Leonard and was pretending to be a commuter. I laugh at the clothes they're dusty from lack of use I brush them off. I leave the house drive to the hotel pick up my parents. We drive to the studio, pull up to the gate, our names are on the proper list, the guard waves us through.

We park start heading toward the theater my Mom and Dad look around as we walk. Studios are large bland ugly places. The one we are on consists of a couple hundred acres of land dotted with what look like airplane hangars, a few simple office buildings built to look like houses, and a big, ugly, black tower. There is an amusement park attached to the studio where tourists pay for the privilege to be driven around the studio in long funny buses that look like giant golf carts. There are trucks and trailers parked outside of the hangars, casually dressed young people walk, ride bikes or drive golf carts, they all look like they're in a hurry. The tourists all stare at them, hope one of them is a star that they recognize from TV or the movies, my Mom asks where all the stars are, I tell her I don't know I've never seen one. My Dad asks what everyone is doing I say most of them are pretending to be busy so they don't get fired.

We get to the theater Liza and Mitch are standing outside. I introduce them to my parents, I take my parents inside and find them seats. People are starting to arrive I'm too nervous to sit down, I find Liza we walk around the back of the theater and smoke cigarettes. Five minutes before the screening is supposed to start we walk back to the front. There is a small crowd of people at the entrance, a few that I know, most I have never seen. Liza goes to talk to Mitch, I stand at the edge of the crowd wait for everyone to go inside, when they do I follow them. I stand at the door, wait for the lights to go out. I don't want anyone to see me I'm ner-

vous, much more self-conscious than I expected to be. When the lights
are out and just before the movie starts I slip in walk to the back row
sit down.

I don't watch the movie, I watch people watching the movie. I watch their
reactions, hope for laughs when laughs are supposed to come, hope to
move them when I want to move them, hope I make them happy sad curious hopeful. The reactions are fine, not great not bad, though I doubt
anything aside from being carried out on the shoulders of a cheering audi-
ence would have made me happy.

The movie ends the crowd claps. I stay in my seat in the back row while
people file out of the theater. When they're gone and I am alone, I stand
and I walk out. My parents, Liza, Leonard and a blond woman with
Leonard are waiting for me. They all hug me congratulate me tell me it
went great, tell me they're proud of me.

We walk to the party, which is at a nearby restaurant. As we walk, I meet
the woman with Leonard, her name is Betty. She's tall, thin, probably in
her forties but looks younger, she's wearing an expensive white silk suit
and large diamond studs in her ears and a Cartier watch. I shake her hand
it's soft, she smiles easily and often.

We arrive at the party. It's crowded Leonard finds a table for himself and
Betty and my parents. I walk around thank people for coming.
Occasionally I stop by the table I hear bits and pieces of conversation. I
hear Leonard talking to my parents he says I see him every week he's
doing great. I hear him say I'm legit now, no more danger, no more illegal-
ity, I'm one hundred percent legit. I hear him say to my father I have a
bunch of idiots working for me, complete and total idiots. I hear him say
it'll be great, I'll pay you a fortune, a fortune, and you can live wherever
you want, anywhere in the world. I watch my parents and Leonard and
Betty from across the room. Leonard and my father look like they're engaged in a serious conversation, my mom and Betty are laughing and smiling. It's strange to see, my mom and dad and my criminal friend from
rehab and his girlfriend sitting at a table together. Fucking strange.

At the end of the night I have a stack of business cards, people who said
great work give me a call maybe we can do something together. My jaw
hurts I'm not used to talking so much, I don't like talking so much. I'm

glad this is over it seems to have been a success. I find Liza and Mitch and I thank them, thank them, thank them. I find my parents and Leonard tell them it's time to go we leave.

We walk to the cars we are all parked in the same place. I thank Leonard for coming he tells me he's proud of me. I tell Betty it was nice to meet her, that I hope we see each other again, she says the same thing to me. They get in Leonard's car and drive away. My Parents and I get in my car, I start driving them to their hotel. My father speaks.

Your friend Leonard is an interesting fellow.

Yeah, but you knew that already.

You know what he was talking to me about?

I'm scared to ask.

My mom starts laughing.

What's so funny, Mom?

She shakes her head, giggles.

What'd he say?

He wants me to come work for him.

I laugh, speak.

What's he want you to do?

Work for his *phone* company.

I laugh again.

You gonna do it?

I'm actually tempted.

No way.

My Mom speaks.

You should have heard his offer.

An offer you couldn't refuse?

My Dad laughs, speaks.

He said he stopped making those.

Yeah. So what was it?

A huge amount of money for six to twelve months of work.

Really?

My mom speaks.

It was a crazy amount of money.

Why only six to twelve months?

My Dad speaks.

He wouldn't say.

What would you do?

He wouldn't say that either.

Did he say anything?

That he needed someone he could trust who was outside of his organization and had extensive international business experience.

That's weird.

My mom speaks.

He's not exactly normal, James.

I chuckle.

Yeah.

I drop them off at their hotel. Leonard calls my Dad again the next day, says he would really love my Dad to reconsider his offer. My Dad says no thank you, Leonard, though I appreciate you thinking about me. I spend the next two days with my parents. We go to the beach, walk around Beverly Hills, eat at nice restaurants. I take them to my house when Jaylen and Tommy aren't there, they both think it sucks, when they say it I laugh. It's a good two days, it gets better with them every time we see each other. I take them to the airport my Mom cries tells me how proud of me she is, my Dad tells me to keep it up.

I call the people who gave me their business cards. Some of them take my calls some of them don't, some of them say they liked the movie, some of them dance around saying anything about the movie.

Tommy and Jaylen run low on funds can't afford weed anymore so they start growing it in our backyard.

Leonard cancels our Wednesday lunch once twice three straight times. He doesn't tell me why, just calls and says he can't make it.

I send my script to a dozen people two dozen people. I call them, follow up with them, a few of them like it, a few of them don't like it, nothing happens either way.

Cassius keeps growing it's shocking how fast he's growing. He still goes everywhere with me rides shotgun in the truck sleeps in my bed. Though he now looks like a large menacing pitbull he is a baby baby baby. He loves to give kisses, play tug-of-war, chase a ball, he'll do anything for a treat he's a huge musclebound baby.

I take a job working as a production assistant. It's shitty work I drive around all day running errands for an asshole director who thinks he's saving the world with a shaving cream commercial.

Leonard cancels a fourth time, fifth time, sixth time. I wonder if something bad is happening or if he's just busy when I ask him he says he can't talk about it yet, he'll tell me when he can.

Tommy and Jaylen start selling the weed they're growing they figure it's easier than working. Our phone rings constantly there is a steady stream of people in and out of the house dull-eyed, slow-speaking, potato-chip-eating people.

A producer calls he read my script says he loves it. I've heard this before heard producers say they love it and I never hear from them again. I ask him if he's going to blow smoke up my ass or actually do something, he says he wants to buy it and make it. I ask him how much he gives me a number I say fucking sold, my friend, it is all yours.

Cassius and I move out.

My new house is in Laurel Canyon, which is a small neighborhood in the Hollywood Hills. There is one road into the canyon. The road is off Sunset, it is a two lane road that twists turns and is lined with huge overhanging trees and walls of rock. Houses built on stilts dot the rock, once you're into the canyon there are two roads that lead up further. The first road sits at a small intersection, there's a stoplight, a convenience store, a pizza place and a real estate office, the second road is several hundred yards up, there is a stoplight and the ruins of a stone mansion. The canyon is heavily wooded with pines oaks maples and cypress. It does not look like the rest of Los Angeles, it's cool dark and quiet, more like a forest than a city.

I live in a small house at the top of the first road. My house is pink stucco it has two bedrooms a bathroom a kitchen a living room. It has a small backyard that is dug out of the side of a hill, three cement walls hold the hill back and enclose the space. I don't have much furniture a mattress and a desk, I buy a futon and a television and a stereo. My neighbors are friendly say hello I recognize one of them as a drummer for a heavy metal band there's always noise coming from his house. I recognize another as a famous female porn performer there is always noise coming from her house. The couple next door are in their thirties, she's an actress, he's a composer. They're a brand of hippie found only in LA, they drive a Mercedes but say things like groovy, far out and dig it, man, dig it hard. Cassius and I are happy here we have a mellow life. I go back to trying to write a book no progress, he sleeps in the backyard chases flies tries to eat them. We take long walks through the hills. We watch TV on our futon. We get food from the store at the bottom of the hill, I like canned ravioli and fruit punch, Cassius likes beef-flavored kibble.

It's afternoon I am sitting at my desk drinking coffee smoking cigarettes trying to work, Cassius is on the futon watching a soap opera. We hear a car stop in front of the house. Cassius looks over at me I shrug tell him I don't know who it is we hear voices. Cassius looks at the door there's a knock. I stand walk to the door, Cassius stands walks to the door, I ask who is it, Cassius barks. Leonard speaks.

Open the door, my son.

I open the door. Leonard and Snapper stand in front of me.

Leonard speaks.

Your new house, it's a fucking palace.

I laugh.

Come on in.

They step inside. Cassius greets them both with a kiss on the hand he knows them they say hello to him. I speak.

You want something to drink?

What do you have?

I got coffee, and I got some beer and cola in the fridge.

Leonard speaks.

Cola please.

I look at Snapper. He speaks.

Why you got beer?

In case someone comes over and wants to drink it.

It don't bother you having it here?

I could give a shit. If I were gonna get drunk, I'd drink something a lot stronger than fucking beer.

He laughs.

I gotta drive. I'll have a cola too.

I get the colas from the fridge, hand them to Leonard and Snapper, speak.

What are you guys doing here?

Leonard speaks.

You never invited us up, so we decided to stop by.

Snapper speaks.

It hurt a little, Kid, the no invite thing.

I speak.

I figured you knew there's an open invitation, and I figured you'd stop by when you wanted to whether there was an invitation or not.

Leonard speaks.

You're right, we would.
Snapper speaks.
Invitations are still nice, though.
I speak.
From now on you're invited whenever you want.
Leonard speaks.
You got any plans tonight?
Nope.
Cassius have any?
I look at Cassius, who is back on the futon.
You got any plans tonight, Big Boy?
Cassius looks up, doesn't say anything. I look back at Leonard, speak.
I think he's free.
Leonard speaks.
Good, you're coming with us.
Where we going?
Las Vegas. I'm getting rid of my place there. I want to show you a night on the town before I leave.
You're moving?
Going to live at the beach house full time.
I look at Snapper.
You moving too?
I got a girlfriend in Vegas. I'm probably gonna split time between the two places.
You've got a girlfriend?
Don't sound so surprised. Lots of women like me.
Leonard speaks.
She's nice, works as an accountant for one of the casinos.
I speak.
Can I meet her?
Snapper speaks.
Maybe. I'll see what she's doing tonight.
Leonard speaks.
If we get there by tonight. Come on, let's go.
And you're sure Cassius can come?

Does he want to come?

I look at Cassius, speak.

You want to go to Vegas, Cassius?

He looks up at me again. I look back at Leonard.

He doesn't know those words. I've got to ask him another way.

I turn back to Cassius.

You want to go bye-bye in the car, Big Boy?

Cassius immediately jumps off the couch, runs over to me, starts panting, turning in circles. I look back at Leonard.

Do I need anything?

Everything will be taken care of.

Cool.

I put Cassius on a leash we walk out of my house get into Leonard's Mercedes start driving. The drive is simple. As soon as we're out of Los Angeles it's one long road that cuts through open, desolate desert. Leonard says he wants to set the mood so we listen to Frank Sinatra. Cassius sticks his face out the window, occasionally brings it back into the car and snorts and sneezes, immediately sticks it back out. The drive takes four and a half hours if you drive the speed limit, after three we start to see a dim glow hovering along the horizon. Leonard points it out, speaks.

There it is, that mean and wondrous wench. The best place and worst place in America, a place where dreams come true, where people are destroyed, a place that doesn't care about the past and is a vision of the future, where capitalism is displayed in all of its glory and horror, where everything and anything can be bought, sold, traded or stolen, where some of the smartest and most ambitious people in the country come to make their fortunes, where some of the absolute worst and most despicable people in the country come to make their fortunes. It is corrupt, dirty and disgusting, and in five hundred years its massive buildings, thought of as garish and ridiculous, will be considered marvels. It is a giant carnival devoted to the glory of money and everything money can do, both good and evil, and there is plenty of both.

The dim grows and starts to form itself, becomes an outline of light. We pass bush league casinos on the side of the highway places for people who can't wait to get to the big casinos or need to make one last bet on their way out, we pass lonely gas stations, a ramshackle souvenir shop, one or two fast food restaurants. The light rises becomes brighter more defined, and very suddenly, we cross a line that separates an empty desert from a manic city.

We turn onto the strip. Both sides of the street are lined with massive, sprawling buildings covered in neon it's night and dark but looks like it's day. Leonard looks back at me.

Welcome to the Strip.

Wow.

When you see someplace you want to stay, let me know.

Aren't we staying at your house?

My house is a mess, all packed-up, boxes everywhere. I've been living in hotels.

Where?

All over the place. I move all the time, think it's nice to mix it up.

What do you recommend?

Whatever catches your eye.

I look out the window. Cassius climbs on my lap he looks out the window I ask him where he wants to stay he licks my face. We drive I see a huge black pyramid bigger than those in Egypt lights twinkling behind it. I see a ridiculous version of King Arthur's castle. I see New York City rebuilt a roller coaster winds its way through skyscrapers. I see what Leonard says is the biggest hotel in the world five thousand rooms every one offering the finest amenities. I see Monte Carlo, New Orleans, a hotel for pirates, a pink flamingo and a palace built in the image of Rome, though it doesn't look like the Rome I saw in Italy. I see the old-timey places, the new-timey places, big places giant places absurdly humongous places, rundown places sparkling places expensive places bottomed-out places. When we reach the end of the Strip we enter a dark area of grimy streets lined with convenience stores, hotels renting rooms by the hour, warehouses and hookers. I see another area of light a mile or so away I ask Leonard what it is, he says downtown Vegas. I ask him what it's like he says faded, lost and forgotten. I turn back look down the strip it is a perpetual wall of light. I look at Leonard, speak.

Which place is the most ridiculous?

Leonard speaks.

That's a tough question. What do you think, Snap?

Snapper speaks.

Excalibur has a magical medieval castle, a moat and a fire-breathing dragon. Circus Circus has exotic performing animals and the AdventureDome theme park. Mirage has the indoor jungle, Barbary Coast and Treasure Island are both full of pirates and buccaneers. They're all fucking ridiculous.

Leonard looks back at me.

They're all fucking ridiculous, my son. All of them.

Where do they have the best food?

Snapper speaks.

The Grand.

Leonard speaks.

I agree. Best food is at the Grand.

Let's go there.

Snapper nods pulls away we start driving back down the strip. I stare back out the window pay less attention to the buildings and more attention to the people, the hundreds of people thousands tens of thousands of people, on the sidewalks on footbridges that lead back and forth over the Strip in front of the casinos walking in and out. I stare at the people some looking around in awe some happily chatting some worried some quickly walking a few crying. I see Elvis, I see a couple just married he's in a tux she's in white, I see hookers lingering. I see a family hand-in-hand mother father four little children. I see a woman in a wheelchair an old man with a cane a blind man tapping a preacher pounding and screaming a hustler dealing cards people know they're going to lose but they play anyway. I see old young white black yellow red rich poor they're all looking for more more more, they're all the same and they all want more.

We pull up to the Grand the entrance lives up to its name. As soon as the car stops it is surrounded by valets. Leonard waves them off, Snapper pulls away, parks the car. Instead of walking toward the doors, Leonard turns and walks toward the sidewalk. I have Cassius on a leash we follow him. He stops, speaks.

I want to tell you something before we go inside.

Okay.

You see all this.

He motions up and down the strip.

Yeah, I see it.

It's all a fucking charade. Built to lure you in, tempt you, tease you, make you starry-eyed and dumb, make you think it's yours for the taking if you just throw down those next few bucks.

He turns to me.

You can do what you want, but the way I do it is I decide on a sum, the sum is an amount I won't miss. I play it until I'm either happy with my winnings, or I lose it all. I never go over, never spend more. The reason I do this is because this . . .

He motions up and down the strip again.

This was not built on losses, it was not built on losses. You understand? The casino always wins.

He nods.

Yeah, the casino always wins. Goddamn sons of bitches. They should let me always win.

I laugh, he smiles. He turns back toward the entrance.

You ready.

Yeah, I'm ready.

We walk to the entrance, step into a huge revolving door it is silent between the swinging panes, for a second or two it's beautiful, light and silent. I step out of the door into the lobby, into flashing lights into noise from slot machines into music into laughing and cheering into the blast of air conditioning into plush carpeting into thirty foot ceilings into madness. Cassius looks around appears slightly confused, Leonard steps in behind us walks toward the reception desk we follow him. He arrives at the desk asks for someone. The woman asks for his name he gives it to her she makes a call. Thirty seconds later a man in a suit steps out of an office behind the desk greets Leonard, shakes his hand, the man says it's great to see you again, how can I help you? Leonard tells him he'd like to stay for the night the man asks if anyone will be with him Leonard says we'll be three. Man asks if we have any bags Leonard says no we'll be purchasing whatever we need the man says excellent, let me know if I can help in any way. Leonard says please order a large porterhouse steak cooked well and a bowl of water and have them sent to our room immediately. The man looks at Cassius and laughs, says of course and steps to the desk, speaks with one of his coworkers. Snapper joins us, the man steps away from the desk, says follow me.

We go to an elevator. We ride to the top floor we need a key to open the elevator door. We step into a hall, a long hall with thick carpet, low lights, subtle neutral paint and two doors, one on each side of the hall just two doors. The man leads us to one of the doors opens it holds the door we go into the room.

It is not a room, not a suite, not an apartment. It is a mansion in the sky a beautiful series of rooms, bedrooms dining room living room multimedia room den kitchen bar sitting room. There are windows in every room offering views of the Strip of Vegas of the desert, the furniture looks like it belongs in a museum, the carpet is soft and thick, the drapes long and thick, the glasses at the bar crystal the refrigerators stocked. The man gives a brief tour gives us a card tells us to please call him if he can do anything for us he leaves. I let Cassius off his leash he starts running around smelling things. I look at Leonard.

This is incredible.

It's not bad.

What's something like this go for?

It doesn't.

It's free?

Yup.

You pay nothing?

Doubt anyone who's stayed here has paid for it.

Suite for high rollers?

High rollers, VIPs and people like me.

You're not a high roller or a VIP?

I'm something else, something that exists here but isn't often acknowledged to exist.

International superstar?

He laughs.

More like someone you don't want to piss off.

I laugh.

Are we expected to spend a bunch of money in the casino?

They're going to take care of us, and provide us with whatever we want, regardless of how much money we blow in the casino.

Whatever we want?

Leonard smiles.

Yeah, and you can get exotic in your requests if you would like.

How exotic?

As exotic as you can imagine.

I laugh again. Snapper walks into the room says he's hungry. Leonard asks if I'm hungry I say yes he asks if we want to eat in the room or in a restaurant. We decide to go to a restaurant. We wait for Cassius' steak. When it arrives I cut it into small pieces he eats it in about two seconds. I give him the bone he takes it runs around the room a couple of times jumps onto a couch starts chewing, he looks happy, like he'll be occupied for hours. We leave the room, take the elevator back downstairs, walk around, try to decide where we are going to eat, there are about twenty different restaurants. We go to a steakhouse. Snapper and I both have huge slabs of prime rib with spinach and hash browns, Leonard has a salad. After dinner we go to the casino Leonard wants to shoot craps. I have no idea how to do it Leonard tries to explain I say don't worry about it, just give me the dice and let me throw. He laughs hands me the dice I start to throw and my oh my do I fucking throw. Leonard handles the betting and we win again and again we start to accumulate a large stack of chips and a crowd around our table. With each throw the crowd either cheers or groans and we get many more cheers I keep throwing throwing we keep accumulating I have no idea how much we have at least ten times what we started with. We look at the pile and laugh. Leonard says you're my good luck charm, my son, let's quit while we're ahead.

We quit, cash out the chips, we have over ten thousand dollars in fifties and hundreds. Leonard asks me if I'm okay with money I say yeah, I'm doing well he says if you don't need it, let's give it away. We leave the casino walk out to the Strip.

We walk, look, we give a thousand dollars to an elderly couple, we give a thousand to a couple who just got married. We find some homeless men they're drunk we give them a few hundred dollars each. We see a family their car is broken-down we give them a couple thousand. We hand out money to whoever we see that looks like they're down, depressed, who looks like a few bucks will make them happier. Some of the people are thrilled thank us can't believe their luck, some of them don't want the money think we want something in exchange, some of them take it and quietly walk away. When we have a thousand or so left Leonard says we're keeping the rest for later we're going to need some throwaway money. I ask him why he says there's big fun coming, my son, big-ass motherfucking fun.

We walk back to the hotel, Snapper is having a drink with his girlfriend, Leonard wants to join them. I say let's give them some privacy, he says no, they're expecting us. We walk to a small quiet bar. Aside from the rooms it is probably the only quiet space in this entire complex. Snapper is sitting at a table for four with a small blond woman. They stand as we enter, Leonard speaks.

Look at Olivia, the most beautiful girl in the world.

The blond woman smiles it is a shy smile. Leonard gives her a hug they separate.

Olivia, this is my son James. James, this is Olivia, the most beautiful girl in the world.

She smiles again the same smile. She's short thin has dark brown eyes sandy blond hair. Her hands are soft, her nails immaculate, she wears a black skirt and a black blouse, she's beautiful in a simple natural way as if her beauty is something that she doesn't think about or let worry her. We shake hands, say hello, sit down. She looks at me speaks.

Dominic has told me a lot about you.

Dominic?

Snapper speaks.

She doesn't like my professional name.

I laugh.

I don't blame her.

She smiles.

Are you having fun in Vegas?

Yeah, I am.

You have good guides.

I laugh again.

Yeah, I do.

We sit talk laugh. Olivia is from Albuquerque, where her parents, Italian immigrants, opened a pizza parlor. She grew up working in the parlor, put herself through school, got her job in the casino when she graduated, has been there for six years. I ask her how she met Dominic she says she has a dog, a big, sweet, dumb as dirt Newfoundland who got off his leash one day and started wandering around her neighborhood. Dominic found him and brought him home. She says he seemed shy and nervous and sweet, and she thought he was handsome so she asked him out. They went to dinner and a movie that night. She took him to a romantic chickflick to see if he could deal with it and he laughed when he was supposed to laugh and clapped at the end. They had coffee afterwards, and when he took her home at the end of the night, Dominic didn't try to kiss her. She hoped he would ask her out again or ask for her number, but it didn't happen, and she went to sleep disappointed. The next day, when she got home from work, there was an envelope at her door. Inside the envelope, on a piece of handmade paper, someone had carefully transcribed a poem by Emily Dickinson called *It's all I have to bring to-day*, and beneath the poem there was a phone number. She called the number and Dominic an-swered and, she smiles and says, we've been together ever since. At the end of the story Leonard laughs, looks at Snapper, speaks.

You still remember the poem, Dominic?

Of course I do.

Recite it for James.

No way.

Come on.

Only for Olivia.

When did that become policy?

Olivia looks at Leonard, speaks.

When I said so.

Leonard laughs.

Since when are you the boss?

When he's with you, you're the boss. When he's with me, I'm the boss.

What about when he's with both of us?

Olivia smiles.

We both know the answer to that one, Leonard.

Everyone laughs, Olivia smiles and nods, holds her hands over her head like she's a champion. We finish our drinks. Olivia says she needs to go home, Snapper asks Leonard if we're okay without him for the night. Leonard says yeah, we're fine, everyone stands Olivia hugs Leonard and me, she and Snapper leave. Leonard looks at me, speaks.

You tired?

What time is it?

Time doesn't matter here. You sleep when you're tired, not when a clock tells you you should sleep.

Is there anything else to do?

A friend of mine owns a strip club. I kept that dough so you could live in lapdance heaven for a couple hours.

You gonna join me?

I'm not much of a lapdance man.

I would have thought you liked them.

Nope.

Fuck it then.

You sure?

Lapdances are fun when your buddy's sitting next to you and everyone's laughing. There's something dark and sad about them when you're there alone hoping for something you're not gonna get.

Leonard laughs.

I could arrange that you get it.

That's dark and sad too.

He laughs again.

So what do you want to do?

Is there anything I've missed?

Is there anything you haven't seen that you want to see?

No.

We could go see a Sinatra imitator, or we could go to an all-night, all-you-can-eat buffet.

I'm good.

What do you want to do with the last thousand?

I don't care.

Let's put it on red or black and go to sleep.

Red.

Fine with me.

We go back to the casino bet red win bet red win we leave with four grand. We go back to the suite. Cassius is sleeping on the couch the bone is resting next to his sizable head. I wake him up we thank Leonard for a great night, a ridiculous night, we thank him. We go to our room the bed is huge the sheets are soft we go to sleep.

Cassius and I go home back to our little house in the hills. I spend my time in front of a computer, he spends his time in front of the TV. We go for walks three times a day, once in the morning, once in the afternoon, once at night. I eat most of my meals at home, I rarely go out with my friends. I read for three or four hours before I go to bed.

I have a good life, a simple life, for the first time in my life I'm happy and secure and stable. My Fury, which has shaped most of the twenty-five years of my life has faded without the fuel of drugs and alcohol, has faded as I have learned not to hate myself. Part of me is humbled by this life, this beautiful life. Another part of me feels incredibly fortunate. Part of me is waiting to fuck it up somehow, waiting to make some dumbass decision that destroys it, waiting for it to end. Part of me feels like it isn't complete without Lilly, this is what she and I dreamed of having together. Sometimes I pretend she's here with me. I talk to an empty chair across the table, I wrap my arms around nothingness and tell her I love her. I tell her I'll be home in a little while when I leave, I tell her I'm tired and want to go to bed at the end of a long day. Even without her I have all I need, my little house, my big funny dog, my legally earned money, my time, my own time, my own precious time to do whatever I want to do. I have simple things, a simple life, all I need.

Leonard goes east for his annual attempt at a tee-time on the golf course where his father worked.

I see a drunk movie star drive his Porsche into a tree going ten miles an hour. He gets out of the car and starts kicking the door starts screaming nobody understands, nobody understands.

Cassius becomes friends with a squirrel who lives in a tree above our yard. He sits and watches the squirrel jump from limb to limb, watches him collect acorns, watches him chatter and squeak, he spends hours watching the squirrel. I think Cassius is lonely.

I see a famous young actress, a shockingly beautiful young actress, gorging at a fast food restaurant, she disappears into the bathroom after eating six cheeseburgers.

I finish another script I like it.

I see a famous director throw an omelet at a waitress while screaming onions aren't mushrooms, onions aren't fucking mushrooms. The waitress walks away with egg in her hair, on her neck, on her shirt, tears in her eyes her hands are shaking. A minute or two later the manager of the restaurant walks over and apologizes to the director says the meal's on us please tell me what else I can get for you.

My friend Danny calls from Chicago tells me he hates his job, wants to do something new. I tell him to come to Los Angeles, it's the land of opportunity. He says what would I do, I say let's raise some money and we'll make a movie. He says that's crazy, I say it's crazier staying in a job you hate, he says you're right, I'm coming to Los Angeles.

Cassius and I are at the veterinarian's office. Cassius is having a regular semi-annual check-up. The vet asks me if I would ever consider having another dog, I look at Cassius, ask him he wags his tail says yes, Daddy, yes, Daddy, let's get another dog, please Daddy, yes. The vet says she has a young female pitbull that she found in a box behind a convenience store. I say bring her out, the vet leaves comes back two minutes later with a small, brindle pitbull her ears are sticking up her tail is wagging. Cassius licks her, they start jumping around barking and yelping. I ask the vet if she has a name the vet tells me she calls the little dog Bella. I say welcome to the family, Bella, I'm your new Dad, the big boy is your new brother.

A girl I know from school calls me asks me if I want to have dinner I say yeah, sure, I'll have dinner. Her name is Conner she's six foot two she likes a nice, strong cocktail and she likes to laugh. I ask her where we're going she tells me it's a bar that serves decent food in an outdoor courtyard. I ask her if anyone is coming with us she asks me if I remember her friend Allison. I ask if it's Allison skinny Allison and she laughs and says yes, that's her and I say yeah, I remember Allison. I ask her what time she says eight.

I work all day take a shower get dressed. I think about Skinny Allison on and off. She was tall, as tall as I am. She had long dark blond hair, olive skin. The first time I saw her she was eighteen, but looked fourteen, and in the two years we were at school together, she never aged. She was thin, long thin, delicate thin, fragile thin, thin like a runway model, thin the type that food wouldn't affect, thin that was somehow natural for her, as if her body would gain weight as she got older. I saw her occasionally she was usually with Conner we never spoke. I never tried to speak to her because I knew she wanted nothing to do with me. She was from a nice, traditional Southern family, she did well in school. I imagined she would find a handsome, successful, stable man and live in a big house and have a beautiful family.

Cassius and Bella are sitting on the couch. I stop say goodbye to them they wag their tails and look up at me. If they could talk they'd say go on and leave, Daddy, we're going to have fun tonight without you, maybe we'll eat a pillow or chew our bones or try to catch squirrels or watch TV, go on, Daddy, leave. I give them hugs walk out to my truck drive down the hill to the bar.

I walk into the bar look around. I see Conner sitting at a table. I walk to-

ward the table Allison is sitting next to Conner they stand as I approach
them. I hesitate as I walk, blink a couple of times, try to keep my jaw
from dropping, my knees from buckling, my eyes from popping out.
Allison is not skinny Allison anymore. She's still thin but her body has
filled out, there are curves beautiful curves. Her hair is longer, more
blond. She's wearing light blue leather pants a white t-shirt. She's no
longer a girl she's become a woman, a gorgeous, voluptuous woman.
Men all over the bar are staring at her. I'm staring at her. I stop at the
table speak.
Hi.
Conner speaks.
Hi. You remember Allison?
I look at Allison.
Hi.
She speaks.
Hi.
Long time.
Yeah.
How you been?
Great. You?
I laugh.
Been a long couple of years.
She nods.
So I've heard.
We sit, they're both drinking white wine, I order a nice cold cola. I talk to
Allison ask her about her life. She's been living in Vail for the last two
years, teaching skiing and working in an art gallery. She loves Vail, but
wants to move, feels like two years in a ski town is long enough, that it's
time to become an adult. I ask her where she wants to go, she says she
isn't sure, maybe San Francisco maybe Santa Fe maybe Washington DC. I
ask her what she wants to do, she says she needs to figure it out, maybe
teach, maybe try to be a painter, maybe go back to school for landscape
architecture. She asks me about my life I say it's good, never been better.
She asks if it's true I got locked-up I tell her yes. She asks what I'm doing
in Los Angeles I tell her, she asks if I like Los Angeles I say more and more

every day. I ask her why it's not on her list of potential residences, she says she just can't imagine living here.

We order dinner they get salads I get a big fat fucking cheeseburger. We keep talking I ask about painting why she does it, she says she does it because when she is actually painting she forgets about the rest of the world, forgets about problems and insecurities, about failures and an uncertain future, about everything she just loses herself and paints. I ask who she paints like, she says she tries to paint like herself. I ask her who she likes, she says Matisse and van Gogh. I ask her why she says because Matisse paints beautifully and van Gogh paints painfully.

When the food comes, I can't eat. Allison intimidates me, makes me nervous, takes away my appetite. I take a few bites of the burger, try to look away from her, try to focus on Conner, try to seem cool and secure and distant even though I don't feel cool or secure, even though I don't want to be distant. What I want is to be next to her, to hold her, to be inside of her, to devour her, to disappear within her, to become part of her somehow, to become part of her. Part of what I feel is purely physical, a desire an urge a desperate clawing need, part of what I feel is something else, something that makes me smile, feel empty and full, makes my heart hurt. We finish dinner. I pay the bill they both thank me, we stand walk out. We wait for our cars at the valet, Conner asks me what I'm doing for the rest of the night, I tell her I'm going home getting in bed reading a book. Allison asks me what I'm reading I tell her Paul Bowles she asks me which book I tell her *The Sheltering Sky*. She smiles says she loves Paul Bowles, loves that book. I tell her I'll give her my report when I'm done she smiles says I'll look forward to it.

Our cars arrive. I ask them what they're doing tomorrow, Conner says she's not sure. I tell her to call me, that I might take my dogs for a walk in the Hills, that they can come if they want, she says cool. We get in our cars we leave.

I drive home and every second of the drive is spent thinking about Allison about how she looked in the first instant I saw her, about how she laughed she has a quiet shy laugh, about her smile she smiles like she's hiding something, about her leather pants her curves about painting I want to watch her paint about her reading I want to watch her read about the skinny girl that isn't skinny anymore, about what she would look like next to me with me beneath me on top of me about how she scares me she fucking terrifies me.

I get home the dogs are already asleep on top of my bed. I get into bed I stare at the ceiling I think about Allison. I close my eyes I think about Allison. I fall asleep thinking about Allison.

I wake up thinking about her. I try to work I can't work. I walk the dogs I want to go home I'm worried Conner might call I don't want to miss it. I brew some coffee my hand quivers as I drink it. I try to read, the words make no sense. I smoke cigarettes and stare at the wall and think about her. I hope Conner calls I want to see Allison again.

Conner calls we agree to go for a hike in the Hills. I ask the dogs if they want to go out, they jump up and down wag their tails run in circles. I ask them if they want to meet a girl Daddy likes they don't care. I ask them if they want to go bye-bye in the car they start barking.

We meet go for our hike. I let the dogs off their leashes they run away. It's hot I take off my shirt. Allison asks about my tattoos. I tell her they're like scars they remind me of things I've done, of how I want to live and how I don't want to live. Allison says I have a lot of scars. She smiles and she reaches out and runs her finger along the top of my left arm, along a faded black outline, she doesn't speak just runs her finger along my arm, along my arm, along my arm.

We agree to meet for dinner. They're going to come to my house I'll drive us all to a nearby restaurant. They arrive we go to a local Italian place we eat, Conner and Allison drink wine I drink cola. We stay for three or four hours. I don't want to leave Allison I want to sit with her for the rest of the night, tomorrow, all of next week, for the next month, year. The bill comes I pay we go back to my house I have a few bottles of wine in the house for people who want to drink. Conner and Allison open one of them. We sit in the backyard it's a beautiful California night, warm still quiet clear. They drink, we smoke, talk about friends from school where they are what they're doing how they're doing, some are doing well some are disasters some have faded away. I ask Allison why we were never friends at school she laughs and says because you were psychotic and I was scared of you. I ask her if she's still scared of me, she says you're like your dogs, you appear kind and sweet and gentle, but I don't think I'd like to make you angry. I ask her if that means she's still scared of me she says she hasn't decided yet. I tell her to let me know if there's anything I can do to ease her fears, she smiles says okay.

It gets late two or three. Conner wants to go home. She's drunk I tell her she shouldn't drive they should stay here they can have my room I'll sleep on the couch. Conner wants to leave she walks out Allison follows her. I hear them arguing. I hear car doors open I hear them close. I hear Conner's car start, pull away. I hear a knock I walk to the door open it. Allison is standing in front of me she speaks.

There's something you can do.

What do you mean?

To help ease my fear of you.

What's that?

She smiles.

Invite me in, I'll show you.

We have breakfast, lunch, dinner she stays the night again, we spend all of the next day together she stays the night again. She changes her flight so she can stay longer she picks up her bags from Conner we spend three more days together. We take the dogs for walks through the hills. We go to a gourmet grocery store Allison cooks a fancy dinner. We go to the movies sit in the back row hold hands share popcorn whisper to each other. We go see a band sit in the back row hold hands whisper to each other. We lie in bed for hours talking kissing exploring each other we lie in bed and stare at each other, her eyes are the same pale green as mine we lie in bed and we look into each other.

I convince her to stay for three more days. We drive up the coast. We get a room in a beachfront hotel we have plans to walk on the sand, swim in the ocean, sit in the sun, eat every meal outside. We never leave the room. We spend three days kissing touching exploring discovering we spend three days talking whispering laughing. We spend three days falling in love and I fall truly, deeply and absolutely in love with her. I fall in love with everything about her. I love her mind body smile, I love her walk long and graceful her voice soft and reserved. I love how she smokes, eats, I love her accent certain words have a faint Southern twang. I love the books she reads Paul Bowles and Jack Kerouac, the painters she admires Matisse, van Gogh and Michelangelo. I love that she went abroad alone lived in Florence and went to school. I love that she loves my dogs, that she's not scared of me anymore, that she makes fun of me and my past, says I'm nothing like what she expected, that I'm soft and sweet that I'm nothing like the monster she heard about. I love that I have never felt anything similar to what I feel when I'm inside of her, it's calm strength peace fulfillment fearlessness abandon satisfaction it's something I never knew with Lilly have never known with anyone. I love when I am near her I have to touch her, have to kiss her, have to have my arms around her, have her close to me next to me touching me. I love that when I am with her everything else disappears, I don't think care wonder or worry about anything but her.

We go back to Los Angeles. Allison says she needs to go home. I ask her to stay tell her I want her to stay please Allison stay with me. She has to go home. She doesn't know when she'll be back.

I drive her to the airport.

I walk her to the gate.

I kiss her goodbye.

I'm in love with her.

Please, Allison.

Stay.

The phone rings I pick it up.
Hello.
My son, MY SON, **MY SON!**
What's up, Leonard?
Where the fuck have you been?
Around.
Around my ass. I've left about ten messages.
I haven't checked 'em. Everything okay?
Yeah, but you missed lunch.
I didn't know you were back, didn't know we were having lunch.
Because you didn't check your fucking messages.
I laugh.
Sorry. How was it out East?
No good.
That sucks.
I've decided I'm going to have the entire course fucking torched. Burned
to the fucking ground.
Really?
No. Fuck no. But I didn't get on and I'm pissed.
Sorry.
What have you been doing?
Met a girl.
Who?
Her name's Allison.
Nice name. How'd you meet her?

I went to school with her, knew who she was there. She was out here visiting a friend of hers and we all had dinner.

And?

And we had dinner the next night, then she stayed with me for five days, then we went to Santa Barbara for three days, then she went home.

My son, oh my son. This sounds serious.

Maybe.

Are you in love with her?

Madly.

Have you told her?

No.

Why didn't you tell her?

I don't know.

Why'd you let her go home?

I don't know.

Are you ready for something like this?

I feel like I am.

You're over Lilly enough to be with someone else?

I feel like I am.

I feel like I am isn't good enough. If you're going to tell this Allison that you love her, you need to be sure.

Who said I'm going to tell her that I love her?

Are you sure?

Why do you need to know?

I don't need to know, you need to know. Are you ready to love someone, and are you sure about her?

Yeah, I'm ready, and yeah, I'm sure.

I assume you have Allison's phone number.

Yeah.

We're going to hang up. You're going to call her. You're going to tell her that you love her, that you want her to move to Los Angeles, that you can't live without her. Then we're having dinner.

I laugh.

What if she doesn't love me, or she doesn't want to move here.

Then we will have a miserable dinner.

I laugh again.
We're hanging up now, my Son.
Okay.
And you're going to call her.
Okay.
And then you're going to call me back and we'll make dinner plans.
Sounds good.

I call Allison my hands are shaking I can see my heart beating I can hardly speak I call her she answers the phone. We talk for a few minutes. I wonder if she can tell I'm nervous scared I wonder if she can tell I'm shaking I hope not. I tell her that I love her. I tell her that I want her to move to Los Angeles. I tell her that I don't want to live without her. I tell her that I love her, I love her, I love her.

I fly to Virginia. I'm going to spend a week with Allison's family, help her pack, drive across the country with her. She picks me up at the airport I see her grab her hold her kiss her tell her I've missed her I'm so happy to see her I love her.

Her parents live in Virginia Beach. They live in a big, beautiful Southern house with white columns and a wide porch, on one side is a golf course on the other side is a quiet inlet of the Atlantic Ocean. They're conservative Southerners, people who believe in God, family, tradition. I like them, they seem to like me. I don't swear around them, never let them see my tattoos, avoid discussions about my past. I stay in a room on the side of the house opposite Allison's room. Every chance I get I drag her into closets into bathrooms into the attic, we sneak out of our rooms at night meet in the kitchen in the living room outside in the grass. I play golf with her father, go shopping with her and her mother, we go to their country club for dinner, Allison and I ride bikes take walks along the beach. It's a nice week, a mellow week, it feels like what our life could be like in a few years if we get married and live somewhere other than Los Angeles. It's an image I like it feels happy, comfortable. It feels right as right as any life I've ever imagined.

At the end of the week we pack the car, have a last breakfast with her parents, they cry and wave as we pull away. We've mapped out our trip in an atlas we're going a zig-zaggy route that takes us through the Southern United States. We're going to take our time at least a week, maybe two. Our first stop is Richmond. We stay with Allison's brother, who is a lawyer for a large tobacco company. I met him in Paris several years ago we had drinks together a few times when I left Paris I ended up in rehab and jail when he left he went to law school. He's tall, blond, handsome, he wears pressed pants, starched shirts, lives in a pristine apartment, I imagine that he keeps an accurate checkbook and pays his taxes on time. He takes us out for dinner says he's tired of Richmond is tired of living in such a conservative environment is thinking of moving. I ask him where he wants to go he's says he's not sure maybe Los Angeles. I offer to throw his shit in Allison's trailer he can come with us. He declines.

From Richmond we go to Washington DC. We walk around Georgetown go to the National Gallery. Allison takes me to a bathing suit store she wants to buy me a leopard print Speedo, I ask her why she says because it's funny. I try one on walk around the store ask the other customers what they think of it. Most ignore me, two gay men tell me I look great, an elderly woman tells me to get away from her before she calls the police. I wear the Speedo as we drive out of town.

We decide to go to Memphis. Halfway there we stop at a cheap motel. We get a big room with a big bed it's the first time we've been truly alone since my arrival we take advantage of it. We arrive in Memphis tour Graceland eat barbeque listen to the blues on Beale Street. I feel bad for Elvis dying on the toilet in his big, silly, lonely house. I eat barbeque until I can hardly walk. I dig the blues and at times have known the blues but not right now, not right now.

We drive south through Tennessee and Mississippi. I walk into a backwater truckstop wearing the Speedo, truckers want to kick my ass, the clerk laughs and asks me if I am going to the beach. Further south to New Orleans we see my friend Miles Davis, not the trumpet player Miles Davis, my friend from rehab the Honorable Miles Davis, Federal Judge. Miles was my roommate at rehab. We spent a lot of sleepless nights talking, listening to music, he plays the clarinet he would play when he couldn't sleep. He helped me deal with my legal problems, talked to people for me, made calls for me and helped me avoid a stretch in prison. Aside from Leonard he's the only person I knew there who is still clean, the rest of our friends are either locked-up or dead. We stay in New Orleans for three days. I meet Miles' wife she's a Doctor we have a huge cajun dinner with her and Miles. We go to a bar in the French Quarter where the waitresses look like beautiful women but are all men. We drink strong coffee eat beignets watch ragged magicians perform and drunk guitarists play and fortune tellers speculate and lie. We listen to jazz at night in dark smoky bars where the best musicians in the world play out their lives in obscurity. We walk through the gardens of former plantations the owners are still white the help is still black doesn't seem like much has changed. We eat Sno-Kones in the ghetto we wander through the zoo, what's up orangutan, I like that crazy hair. I'm sad to leave, sad to say goodbye to Miles. I could live in New Orleans, I don't mind the heat and noise and dirt, it's a beautiful decrepit debauched disintegrating paradise. We drive north cross into Texas decide to try and make it across in one shot. Allison buys some books we turn off the radio she starts reading to me. Fourteen hours later we're through two books both Paul Bowles a gallon of coffee three packs of cigarettes and I can't see straight. Four more hours and we're in Santa Fe we see Allison's friends walk through the mountains spend a day at a spa get massages swim in a hot springs Allison gets treatments I have no idea what I just sit and read a book.

We go to Vegas. We're both tired we don't leave the room.

We drive from Vegas to Los Angeles. We pull up to the house. Cassius and Bella have been staying with a friend he dropped them at the house earlier in the day. As I walk to the door I can hear them barking I don't know if they smell me or hear me but they know I'm home. I open the door they jump up and down run in circles, Cassius pees himself they give us kisses. I tell them Daddy's home now he isn't going away again. I tell them Daddy has Mommy with him she isn't going away again. Allison smiles I look at her put my arms around her, kiss her neck, speak.

I love you and I'm happy you're here and I don't want you going away again.

Allison's parents don't want her living with me until we're engaged we're not ready to get engaged she moves in with Conner. Their apartment is at the bottom of the hill about five minutes from my house. Danny and I start trying to raise money for a movie. We call every wealthy person we know we tell them we have a great investment opportunity for them, some of them actually write us checks.

Allison starts working as an assistant for a producer at a studio. The producer is the son of the head of the studio, and has never actually produced anything, but has a big office and a large expense account.

I keep trying to write a book I spend most of my time smoking and drinking coffee and playing with the dogs and swearing.

Allison and I walk into a coffee shop. We see an ex-girlfriend of mine sitting at a table, the ex-girlfriend sees us. We all went to school together, the ex-girlfriend and Allison know each other. I have not seen the ex for three years, we split on terrible terms. The last time we saw each other I was bleeding, beaten, in handcuffs, on my way to jail. I look at her she looks the same, arctic blue eyes long thick blond hair. I say hello she says hello, Allison says hello she says hello to Allison. I have wondered what happened to her, where she was, what it would be like to see her. I feel nothing. I could give two shits about her. Allison and I order our coffees and we sit outside and smoke and laugh and look at each other and when the ex leaves none of us bother to say goodbye.

A yappy little beagle bites Cassius on the ass while I'm walking him and Bella down our street. The beagle snarls and barks jumps at Cassius, looks like he's going to bite him again. Cassius tries to ignore the beagle but the beagle keeps coming until Cassius lunges at him, puts his entire head in his mouth, shakes him a couple of times and tosses him a few feet away. The beagle shakes it off, appears to be fine, and runs away.

Allison and I are together every night. Most of the time we're at my house, once in a while we're at her apartment. She is the first person I have completely loved. I love her physically, emotionally, I love everything about her I love her more every day, more every day. Sometimes I wonder if this is it what my life would have been like if Lilly had lived. Sometimes I feel guilty because I'm happy. Sometimes I hate myself because when I'm with Allison, I stop thinking about Lilly, and I stop missing her.

Leonard wants to meet Allison. I invite him over for dinner, tell him we'll cook for him. He laughs, calls me a domesticated motherfucker, asks me what I know how to cook, I tell him absolutely nothing, Allison's in charge. He laughs again says he'd love to come I ask him if tomorrow is cool he says yeah.

Allison and I go to the fancy gourmet grocery store. She has a list she tells me what to get she checks to make sure I've picked up the right items she double checks as we wait in line.

She starts preparing the food in the afternoon. She makes a salad, mashed potatoes, an apple pie. While she's in the kitchen, I clean the house. I sweep the floors mop the floors, scrub every surface in the bathroom, wash the sheets wash the futon cover, pick up all the dogshit in the backyard and throw it in the woods. The smells coming from the kitchen make me hungry make me want to eat I take regular breaks to go into the kitchen and try to snack. Allison kicks me out I try again she kicks me out again. We take showers put on nice clothes survey the house to make sure everything is in order survey the kitchen to make sure everything is on schedule. Allison knows about Leonard knows what he does and who he is knows about my relationship with him knows how much he means to me. We both want tonight to go well she's nervous. I know Leonard will like her, I know she'll like him though she may be slightly intimidated by him. We hear a car pull up the dogs start barking car door opens knock knock knock. I open the door, Leonard is standing there with a huge bouquet of flowers, two bottles of wine one white one red. He speaks.

My son.

Come on in, Leonard.

Leonard steps into the house. Allison is in my bedroom. Leonard looks around, speaks loudly so that Allison can hear him.

I knew it, I knew it. This beautiful perfect woman was all a delusion, an invention, she doesn't exist.

I laugh.

I was always suspicious. This Allison sounded too good to be true. No one can be everything you said she is, gorgeous, smart, well-read, knowledgeable in the history of art, and willing to tolerate you. It's impossible, impossible.

Allison walks out of the bedroom. Leonard sees her.

Oh my.

Allison smiles.

Hi, Leonard. I'm Allison. I've heard a lot about you, it's nice to meet you.

Leonard drops to one knee.

My Lady, you're a vision. May I offer you flowers, and may I offer you wine, red if you please, white if you please.

Allison laughs, takes the flowers and wine.

Thank you.

May I stand?

She laughs again.

Of course.

Leonard stands, Allison walks into the kitchen puts the flowers in a vase. I follow her ask her what kind of wine she wants she says red I open the bottle ask Leonard if he wants a cola he says no, I stopped drinking cola, just water for me. I pour Allison a glass of wine, Leonard a glass of water, a glass of cola for me. Allison puts dinner in the oven, Leonard sits down on the couch. He looks at Allison, speaks.

Pretty Lady. Come sit with me.

Allison smiles, looks at me.

Can you handle yourself in here?

Yeah.

Allison sits with Leonard. I set the table, warm up the potatoes, put dressing on the salad. I hear bits of their conversation I hear them talking about Allison's hometown about women's clothing, which Leonard seems to know about for some reason. I hear them talking about art about wine I hear them laughing I hear them talking about me I try not to listen. I finish in the kitchen put the salads on the table tell them dinner is ready.

They walk over, Leonard pulls out Allison's chair, we all sit down. Leonard raises a glass, speaks.

To my son, and to the beautiful, charming, intelligent young woman he has somehow convinced to spend time with him.

Allison and I laugh we all clink glasses we each take a sip. We eat the salad, eat dinner Allison makes beef tenderloin, eat dessert. Leonard asks Allison what I was like before rehab, she laughs and says she doesn't really know because she tried to avoid me as much as possible. Allison asks Leonard what rehab was like, he laughs and says it was great and awful at the same time. She asks how it was great, he says as ridiculous as it may sound, it was fun being institutionalized with a bunch of crazy drug addicts and alcoholics, we laughed a lot and told each other all kinds of crazy stories and became great friends. She asks why it was awful he says because nobody ends up there because they're healthy or sane or stable, nobody ends up there because they have a good life, and it's pretty miserable dealing with all the shit we've done to ourselves and other people and it's pretty miserable trying to figure out how not to do it again. She asks about our friends there Leonard tells her about Ed and Ted, Ed died in a fight and Ted is in prison for the rest of his life, about Matty the boxer shot dead outside a crackhouse, about Michael he blew his brains out with a shotgun, about John also now in prison for the rest of his life. Allison asks if Leonard knows Miles, Leonard says of course I do, he's a fine, fine man, I wish I could be friends with him. Allison asks why he can't, Leonard says our positions on opposite ends of the legal spectrum prevent any such friendship. Allison asks about his job, Leonard laughs, says if you're asking, you know, and that's all I'm going to tell you.

As I am clearing the table, Allison gets up goes to the bathroom. Leonard stands, starts helping me, speaks.

If she was my type I'd try to steal her from you.

That'd be a problem.

Thankfully she's not my type.

Do I have your approval?

Buy the ring tomorrow.

I guess that means yes.

That means yes yes yes yes yes, you're fucking crazy if you let her go.

I don't want to, but who knows.

What would stop you?

I don't know.

Lilly?

No.

Does she know about her?

Sort of.

What's that mean?

She knows of her, but she doesn't know details.

Why not?

I don't like talking about Lilly, and I don't with anyone but you, and I don't want Allison to feel like she has to live up to my memories of my dead girlfriend.

That might be a burden.

It would suck for her.

Yes, it would.

I love her and want her to feel comfortable.

I think you're being smart.

Thank you.

Allison returns, Leonard turns around.

Ah, pretty lady, we were just talking about you.

Allison smiles.

What were you saying?

James was telling me how much he loves you.

She smiles again.

I love him.

And I was telling him that if you were my type, I would try to steal you from him.

Oh yeah?

Yeah.

You're charming, Leonard, but you wouldn't get me.

I'm handsome too. Don't forget handsome.

Allison laughs.

Yeah, you're handsome too, Leonard, but I love him.

Leonard looks at me.

You're lucky man, my son, lucky motherfucky.

I laugh.

A motherfucky?

Leonard nods.

Yeah.

What's a motherfucky?

That's you. You're a lucky motherfucky.

You ever use that one before?

Nope, just invented it, just for you, lucky motherfucky.

I laugh again, look at beautiful Allison, look at my friend Leonard, look at my doggies asleep on the floor, they're all in my house in Laurel Canyon in the hills above Los Angeles. I just had a great meal. I'm in love. I know I'm going to wake up tomorrow. I'm a lucky man. A lucky man.

Lucky motherfucky.

Allison, Kevin and I are walking the dogs up the hill toward my house. It's early Saturday morning, the sky is clear, the sun is shining. Allison has Bella I have Cassius Kevin is telling us about his job, he works for a former television star who now spends most of his life in the gym on the phone in front of the mirror. As we walk we hear a car coming up the hill behind us, we can hear it moving fast, we step toward the curb keep walking. A small blue convertible roars past us, slams on its brakes about fifty feet in front of us. We walk toward it we see a man a light-skinned black man sitting behind the wheel he's staring at us. We keep walking when we're about ten feet away the man pulls thirty feet in front of us, stops, keeps staring. When we get closer he does it again. Closer he does it again. Allison and Kevin are confused wonder why this is happening my instincts tell me that something unpleasant is about to happen. I pass Cassius' leash to Kevin walk toward the car the man is staring at me I speak.

Is there a problem?

The man pulls the brake on his car, opens the door, steps out. He's taller than me bigger than me he looks pissed. Allison and Kevin stop a few feet behind me. The man speaks.

Yeah, there's a problem.

What?

That your dog?

He motions toward Cassius.

Yeah.

Your dog bit my dog. Hurt 'im real bad.

What kind of dog do you have?

Got a little beagle named Elron.

I nod.

Yeah, my dog bit your dog after your dog bit him.

That's not what happened.

Yeah, it is.

No, it's not.

I was standing there. Your dog came running up, started snarling and barking, bit my dog, then came after him again, and my dog bit him back.

I got two hundred and fifty dollars in vet bills. What are you gonna do
about it?

Show me the bills and we can try to work something out.

What's that mean?

It means I'll give you my address and phone number, and you can show
me the bills and we'll work something out.

The man stares at me, I stare back. I'm not scared of him, but have no interest in fighting him, or making anything out of this situation. We're
neighbors. His dog, a twenty pound beagle, bit my dog, a ninety-five
pound pitbull. My dog bit his dog back, and I don't doubt he hurt him,
and the right thing to do is try to settle this amicably. The man turns
around, opens his car door. He sits in the driver's seat, takes a pen and a
pad of paper out of a backpack sitting on the passenger's seat, hands them
to me. I write down my name, address, phone number, hand the pad back
to him. He stares at me, speaks.

I'm glad you did that.

No problem.

He puts the pad and pen back into the backpack, takes out a pistol, looks
up at me.

I said I'm glad you did that because I didn't want to go shooting anybody
and I didn't want to go killing anybody.

What?

He shuts the door of his car.

You heard me.

I'm shocked. The gun is sitting on the seat, the man is staring at me, I
speak.

Just show me the bill and we'll work something out.

He stares at me for another moment, starts the car, quickly pulls away. I
turn around, look at Allison and Kevin. Allison is pale, looks terrified.
Kevin is staring up the street.

You okay?

279

Kevin shakes his head, speaks.

What was that?

The guy is obviously not right.

That's putting it mildly.

I look at Allison.

You okay?

She shakes her head, I step forward, take her hand it's shaking.

He was going to shoot us.

He wasn't going to shoot us.

I want to call the police.

We don't need to call the police.

I want to go home and call the police.

We'll go home. We're not calling the police.

We start walking up the hill. I know where the man lives I've seen his car in the driveway. We're going to have to walk past his house to get to my house, I'm hoping the car isn't there. It isn't we get to my house Allison has become increasingly more upset almost frantic. She speaks.

Call the police.

The police aren't going to do anything, Allison.

He threatened to kill us.

And if they go see him he'll deny it and nothing will happen.

Please, just call them.

It's a waste of time.

Kevin speaks.

I think you should call them.

I'll make a call, but it's not going to be to the police.

Allison speaks.

Who are you going to call?

Leonard.

What's he going to do?

I don't know. We'll see.

I pick up the phone, dial, wait, Leonard answers the phone.

Hello?

Leonard.

My son. Happy day to you.

Not really.

What's wrong?

Some motherfucker just threatened to shoot me, and maybe Allison, and maybe my friend Kevin.

What?

I tell Leonard what happened. Tell him about the car, the man, the gun, the threat. When I finish telling him, he laughs.

This is not funny, Leonard.

It's sort of funny.

Motherfucker had a gun. It wasn't funny.

Motherfucker might have had a gun, but he's nothing to worry about. He's not a tough guy.

He looked tough enough to me.

He might have looked tough, but he's no tough guy.

What's the difference?

A tough guy would have shot you, he wouldn't have threatened to shoot you. And he also violated one of the primary rules of a tough guy.

What's that?

Never show your gun, just empty it.

That's very comforting to know, Leonard.

It should be. The guy's probably not dangerous, just a bully.

How do you suggest I deal with him?

Your instincts were right. Pay the bill, settle the situation amicably, make it go away.

And what if that doesn't work?

Leonard laughs.

If there are any problems, call me.

Thank you, Leonard.

Tell Allison not worry.

I will.

I hang up the phone, turn to Allison and Kevin. Allison speaks.

What'd he say?

He told me to tell you not to worry.

What's he going to do?

Nothing.

What are you going to do?

When the guy brings me the bill, I'll work something out with him.

You should just pay it.
I probably will.
He scares me, James. I still think we should call the police.
Leonard is better than the police.
You promise?
We're going to be fine. I promise.

I don't hear from the man. No bill, no phone call, nothing. I stop by his house a couple of times when I see the car in the driveway. I knock on the door no one answers.

Leonard cancels three lunches in a row, switches our weekly lunch to every other week, starts arriving without Snapper.

Danny and I raise enough money to shoot our movie. We hire a crew, a cast, start pre-production, start shooting. Neither of us has any idea what we're doing, and because we don't have much money in Hollywood terms, almost no one on our crew has any idea what they're doing.

Allison hates her job wants to quit. I tell her she should quit, tell her she should take her time figure something else out, tell her she doesn't need to worry about money she can have mine. She says she doesn't want or need me to support her that she's fine on her own that she can pay her own bills. I tell her she can have whatever I have, take whatever she needs from me, that I don't care about money as much as her happiness, that I don't see it as support I see it as giving someone I love a chance to make a change in their life. She's stubborn won't take anything from me she wants to do it on her own.

We keep shooting the movie the days are twenty hours long nothing goes right we fall behind schedule go over budget. Allison gets mad because we never see each other and when we do see each other I'm too tired to talk eat go out I'm too tired to do anything but sleep.

I see footage from the film realize that the film isn't very good realize that I'm no film director think that if I work harder I can somehow save my sinking ship I work harder harder harder every minute of every day is consumed with somehow saving what I've tried to create what Danny and I have spent other people's money to realize.

I spend less and less time with Allison she gets more and more angry.

I don't see Leonard at all.

Work harder and harder.

Sleep less and less.

We finish shooting the movie thank fucking god it's over.

Allison's parents come to Los Angeles they want to see where she's living how she's doing. We pick them up at the airport show them Allison's apartment take them out for a fancy dinner. Next day we go to the beach show them Beverly Hills have them to my house I cook a chicken for them it's not very good. They're nice, polite people they play with Cassius and Bella, both of whom got baths prior to the parents' arrival, they pretend the food I make is edible.

Next day we drive to Newport Beach, an affluent community in Orange County. Close friends of Allison's parents live on an Island near there, we spend the day with them. We walk through the little town on the Island, sit on the sand, swim in the ocean, go for a boat ride. I do not take off my shirt in their presence, do not want them to see my tattoos. I do not swear try not to smoke.

Evening arrives we can either go back to Los Angeles or stay for dinner. Allison's parents want to stay we decide to go to a restaurant in Laguna, which is where Leonard lives. I want to call him, see him, I ask Allison, she doesn't think it would be appropriate, her parents want to spend time with her and me and their friends.

We drive south drive into Laguna we drive past the bluff where I can see Leonard's house we drive past a billboard for the Pageant of the Masters it's a photo of a living Seurat I laugh at the idea of Leonard and Snapper sitting in the crowd oohing and aahing. We drive past a restaurant I've heard them mention I can imagine them sitting on the front deck. I scan the sidewalks hoping to see them, the sidewalks are crowded no luck for me.

We pull up to the restaurant, valet my truck, wait for Allison's parents and their friends. They arrive, we walk into the restaurant. It has a tropical theme, looks like what I imagine a restaurant in Thailand would look like,

wicker chairs with dark comfortable cushions, overhead fans, palm trees
and large exotic flowers, candles everywhere. We're led to a table in a cor-
ner it's a large table with room for a couple more chairs. Almost immedi-
ately after we sit, I hear Leonard. I don't see him I hear him.
MY SON, MY SON.
I look around, don't see him.
I'M OVER HERE, GODDAMNIT. I'M OVER HERE, MY SON.
I laugh, continue to look around.
HERE HERE HERE HERE HERE.
I look toward the voice, see Leonard and Snapper walking toward our
table. They're both wearing Hawaiian shirts, khaki shorts, docksiders.
Snapper has a pair of black socks with his docksiders. They're both smil-
ing, Leonard is waving.
My son, what are you doing here?
I stand up. Allison is smiling, shaking her head she's not angry just sur-
prised, her parents and their friends look confused. I speak.
What's up, Leonard?
What's up? What's up? What's up is you're right in front of me, in my
town. What a surprise.
I laugh, give him a hug, give Snapper a hug. Leonard looks at
Allison, bows.
Beautiful lady, it's always a pleasure to see you.
Allison laughs.
You too, Leonard.
Leonard looks at Allison's parents and their friends, speaks.
And who do we have here?
Allison introduces everyone, Leonard bows to the women, shakes hands
with the men, Snapper smiles and says hello. Leonard looks to the
men, speaks.
Do you mind if we sit with you for a few moments?
Allison's dad says sure, Leonard motions to a busboy, shouts.
Garçon. Two more chairs. Immediately.
The busboy pulls over two chairs, Leonard and Snapper sit down. Allison's
parents seem confused her mother looks at Leonard, speaks.
Your name is Leonard?
Yes, it is.

She looks at Snapper.
And your name is Snapper?
Yes, Ma'am.
What kind of name is that?
It's a nickname, Ma'am.
How did you get it?
I like to fish. I am an expert snapper fisherman. Thus the name.
She nods, and looks at Leonard.
And how do you know James?
We met several years ago. We were both on vacation at a luxury resort. We
had lunch together one day, and we've been great friends ever since.
I try not to laugh, I look at Allison, she seems to be both amused and hor-
rified. Her parents keep talking with Leonard we sit and listen to them.
Her mother asks.
Why do you call James your son?
If I had a son I would like him to be like James. Because I don't have a
son, I have made James a son of sorts, and I like to call him my son.
Why don't you have children?
I've never been married, and didn't want to have a child out of wedlock.
Why didn't you get married?
I would have liked to, and I would have liked to have children, it just
didn't work out for me, and I'm probably not suited for marriage.
Thankfully I met James and have experienced a form of fatherhood that
has made me very happy.
Allison's father asks.
What do you do, Leonard?
I am a semi-retired business executive.
What type of business?
I'm the West Coast Director for a large Italian finance firm.
What type of finance?
We have interests in entertainment, telecommunications, we work with
some unions, do some short-term, high-interest loans.
He looks at Snapper.
What do you do, Snapper?
I was a security guard, I became a collections officer, now I'm an
executive assistant.

What do you assist with?

Whatever's necessary.

Her mother asks.

Do you see James often?

All the time, as much as possible.

Do you know his parents?

Wonderful people. Absolutely the best. I tried to get his father to work with me but he wouldn't do it. They're a class act, you'll love them.

Her father asks.

Are you able to discuss any of the deals you've done?

I could, of course, but our firm's policy is to be as discreet as possible. We do not like attention.

Allison's parents' friends seem confused and fascinated. Leonard tries to change the direction of the conversation, starts commenting on the women's hair, clothing, jewelry, starts flooding them with compliments. He asks the friends if they've been to the restaurant before they say no, he smiles and says it's great you're going to love it. After a few minutes he looks at Snapper, nods, they both stand up. Leonard looks at me, speaks.

A wonderful surprise, my son.

I smile.

Yeah it was.

Lunch this week?

Yeah.

He turns to Allison.

You break my heart every time I see you.

She smiles.

Good to see you too, Leonard.

He turns to Allison's parents.

You are to be commended for having such a beautiful, intelligent, well-mannered daughter.

They both smile. Allison's mom speaks.

Thank you.

I hope to see you again, perhaps at a wedding.

They both laugh. Allison speaks.

Easy now, Leonard.

He laughs, steps back.

I hope you have a wonderful dinner.

Snapper speaks.

Nice to meet all of you.

They turn and walk away. I watch them walk away everyone at our table turns and watches them walk away, and when they're gone from view, Allison's mom laughs and says I'm not sure how to top that, and we all laugh with her.

We start looking at the menus. Before a waiter arrives, the manager comes to our table with a bottle of wine. He speaks.

Your meal, with accompanying bottles of wine, has already been ordered for you.

He opens the bottle, pours some in a glass for Allison's dad, who sniffs it, tastes it, nods, says very good. The manager fills everyone's glass but mine. When he's done he looks at me, speaks.

A cola will be here for you in a moment.

I laugh, say thank you. The friend of Allison's parents picks up the bottle of wine, looks at it, says wow, this is nice. As he hands the bottle to Allison's father, food starts arriving. There are plates of skewers beef chicken and shrimp, oysters with spicy salsa, seaweed salad, spinach salad with yellowtail, seviche. We share everything pass the plates amongst each other. As soon as we finish more food arrives bigger portions on bigger plates shrimp tempura, lobster tempura, black cod with miso sauce, whole fried snapper which makes me laugh, salmon teriyaki, beef tenderloin with pepper sauce. Whenever a bottle of wine is empty another appears immediately, whenever my glass of cola is empty, I get a refill. A waiter stands next to our table to take care of whatever we want, whatever we need. Allison's parents and their friends are overwhelmed by all the food the wine the service. I've told Allison about meals like this with Leonard it's her first experience she thinks it's wonderful. When the entrees are gone and cleared we get dessert, chocolate cake, mango banana ginger and coconut ice cream, rice pudding and fresh fruit and strong coffee and subtle tea. After dessert Allison's father asks for a bill. The waiter leaves to get the manager. The manager comes to our table, speaks.

How was your meal?

Around the table he hears great, wonderful, amazing. He speaks again.

Is there anything else I can get for you?

Allison's father speaks.

The bill please.

That has been taken care of, sir.

I would like to take care of it, please.

I'm sorry, sir, but that's not possible.

I look at the manager, speak.

Thank you.

Certainly. Please let me know if you'd like anything else before you leave.

The manager leaves, we stand up and leave. We say goodbye to the friends they get in their car and drive away, we get in my truck and drive away. Allison and her mother sit in the backseats, her father sits in the passenger seat. About halfway to Los Angeles, Allison and her mother are both asleep. Her father looks at me, speaks.

James.

Yeah.

I need to speak to you about something.

Okay.

And I need you to be honest with me.

Of course.

Your friend Leonard.

Yeah.

You didn't meet him at a luxury resort, did you?

No.

Did you meet him in jail or rehab?

I met him in rehab.

Why was he there?

Cocaine.

Does he still use it?

No, he's clean. Same as me.

And does West Coast Director of a large Italian finance firm mean what I think it means?

Probably.

Is that a good thing or a bad thing?

It is what it is.

And his executive assistant?

A wonderful man but also probably what you think he is.

The name Snapper doesn't have anything to do with fish, does it?
No, not a fishing reference.
Is my daughter in any danger?
Absolutely not.
Are you sure of that?
If anything, your daughter lives under a veil of protection. Leonard loves her, and would never allow anything to happen to her.
Are you involved in what he does?
No.
Does he really know your parents?
Yeah, they love him.
Allison's father looks out the window. It's dark, the highway is empty. He takes a deep breath, speaks.
It's a strange world we live in.
Yeah, it is.
He stares out the window. I drive. He turns back to me.
Will you please thank your friend Leonard for dinner, and tell him and his friend Snapper that we enjoyed meeting them.
I smile.
Yeah, I will.

We finish our movie it's not very good. We have a big premiere my parents come my brother comes Leonard comes there's a big crowd. At the after party people shake my hand pat me on the back give me their business cards tell me the movie was amazing, incredible, great. I smile say thank you but I know it wasn't very good. It hurts me to admit it, and it hurts me to accept it, my movie wasn't very good.

Allison hates her job more and more with every passing day and is more and more miserable with every passing day she comes home angry every night.

Leonard goes back to the East Coast to try to play the golf course. He says this time he's taking a briefcase full of cash with him. As I always do before his pilgrimage, I wish him luck, good luck Leonard good luck.

The script I sold goes into production, an actor from a popular television show about a group of friends in New York is the star. He hires his best friend to rewrite my script I read the new version and I hate it. I call a lawyer and I ask him if there's anything I can do about it, he reads my contract and says no and he tells me that when you take Hollywood's money you have to be prepared to eat Hollywood's shit. I don't like eating shit but I know I'm going to have to this time, so I go to my kitchen and I get a napkin.

I'm asleep. I hear the phone ring I'm asleep I hear the phone ring. Allison is sleeping next to me it's early Saturday morning we were out late last night. I hear her pick up the phone say hello. I open my eyes turn over. She has the phone to her ear I see her lose color I see fear register on her face I see her lips start to quiver she passes the phone to me her hand is shaking. I put my hand over it, speak.

What's wrong?

She shakes her head.

What's wrong?

She points to the phone.

Take it.

I put the phone to my ear, speak.

Hello.

You never paid my fucking bill.

I've heard the voice it's early I'm not awake yet.

What?

You never paid my fucking bill.

I sit up. I know the voice it's my neighbor with the beagle, the blue car, the gun.

What are you talking about?

You never paid my fucking bill.

You never showed me the bill.

You knew how much the bill was, you know where I live, you should've fucking paid it.

I said if you showed it to me, we'd work something out. I'll still do that.

Too fucking late now.

What's that supposed to mean?

It means my cousin in the 68th Street Crips is on his way to your house right now to kill your fucking dogs and kick your ass.

What?

You heard me.

This is a huge fucking over-reaction.

Not the way I see it.

Just show me the bill and we'll work something out.

Too late for that.

He hangs up. I hang up. I look at Allison, who still looks terrified.

What'd he say to you?

He said put your boyfriend on the phone, bitch.

She takes a deep breath.

And I said what and he yelled put your fucking boyfriend on the phone you dumb fucking bitch.

You okay?

She shakes her head.

No.

Take a deep breath, calm down, everything is going to be fine.

What'd he say to you?

Doesn't matter.

I start dialing the phone.

Are you calling the police?

No.

Call the police.

No.

Phone starts ringing. Allison looks panicked.

Call the police, please.

Ringing. I take her hand.

No.

Ringing. She starts crying.

Please.

Leonard picks up.

Who dares to call me at this hour?

It's me. Did I wake you?

I've been riding my exercise bike for the last hour. What's going on?

I've got a problem, Leonard.

What's wrong?

I tell him about my conversation with my neighbor. When I'm finished he laughs. I speak.

This is not fucking funny, Leonard.

The guy's full of shit, my son. It's laughable how full of shit he is.

Sure didn't sound like he was full of shit.

He's definitely full of shit.

And how do you know that?

I've never heard of the 68th Street Crips. Now that doesn't mean they don't exist, but if they do, I can promise you that not one of them is going to risk serious fucking prison time to come up to nice, safe, leafy, lily-white, full of movie stars Laurel Canyon to break into your house, shoot your dogs, beat your ass and somehow have to deal with your girlfriend. Gangbangers are crazy and dangerous, but they're not fucking stupid. Your obvious move here would be to call the police, who would roar up there and be sitting in your living room waiting for said supposed dog assassin to show up, at which point he would be arrested. A gang member would know that, and no gangster would be willing to risk it.

So what do I do?

Well, this guy is obviously fucked-up. And he may very well try to hurt you or the dogs, and if Allison is around, he may try to hurt her. That's not acceptable to me. I want you and Allison and the dogs to get in that shit-box truck of yours and drive down to the Four Seasons. I think Four Seasons are dog-friendly, and if they're not, they will be for you. By the time you get there, I will have called and gotten you a room. I'll try to get a big room if possible. Stay there until Monday. Do not leave. Eat your meals there, and if you need anything, clothes or books or whatever, have the concierge get it for you and charge it to the room. Have a nice time. Think of this as a little vacation. Take baths and swim in the pool and get massages and eat room service. Don't think about your asshole neighbor. When you get home on Monday, I will have taken care of your problem with him.

Thank you, Leonard.

I need you to do something for me.

Okay.

Get his address.

Okay.

And call me when you get to the hotel, so I know you're safe.

Okay.

I hang up the phone. Allison has been watching me listening to me she's still terrified I turn to her speak.

We're leaving.

Where we going?

Four Seasons.

The hotel?

Yeah.

Why are we going there?

We're going to spend the weekend there.

Why?

Leonard says it will be safe for us there.

And what do we do when we leave?

The problem will be taken care of.

What's that mean?

I didn't ask, and I'm not going to ask.

This is fucking crazy, James.

Do you want to stay here, see what happens?

No.

Then let's go.

We get up we move quickly we brush our teeth get dressed. Allison keeps some clothes at my house she packs them into a small bag with a tooth-brush, some toothpaste. I get the dogs on their leashes we get in the truck drive down the hill. The blue car is in the driveway of the house Allison won't look at it I get the address. We drive to the Four Seasons, pull into the drive. The valet comes to my truck. He smiles at me like most valets smile at me and my truck, I'm not sure if they think the truck is cool or feel sorry for me for driving it. I don't really care either way.

We walk into the lobby. The dogs are excited, Cassius tries to take a piss in a potted plant. I pull him away we walk up to the reception desk. An attractive woman in her early thirties smiles at us and speaks.

Mr. Frey.

Hi.

We have your room ready for you.

I laugh.

Thank you.

She hands me a small envelope with a keycard and mini-bar key.

If we can do anything to make your stay more pleasurable, please let us know.

Thank you.

We turn around walk to the elevators, take an elevator up, find our room, go inside. It's a small suite, with a bedroom and a sitting room with a couch and two chairs and a desk and a large bathroom with a marble tub and a shower and two sinks and soaps and lotions and big fat towels and thick robes. I let the dogs off their leashes they start running around smelling everything. I sit down on the couch, look at Allison, speak.

You okay?

She nods.

Yeah.

I look around the room.

Not bad.

She laughs.

Yeah, not bad.

I stand put my arms around her kiss her softly on the neck tell her I love her, she puts her arms around me tells me she loves me and we stand in the middle of the room silently holding each other.

We spend the rest of the weekend relaxing eating room service sitting by the pool watching pay-per-view movies taking baths lounging around in the robes. I get the dogs steaks cut them into little pieces, I take them for walks in the underground parking garage. They sleep in the bed with us we sleep well, easily, without worry.

Monday morning Allison and I have breakfast together, I drive her to work. I'm nervous as I go home start driving up the hill toward my house. I approach the man's house. I see a moving van parked on the curb. Men are moving furniture from the house to the truck. The blue convertible is filled with boxes. The man is standing in the door he is speaking into a cell phone. He looks nervous, scared. He sees my truck he immediately turns and walks into the house.

Two days later there is a For Sale sign in the front yard.

I don't see Leonard for two months. He calls me twice he doesn't sound well I ask him if he's okay he says yes, just busy, got some shit going on. I ask him if I can help in any way he says no.

The movie I shot doesn't sell we lose all of the investors' money.

Allison and I start fighting. We fight over everything. There's no good reason for the fighting, and neither of us wants to fight, but we can't seem to stop, and every day my heart breaks a little more, with each fight my heart breaks a little more.

I take a job writing a script for a children's movie. It's an idiotic job and I only do it for the money. I don't give a shit about it and after I turn in my first draft, I get fired.

Cassius and Bella get in a fight and tear each other up. I have to take them both to the vet they both get stitched, they both get infections, they both end up on antibiotics, they both end up with scars. I have no idea why they started fighting, and five minutes after I break it up, they're licking each other's wounds. Aside from Leonard and Allison, they're the best friends I've got, and when they hurt I hurt, and I can't imagine living without them, and the entire incident scares the shit out of me.

There's a huge storm with huge winds a huge tree in my backyard falls it falls through my fucking roof. I'm sleeping when it happens, it sounds like a fucking bomb exploded in my living room. I jump out of bed run into the living room there are tree branches and sticks and leaves everywhere I look up and I can see a black, black sky. I stand there and I look up and it rains on me and I stare up at a black, black sky.

Just before noon. I'm sitting in my living room. It took two weeks to fix the roof I stayed at Allison's we fought the entire time. I'm sitting in front of the television. I'm smoking a cigarette I'm drinking a cola the dogs are on either side of me. We're watching a talk show. Two sisters who are both married to their cousin, the same cousin, are fighting each other. They're throwing punches, screaming, scratching, pulling each other's hair. It's sick, but I enjoy watching it. The phone rings I pick it up. Leonard speaks.

My son.

What's up, Leonard?

I need to see you.

Okay.

I need to see you right now.

Where are you?

At a diner in Hollywood.

What are you doing there?

Doesn't matter, I just need to see you.

Okay.

Can you come now?

Sure.

He gives me the name of the diner I know where it is, I get in the truck drive down, park on the street, which is in a dangerous, rundown neighborhood. I walk into the diner see Leonard sitting in a corner facing the door. He stands as I walk toward him. He looks nervous, anxious.

He speaks.

Thanks for coming.

Of course.

He steps around the table, gives me a hug. We separate. I speak.

What's wrong?

Let's sit.

We sit down. He speaks.

Do you want anything?

No.

Everything okay with you?

Yeah.

Allison?

She's fine.

The dogs?

They're fine.

Work?

It's fine, Leonard, everything's fine.

Good.

What's wrong?

What makes you think something is wrong?

You've been away, I haven't heard from you. We're sitting in this shithole diner in a shithole neighborhood. You look nervous and you seem anxious and I can see your hand is shaking, which is something I've never seen before.

He nods.

You're good, my son, real good.

I laugh.

What's wrong, Leonard? Are you doing coke?

Fuck no. Never. You should know I'm done with that.

Then what's wrong?

I'm going away for a while.

Where you going?

I can't tell you.

Why?

I just can't.

Is this why I haven't seen you, and why when I've spoken to you, you've seemed fucking weird?

Yes.

Where you going?

I can't tell you.
Is someone trying to kill you?
No.
Are you going to jail?
No.
What the fuck, Leonard.
I'm sorry.
I don't understand this.
At some point you will.
When?
When I can, and I don't know when that will be, I'll get in touch
with you.
And that's it?
Trust that I have to do what I'm doing, and that when I can, I will be in
touch with you.
I look away, shake my head, bite my lip. I'm confused and angry and hurt I
don't understand what's happening. I'm scared because Leonard is scared,
nervous because he's nervous. I've never seen him scared or nervous be-
fore something bad is happening, something bad is happening. He speaks.
Do you trust me?
Of course I do.
I've got to go.
I don't want you to get killed, Leonard. And if you're locked up I want to
come see you.
You said you trusted me.
I do.
Then trust that's not what's happening, and trust that I'll be in touch.
I look at him, nod. He stands.
Give me a hug, my son
I stand, give him a hug. I don't want to cry I force myself not to cry. We
separate, he steps away, speaks.
Don't be a dumbfuck.
I laugh.
No drinking, no drugs, no stupid bullshit.
I laugh again.

Okay.

Give Allison a kiss for me, and give those damn doggies some nice pats on the head.

I will.

Goodbye, my son.

He turns and walks out of the diner.

First month second month I pretend he's away on one of his trips, that he's busy, that our conversation at the diner didn't take place. That life is as it has been for the last three years, that he's going to call or start banging on my door or just appear in my living room. I pretend that life is as it has been.

I fail upward, only in Hollywood is failure rewarded. Often the bigger the failure, the bigger the reward. In my case, I wrote an awful movie made worse by a lame television star and his dumbass director best friend that was produced by a big studio and released in several thousand theaters all over America to resoundingly awful reviews and huge numbers of empty seats. I wrote, produced and directed a second movie that was so bad that it was deemed unreleasable by every distributor in America. I wrote a children's movie for a studio and the first draft was so awful that it immediately got me fired. Somehow, I keep getting work, and I keep getting work that pays me more and more money.

I re-write a thriller script. The script is terrible when I start, and is only slightly less terrible when I finish. I get fired again.

Danny meets an incredibly wealthy guy about the same age as us he's from an incredibly wealthy family. The guy wants to get into the movie business. Danny convinces him to fund a company for us. We open an office, hire a staff. I laugh every time I walk through the front door.

Three months nothing, four months nothing. I wonder where he is what he's doing, if he's running from someone, if he's in jail, if he's alive. I wonder if he's happy and laughing I doubt it, if he's pissed maybe, if he's scared yes, I think he's scared. I wonder if he's safe I don't know, I doubt it. Part of me clings to the notion that this is some sort of joke, that he's going to come through my door in a minute and yell my son, My Son, MY SON, that we'll laugh and laugh and laugh about how he fooled me. Part of me knows it's a defense mechanism, that I lost Lilly and though I've moved on, I've never recovered from it, and may never recover from it. I don't want to lose my friend Leonard. I don't want to lose him.

I decide to buy a house I want to live near the ocean. My mom comes to town to help me look for a house, Allison helps me look for a house. We find an old bungalow in Venice half a block from the beach. I take Cassius and Bella out to see the house they approve, Cassius asks if he can take surfing lessons, Bella wants a bikini. I buy the house move in. I hardly have any furniture so the house is almost entirely empty.

Allison and I keep fighting every fucking day there's a new fucking fight. She's mad at me because she wants to move into my house and I want her to move into my house but her parents won't approve of her moving in until we're engaged and I'm not ready to be engaged. All we do is fucking fight. I hate the fights. Hate myself for engaging in them. I try to stop, try to get her to stop, and for whatever reason, we can't stop.

Cassius and Bella have two more altercations. They hurt each other badly each time. I have their vet help me, I hire a trainer to help me, I hire an animal behavior specialist to help me. I love my dogs and I want them to be happy, I do everything I can to try to solve the problem. I talk to everyone I can who might be able to help me.

Five six seven eight. Nine·months. Nothing. Absolutely nothing. I check my mail nothing, voicemails nothing. I drive down to his house in Laguna someone else is living there. I call the customer service number on the back of one of his phonecards. I ask if he's available or if there is a contact number, they say they've never heard of him, I speak to a supervisor, they say they've never heard of him. I have no way of reaching Snapper. I know his first name is Dominic, I don't know his last name. I have no way of reaching Olivia, I know she works at a casino, I don't know which casino. I go to the steakhouse where we used to eat lunch, the Maitre d' greets me, says hello I haven't seen you in a while, I ask him if he's seen Leonard, he says no.

Allison and I break up. It isn't her fault and it isn't my fault. We still love each other but we can't get along and we're tired of fighting and we're tired of hurting each other and we need to be apart. I miss her. I miss everything about her. My life my heart my house my bed is empty without her, I'm empty without her. I cry myself to sleep at night. She's on the other side of town it might as well be the other side of the earth. I cry myself to sleep at night.

Ten months, eleven months, a year I haven't heard from him. I start to wonder if I ever will. I start to wonder if he's dead. If he is, I assume someone killed him. If someone killed him, I hope they did it quickly.

I want to get out of Los Angeles. I think it will be good for me to get out of town, get away from my memories of Allison and Leonard, away from my unhappiness, away from my emptiness. Danny and I decide to make a movie in Seattle. After my previous failures as a writer and a director, I decide that on this movie I'll function only as a producer. I move up there, bring the doggies with me, we live in a hotel.

Two days after we arrive it starts raining. It rains for sixty-three straight days. I hate it. The dogs hate it. We walk outside it's cold and gray we're immediately wet it fucking sucks. I made a mistake coming up here. I shouldn't have run away from my loss, I should have known it would run with me. If I could, I would go back. Go back to Los Angeles to Venice to my house to my life to whatever else I have and have to deal with, be it good, be it bad. I have to stay here for this movie there is too much of someone else's money involved to leave, I have to stay here for five or six months.

The movie is an absolute disaster. The actors are difficult, the crew hates each other, one of the cameramen gets hit by a truck and breaks his arm, leg, jaw and cheekbone, one of our RV's gets stolen, we total a Seattle City Police cruiser, and, after a week, we're over-budget and behind-schedule.

Thirteen fourteen, fifteen sixteen. I assume he's gone, not coming back, dead, killed by someone for something in his past. I would have heard something by now. I would have heard something.

Cassius and Bella get in another fight. It's in the hotel room there's no rhyme or reason for it they just start fighting. Bella gets her throat torn I get my finger bitten. Bella ends up in the vet hospital my fingers swell they look like sausages I end up in the human hospital. When I get out I take Cassius to another vet who is also a behavioral specialist and a pitbull breeder. I just want my little boy, my mister big man, my best buddy to be better and to be happy.

The vet asks me about Cassius' history, his breeding, his life. He examines Cassius, takes him to his home for two days, brings him back, we meet in his office.

Cassius is three years old. He tells me that three is the age where male dogs reach full maturity. Cassius, the Son of Cholo, comes from a gene line of fighting dogs. Not all pitbulls are fighting dogs but Cassius is absolutely a fighting dog. He is genetically pre-programmed to be aggressive, to want to fight, to seek out fights. He will not change, and there is no way to change him, and the older he gets, the more aggressive he will become. Cassius has grown to be almost one hundred pounds. He is all muscle, he is incredibly strong. The vet tells me I can try to micromanage his life, and keep him in the situations where he will not have outlets for his aggression, but that he will be unhappy and frustrated because he will not be allowed to do what his instincts are telling him he should do. I look at Cassius, who is sitting at my feet wagging his tail looking up at me.

I ask the vet what he thinks I should do, he tells me that he thinks I should put Cassius down, that it will be best for him, for me, for Bella. I don't want to accept the vet's opinion, but I know he's right. I look down at Cassius he's still sitting at my feet, I start to cry. He senses something is wrong he wants to make me feel better he jumps up starts licking my face. I put my arms around him and I cry and I tell him I love him, I love him so much, I tell him I'm sorry, I'm so sorry, I'm so sorry.

The vet tells me it will be painless, that I can be with him. We walk into an operating room Cassius jumps up on a steel table. The vet prepares the needle. I hold Cassius and I tell him over and over that I love him and that I'm sorry and that I'll miss him and he kisses me, kisses me, kisses me, he tries to make me feel better he has no idea. The vet inserts the needle, depresses the plunger. Cassius yelps like a little puppy, my big tough pit-bull feels the sting, I hold him as his blood courses through his veins I hold him as he stumbles, as he falls, I hold him as he dies. I look into his eyes and I tell him I love him and I'll miss him and I'm so so so sorry. He dies in my arms and I hold him and I cry, I cry, I cry.

I am lonely and I am lost and I hate what I'm doing and I hate my life. I miss Lilly I still miss her. I miss Leonard I'm allowing myself to mourn him. I miss Allison I wish it could have worked with her I still love her. I miss Cassius and I hate myself for what happened with him. I am lonely and I am lost and I want to go home. I've spent my whole life moving, running, trying to escape, it doesn't fucking work. I want to go back to Los Angeles, I want to go home.

We finish shooting the movie. I have a week or two of work before I can leave, we have to shut everything down, return all of the equipment, clear the payroll, clear the bills. At the end of another long, shitty day I go back to the hotel to go to sleep. Bella and I walk in there's a stack of mail, most of it forwarded to me from Los Angeles. I start going through it bill, offer for a credit card, bill, another offer for another credit card. There's a post-card. It's a picture of the Golden Gate Bridge in San Francisco. I look at it, I don't know anyone in San Francisco who would be sending me this post-card, I look at it.

I have an idea maybe he's alive, maybe he's alive. I smile, you mother-fucker Leonard, why did you wait so long, I smile.

I turn it over. It has my name on it, the address of the hotel where I'm staying, there is no note, just another address in the section where a note would be, an address in San Francisco.

I smile.

You motherfucker.

Why'd you wait so long.

I smile.

san francisco

I pack my shit there isn't much. I'm leaving Seattle as soon as I can. Danny can handle the rest of the work without me.

I drive south through Washington, Oregon, Northern California. Bella rides shotgun, we stop for food, coffee, cigarettes, a walk every few hours, a bathroom break every few hours.

I cross the Bay Bridge into San Francisco. I'm staying with a friend from Paris, a woman named Colleen. Colleen has black hair, black eyes, always wears black clothes, looks like a movie star from the forties. She's seven years older than me, works at an Internet company during the day, makes paintings and collages at night. In Paris she made hats, shoes, clothes, worked at an advertising agency, and she was my only friend who wasn't a degenerate.

I find her house, which is in one of San Francisco's valleys. She gives me a hug, a big kiss, says James is in San Francisco, I'm so happy to see him. I laugh give her a hug, a big kiss. I drop my bags in her place, she wants to take me to lunch I tell her I need to go somewhere first, I give her the address. We get in my truck I bring Bella with us she'll be happy to see Leonard he'll be happy to see her. The address is on the other side of town, Colleen knows the general area. We drive up hills and down hills, up and down up a hill. We're on the street I look at the numbers on the houses. We're two blocks away, a block away. I see a white Mercedes sitting in a driveway I laugh. It's an old Mercedes, from sometime in the fifties or sixties, it's a small convertible in perfect condition. Colleen asks me why I'm laughing I just smile.

I pull over. I tell Colleen we may have to delay lunch, or at least switch the venue, I tell her I'll know in a minute. I get out of the car, Bella comes with me.

We walk toward the front door. The house is a small, two-story, white frame house with black shutters. The lawn is well-tended, there are flower beds on both sides of the front door. It is a nice, clean house, it's inconspicuous, there's no reason to give it a second look.

I step to the door, ring the bell. I'm excited to see my friend, my old friend Leonard. I wait for someone to answer, push the bell again. I wait, wait, no one comes to the door. I wonder if the bell is broken. I close my fist and I knock. I wait, nothing, knock again, nothing. I think about leaving a note, decide against it, I don't know the details of this situation. Bella and I walk back to the car. I'm not disappointed, I know he's here because of the Mercedes. I'll come back until someone answers the door. I'll keep coming back.

We go to lunch. I try again after lunch, there's no one home.

I try again before dinner, there's no one home.

I try again after dinner.

No one home.

I leave Colleen's house I tell her I'm going back to Los Angeles. If I don't find Leonard, I will go back, wait a few days, come back here.

I pull up to the house. It's a beautiful, clear, warm, sunny day. The convertible is sitting at the curb the top is down.

He's alive.

I look toward the front door it's open. I can see through a screen door into the house.

My friend Leonard is alive.

Windows are wide open.

Motherfucker disappeared for eighteen months, didn't say shit about where he was or what he was doing, I thought he was dead.

Curtains fluttering.

He's alive.

I hear the faint sounds of classical music. Bella's on a leash we walk to the door I press the bell. I wait. I see movement.

I smile, my friend Leonard is alive.

A man comes to the door. He's not Leonard. He looks like he's about thirty. He's tall, thin, has short blond hair parted to one side. He's wearing khakis, black leather sandals, a white oxford. He looks very clean. He stands at the door, speaks in a bitchy, effeminate way.

May I help you?

Leonard here?

How may I help you?

I have the postcard in my back pocket, I take it out, hold it up.

I got this postcard in the mail. It has this address on the back, I thought it might be from my friend Leonard.

May I see it?

Sure.

He opens the door enough for me to pass him the card. He looks at it, looks back at me, speaks.

Your name is?

James.

He motions to Bella.

And who is that?

Bella.

He looks at Bella, speaks.

Hi, Bella.

She wags her tail.

Isn't there another one? Cassius?

He died.

I'm sorry.

It sucked.

I'm sure it did. I know you loved him.

Who are you?

He opens the door.

My name's Freddie. I sent you that card. We've been waiting for you.

Is Leonard here.

Yes.

I step inside the house. There are pristine, pale wood floors. All of the fur-niture is white, there are thick, soft, white couches and chairs. There are impressionist prints on the walls, there are flowers everywhere. Freddie leads me through the foyer, the living room, I can see a deck. I can see Leonard, or what appears to be a faded version of Leonard, sitting on a chaise lounge on the deck, he's wrapped in a white cotton blanket.

As I walk toward him he turns to me. He smiles, lifts his hand, speaks, his voice is weak and scratchy.

My son. My son has arrived.

I walk onto the deck. Freddie stays behind, leaves us alone. I look at Leonard I'm shocked, speechless. He's lost thirty or forty pounds. There are open sores on his arms and neck. His hair looks dry and brittle, his skin is gray and sallow. He looks like he hasn't eaten in a month, like a skele-ton, like a dead man. The only thing that remains unchanged are his eyes, which are clear and fixed, dark brown, alive.

My son, you found me.

I'm happy to see him but shocked. I smile.

You sent for me.

I lean down to hug him.

You don't have to touch me if you don't want to.

Fuck that, Leonard.

He laughs, I give him a hug, a strong hug. He feels small and fragile in my arms, feels like a child. He's skin and bones, smells like medicine, sickness, decay. He hugs me back, his arms are weak, incredibly weak.

It's good to see you, Leonard.

My son. It's good to see you too.

I pull away. Bella puts her front legs on the edge of the lounge, kisses Leonard's hand. He looks down at her, smiles.

Ooh, Bella, you little angel.

He leans down, she kisses his face.

Where's your brother? Where's the Big Boy?

He died.

Leonard looks up. He looks hurt.

What happened?

I shake my head. Leonard speaks.

Bad?

Yeah.

And how's Allison?

I laugh.

That was bad too.

She's okay, isn't she?

I assume so, though I haven't spoken to her in a while.

Big changes, my son.

I've been through worse, but it wasn't fun.

Big change never is.

Looks like you're experiencing some big changes too.

He laughs.

That's one way of putting it.

What's going on here, Leonard?

He laughs.

What's going on? Isn't that the fucking question.

You look fucking awful.

He laughs, coughs, speaks.

Pull up a chair.

I look around the deck there are a couple of other chairs I pull one of them over sit down.

You want the long version or the short version?

I'm not going anywhere.

He laughs, coughs, the cough gets worse. I look at him and I'm scared, I put my arms around him pat him on the back. He stops coughing, I pull away, he spits something unpleasant off the deck and into the yard. He laughs, speaks.

Pretty nice, huh?

What's wrong?

You ready?

Yeah, I'm ready.

He looks at me, takes a deep breath.

I'm gay, and I'm dying of AIDS.

I look at him. I don't know what to say. He speaks.

You okay?

I nod.

Yeah.

I'm gay, my son, and I'm dying of AIDS.

I heard you.

Surprised?

That would be one way to put it.

You can leave if you want.

Why would I leave?

I don't know what your position is on being gay, and I don't know what your position is on AIDS.

My position is that you're my friend, and if you're gay, you're gay, it doesn't make any difference to me, and if you've got AIDS, I'm sorry, and I'm going to do whatever I can to help you.

He smiles.

Thank you, my son.

You gonna give me the long version or the short version?

He smiles again, looks away, looks out across the deck. He closes his eyes, takes a deep breath as if he's gathering his strength, looks back.

I've always known. For as long as I've had memories, I've known. When I was a kid, I liked playing with girls more than boys and liked looking at boys more than girls. At the time I didn't know what that meant, though I did know that in a Roman Catholic Italian family, it wasn't considered right. As I grew up, got older, whatever it was I felt got stronger, and I had to work harder to ignore it. I went on dates. When I was old enough, I slept with women, I got engaged a couple of times, and just kept putting the weddings off. Although I love women, I love their company and their beauty, and could perform with them, I just couldn't follow through because it wasn't right for me. All the way through I overcompensated for what I felt, which was a love for men, by being the meanest, craziest, most violent motherfucker anybody knew, that way nobody could question me or doubt me or even suspect me, because a person who did some of the things I did could never be a fairy, even though I was, and I am. What happened, because of the world I lived in, was that my violence made me more respected, and ultimately, more successful. That success locked me into my charade even more, because I was around more people, and they watched me more carefully.

I was in my early twenties the first time I slept with a man. He was a cab driver in New York. We were driving, talking, and he could tell somehow, and he propositioned me and I accepted, and it happened in the back of his cab, which we parked in an alley. I hated myself for it, fucking hated myself, and I hated him for being with me. I knew, though, that I would do it again, and I did, over and over and over, for the rest of my life, always with random men in random places, always with men who had no idea who I was or had any connection to me. I kept hating myself for a while, then I just accepted what I was, and I also accepted that I could never be open about it. If I was ever open, or if I got caught, I would get killed, because my business doesn't allow for weakness. Even though being gay isn't weak, that would have been the perception. Violent men, criminals, people like me, would have never allowed or tolerated or trusted or respected me, and at the first chance they got, they'd have put me in the fucking ground.

Somewhere along the way I picked up HIV. I have no idea from who or when. About six years ago I woke up one day and felt like something was wrong, so I took a test and it came back positive. When I got the result I left the doctor's office and I never went back. I know there are things I could have done with a doctor and drugs and combinations of drugs I could have taken to slow down the virus, and at this point they say there are things that can almost stop it, but if I had started going to a doctor, and had gone on a drug regimen, people would have found out. And again, if my associates had found out, they would have killed me.

I started thinking about what I have done, and I'll explain exactly what I've done soon, a few months after I met you and after you met Lilly. I remember very vividly you telling me about Lilly's desire to feel free from her addictions and the hell of her life, and her telling you that to her, a second of freedom was worth more than a lifetime of bondage. I thought about that every day, every fucking day, and then I started watching you and watching how you took responsibility for the mess you had made of your life, and how you rejected everything you were told would save you in favor of what you believed, which was that you had the power to make the decisions that would decide the course of your existence. What I learned from the two of you was that freedom is worth sacrifice, and that I was in charge of my life and how I lived it and that I could decide to do anything I wanted to do. I wanted to escape, and be free, free of my job, of my position, of my role. I wanted out of the prison I built around myself. I wanted to get the fuck out.

I started taking steps to do it when you were in Chicago. I knew the virus would get me sooner or later, so I was on a time schedule. My plan was to try to legitimize some of my businesses, so that I could make more money and hide it easier. I also read that if I started living better by exercising, eating properly and living as cleanly as possible, it might slow the virus down. That's what all my diets were about, all my exercise plans, and I don't know if they did anything or not. Once the virus started mutating, I was going to disappear, which is what I did, so that, before I died, I could live part of my life as a normal gay man, albeit a normal gay man who was dying of AIDS.

That's what I've been doing since I last saw you. First thing I did was get a fake passport and leave the country. I knew once I was gone that people would be looking for me, though not because I was gay, they probably still don't know that, but because I disappeared with a big pile of money. I knew if they found me they would kill me. Being far away, where no one knew me or would recognize me, was important. I went to London, Paris, Rome, Athens, Madrid, Moscow and St. Petersburg. I looked at beautiful art and saw the sights and went to gay bars at night and looked at beautiful men. I went to India and saw the Taj Mahal, went to China and saw the Wall, went to Japan and saw all sorts of weirdness. After seven months I came back to the States and settled here. I've been very careful since I've been here. I don't usually go out during the day. When I go out at night, I go to gay bars and restaurants with a predominantly gay clientele. I've been out on a few dates, I fell in love briefly, I've done some of the things I've always dreamed of being able to do.

Over the course of time I've also gotten sicker and sicker. As you can see, I'm not in good shape. I hesitated to contact you until recently because I didn't want you followed, and I'm sure at various points over the last year and a half you have been watched very carefully. Snapper, who is a wonderful man, but who is also a man with a nasty job that he does very well, would have known that you might be able to lead him to me, and that's probably what he's been doing since I left, trying to find me and kill me. I don't have much time left. If you leave when I'm finished talking, I'll understand, and I'll be grateful to you for coming at all. What I did was fucked-up, but it's what I did to complete my life, to be able to die happy. Now that I've seen you, I have only one thing left on my list of things to do before I die, which is play the golf course where my father worked and where I promised him I would play. To pull up, park my car in the lot, walk through the front door, and play that fucking course just like one of the members. I know that it isn't going to happen, and if that's all I haven't done, I'm fine with it.

Leonard stops speaking, slumps into his chair as if speaking has taken all of his strength. I look at him broken and dying, wasting away, sores all over his body, wrapped in his blanket, he looks at me I speak.

A lot of things make more sense now.

Like what?

No wife, no girlfriends. Your love of clothes and white cars. Why all of my girlfriends, romantic and platonic, wanted to be your best friend. The house in Laguna Beach, which is a gay town, that I thought you loved because of the view. Why you said Allison, who drops jaws everywhere she goes, wasn't your type. The Speedo bikini you used to wear when you went swimming.

He laughs.

The signs were there. It's fucking amazing nobody ever figured it out. And I still have that suit.

I understand it now.

He laughs again, it is a weak laugh.

Straight or gay I stick to my guns on it, it's for swimmers, Europeans, and motherfuckers with style.

I laugh.

I'm still not any of them.

Your loss. Someday you'll realize. Your loss.

Is Freddie your boyfriend?

No, though in a different situation I might want him to be. He's my caregiver, a nurse of sorts. He helps me deal with what's happening to me.

I look at him.

I'm sorry, Leonard.

For what?

I'm sorry you had to live like that for so long, sorry that you had to hide, and I'm sorry that you're dying.

I chose how to live as I've lived, and I'm choosing how to die as I'm going to die. You shouldn't be sorry. If anything I should be sorry, for keeping the secret from you and for disappearing on you.

No apology necessary.

Thank you.

Is there anything I can do?

Hang out with me. That's all I want. Some time with my son.

That's why I'm here.

Thank you, James, thank you.

Freddie orders lunch from an Italian restaurant. He sets up a table on the deck. We have mozzarella and tomato, pappardelle with boar ragu, veal chops, gelato. I eat like a pig, Leonard hardly eats at all. He feeds most of his lunch to Bella, pretends to eat the rest by pushing his food around the plate. I ask him about his travels, he smiles, calls for Freddie, asks him to get his books.

Freddie brings out a stack of books, sets them on a table. There are a few art books, a couple of photo albums, four or five weathered travel guides. Freddie starts to walk away, Leonard speaks.

Don't you want to look at them with us?

Freddie turns around, smiles.

You've shown them to me about seventy-five times, Leonard. I think I can skip this viewing.

They both laugh, Freddie goes back into the house. Leonard stares at the books for a moment, smiles. He reaches for one of the travel guides.

Move your chair over here, my son.

I move my chair so that I'm sitting next to him.

We'll start with London.

London is a good place.

A great place. Much, much better than I expected. Everyone says the food is bad and that the English have terrible teeth, but I ate like a king and saw plenty of nice choppers.

I laugh.

And the accents. They're everywhere. Wonderful British accents.

Laugh.

He opens the book, opens one of the photo albums. There is a picture of him at a stadium surrounded by fans in red and white jerseys, with banners, hats, horns and beers.

I open to Wembley, where I saw the FA Cup final, which is sort of like the English version of the Super Bowl.

For soccer.

Yes, for soccer, though they call it football.

How was it?

Great. They're crazy about their football. They have to keep the fans of the teams separated by big fences or they'll attack each other. They make our fans look like poodles.

He keeps flipping through the books, opening a passage in a guide book to a corresponding photo, he starts showing me the highlights of his trip to London. He shows me his hotel, the Covent Garden, which he calls delightful. He reads me a passage about his favorite restaurant, which is the oldest fish and chips stand in the city. He talks about the London Dungeon Museum, there were fucking rats running in circles around the iron maiden, about the British National Museum, half of civilization under one big fucking roof, about the National Portrait Gallery and the Tate, my oh my they took my breath away. He talks about the weather it sucked but I didn't mind, about the friendly disposition of the city, it's like a cleaner, nicer version of New York.

He closes London we work our way through France. He says France is like a beautiful woman who knows she's beautiful, some people will love her beauty and arrogance, some people will hate it. Leonard loves it, says he spent two weeks wandering aimlessly around Paris drinking coffee and shopping and watching people and looking at the antique stands along the Seine, he spent two days in the Louvre and two in the D'Orsay, he spent another at the Musée Rodin. He ate every meal in a different restaurant, would just stop as he walked, pick places at random, he was never disappointed.

We move through the rest of Western Europe he says I loved it all, LOVED IT ALL. We move to Eastern Europe he says man, it's wonderful over there, we should have never been enemies with those people. We skip Italy he says he has another book for that part of his trip. I ask him if there's anything he didn't like about Europe he says the Greeks were mean and the weather in Russia sucked, other than that, I fucking loved it all. He opens the Asian guides, starts taking me through his Indian trip. He says India is a different world, one every American should be required to visit so that we understand how fortunate we are and how stupid we are. He says that despite the crushing poverty, the people are happy and hopeful and optimistic, and despite our own ludicrous wealth, we're depressed and unsatisfied and pessimistic. He talks about the cities you can't believe how many fucking people there are, the food it gave me the fucking shits, the art it's all religious, totally simple and pure, like early renaissance art, which may never have been exceeded. He says the Taj Mahal, the greatest and most magnificent monument to love the world has ever seen, is a fitting symbol for the country as a whole.

We open the book on China he tells me about Beijing it's huge and dirty and it smells and there are bikes everywhere, the wall it's so cool I can't even fucking believe it actually exists, the Forbidden City it makes every other palace in the world look like a steaming pile of dogshit. He tells me about Japan it's weird and noble and somehow simultaneously stuck in the past and in some version of the future, it's like everything is turned up to eleven.

We finish with the guide books and the photo albums, the last picture in the album is of a smiling Leonard sitting at a dinner table with a group of five hundred pound sumo wrestlers, there is enough food to feed fifty people. Leonard is still Leonard wherever he goes under whatever conditions, I laugh at the picture, he closes the albums.

He reaches for the art books, speaks.

Are you ready?

For what?

God, beauty, love. Perfection in multiple forms.

I motion to the books.

In those books?

He nods.

In these books.

That's a tall order, Leonard.

He smiles.

Order filled.

He opens the first book. The text is in Italian, there isn't much of it. Leonard stops talking, starts slowly turning the pages, the pages are filled with color reproductions of paintings, frescoes, altars. I don't know or recognize many of the paintings, though I do recognize names: Botticelli, da

Vinci, Caravaggio, Correggio, Ghirlandaio, Raphael, Tiepolo, Tintoretto, Titian. We spend a couple of minutes on each page. Sometimes Leonard will say where the piece exists, the Uffizi, Galleria Borghese, Santi Apostoli, the Pope's rooms at the Vatican, sometimes he'll point to a small detail, a drifting lock of hair, the reflection of a glass, a shading, a shadow, the look of a face.

We close the first book. Leonard carefully sets it apart from the guide books and photo albums. He opens the second book, which is on the work of Michelangelo. He moves more slowly through the pages, some of which appear to be stained in some way. We see the Pietà, David from twenty angles. We see the sketches for the Tomb of Julius II, the plans and corresponding photographs of the Laurentian Library. There is a page for each of the panels of the Sistine Chapel, the entire ceiling is spread across two pages. There are pages devoted to the details of the Last Judgment, the entire wall is spread across two pages. As we stare at the Last Judgment, tears start falling onto the pages. Leonard doesn't bother to wipe them away.

God, beauty, love. Perfection in multiple forms.

We stare at the pages and tears fall from Leonard's cheeks.

God, beauty, love.

Perfection in multiple forms.

I stay at Leonard's house. Bella and I stay in a guest room on the second floor. Freddie stays in another room on the second floor. Leonard has a bedroom set up in what used to be the dining room on the first floor.
I carry Leonard to bed at night, carry him from his bed to the deck in the morning. We eat breakfast on the deck, he has sores in his mouth and all he wants is bread and water, he has trouble taking it down.
We play cards.
We watch baseball games, sports highlight shows. We rent movies Leonard has a list of movies he wants to see before he's gone *The Graduate, The Bridge on the River Kwai, E.T.—The Extra-Terrestrial, Annie Hall, Snow White and the Seven Dwarfs.*
We go out to a couple of gay bars. We go at night. We go to bars that are quieter, where they have seating Leonard can't stand up for very long. He drinks water, dances in his seat to the music, talks to other men, flirts with them, kicks me under the table when I tell him I think one of them likes him.
We take the convertible for drives through Marin late at night. We drive with the top down Leonard stares at the hills the trees the vineyards the stars the moon the sky.
We make crank calls, pick up the phone dial random numbers start speaking absolute gibberish to whoever answers. They always hang up on us, we laugh and laugh and laugh and laugh.
I take him to San Francisco's art museum. It's early we're the first ones in line. He has trouble walking, I hold his hand as we wander through the galleries, he cries when we leave.
He asks me about my work I tell him I hate it. He laughs says you have discovered the ventriloquist that hides behind Hollywood's doll. I tell him no, I hate what I do because I went to Los Angeles to make some money

so that I could try to write a book and somewhere along the way I got lost. He says quit, write a book, I tell him it's not that easy I have bills and responsibilities he laughs again and says it is that easy, quit your fucking job and write a fucking book. He asks about Allison I tell him that we still love each other but we're through, he asks if there's anyone else I say maybe, he asks who I tell him about one of my neighbors her name is Maya we're friends but nothing more. He says he likes the name Maya, it's a noble beautiful name.

We go to the beach at sunset. He sits wrapped in blankets shivering. I offer to take him home he says no, he wants to stay. We watch the waves crash, we listen to the wind scream, we watch the sun go down, we watch the sun go down.

Leonard asks me if there's anything I need to know before he dies, I think about it for a minute, turn to him, say what's the meaning of life, Leonard? He laughs, says that's an easy one, my son, it's whatever you want it to be.

We finish dinner we ordered Chinese. Leonard hardly ate, he eats less and less every day. Leonard seems distant, distracted, I ask him if he's okay.

I was thinking about my friend Andrew.

Who's he?

He was my lover.

Your lover?

Yeah, my lover.

I laugh.

The person you fell in love with?

Yeah.

You should call him your boyfriend, not your lover.

Why?

Lover is cheesy.

Leonard laughs.

You better watch out.

Why?

You're not allowed to call me cheesy.

I am if you use the word lover.

How many years have I been listening to you wax poetic about your various girlfriends, oh I love her and I can't live without her, oh she's so beautiful, oh her eyes, her eyes, her eyes.

I laugh.

A lot of years.

I'm going to call him my lover, Cheddar Boy, and you're not going to say shit about it.

I laugh again.

Okay, Leonard, call him whatever you want.

My lover.

Where is he?

Across town.

Really?

Yeah.

Why don't you see him?

I don't want to.

Why?

It hurts too much.

Why?

Because love hurts sometimes, and it hurts more if you know it's not going to work out.

How do you know it wasn't going to work out?

Look at me. It wasn't going to work out.

Who is he?

Just a guy. He's a lawyer. He's a little older than me.

A lawyer?

A lawyer. A corporate lawyer. He does work for technology companies.

And older?

I like older men. They make me feel young.

I laugh.

How'd you meet?

Freddie and I went out to dinner. He was sitting alone at a table. We asked him to join us.

Love at first sight?

Leonard smiles.

Yes.

First time?

No, but the first time I ever did anything about it.

What happened?

We ate dinner. He gave me his card. I called him the next day and asked him out. We ate dinner again that night. We talked about art, books, about each other's lives, about our childhoods, he grew up in an upper-middle-class family in San Diego and spent his childhood surfing and playing Little League. He came back here with me that night and stayed with me. We had dinner and he stayed with me every night for the next two weeks.

And then?

I sent him away. Told him not to call or ever come back here.

Why?

Leonard starts to tear up.

I'm already in too much pain. I didn't want to hurt that way anymore.

I'm sorry.

Leonard stares at the floor, starts to cry, starts to sob. I sit next to him, hug him, let him sob in my arms.

It's morning I get out of bed walk downstairs. In the week I have been here we've established a routine, I wake Leonard up, help him brush his teeth, wash his face, shave, help him out to the veranda, where I drink coffee and he drinks water. Leonard isn't in his room I walk out to the deck he's sitting on his chair. He's smoking a cigar, staring out across the backyard. He speaks.

My son.

What's going on, Leonard?

Sitting here, enjoying the morning, smoking a fine cigar.

Big day ahead?

You could say that.

You got plans?

You could say that.

Where's Freddie?

He'll be here in a little while. I told him I needed some time alone with you.

What's up?

He turns to me.

You still think about Lilly?

Of course. Every day.

What do you think about when you think about her?

I remember our time together. How she felt when I held her, how she kissed me, how she smiled, what her laugh sounded like. I remember holding her when she'd cry. I remember talking to her and writing her in jail. I think a lot about what our life might have been like, I invent scenarios that we would have experienced together. Sometimes I think about what it must have been like for her when she died. What she was thinking and feeling, why she did it.

Why do you think she did it?

She felt too much pain. She just couldn't deal with it.

And how do you feel about what she did?

A small part of me still hates her for it. A part of my heart is still broken. Most of me accepts that she did what she did because she thought it was right, and I respect her decision.

He nods, looks back across the yard. He takes a drag of his cigar, exhales, puts the cigar out in an ashtray.

That was a great cigar.

I smile.

Good.

My last one.

You want me to get you more?

I mean it's the last one I'll ever smoke.

Why?

He stares at me for a moment.

I'm going to ask you to respect the decision I'm making.

What are you talking about, Leonard?

I'm in too much pain, my son. I don't want to waste away anymore. I want to go out on my terms, with some dignity, before I turn into a wailing, delirious, drugged-up skeleton.

Don't do this.

We've had a good time here together, and this has probably been the best week of my life. It's only gonna get worse, and I'm not gonna let it.

No.

Are you going to respect what I'm going to do?

I shake my head.

No.

Please understand this, and respect it, and accept it, the same way you did with Lilly.

No fucking way, Leonard. You're not gonna kill yourself.

He stares at me, into my eyes, they are the only part of him that still has life, he stares at me, stares at me.

Please, my son. It's time for me to go.

What are you going to do?

I'm going to ask you to take Bella out for a walk. Stay away for a couple of hours. When you come back, I'll be gone.

I shake my head.

No way, Leonard.

I have a bottle of pills. They're pain pills that I received to deal with what's happening to me. I'm going to take the entire bottle. I'll go to sleep, and I won't hurt anymore.

Please, Leonard. No.

I'm not doing this to hurt you. You're the most important person in my life, the only person I've got in this world, the only person I love. You're my son, my motherfucking son, and I'm proud of you, and who you've become and how you conduct yourself, and I know you don't believe in this, but I'll continue to watch over you, and protect you, and I'll look forward to seeing you again.

He stares at me, into my eyes. He opens his arms.

Give me a hug, my son.

I step forward, let him hug me, start to cry. I don't want this to happen and I don't want to let it happen, I don't want to lose my friend, my best friend, the man who saved me, who helped me, guided me protected me watched over me took care of me I don't want him to die, I don't want him to die, I don't want him to die. He pushes me away I don't want to let go of him he pushes me away.

Be proud, be strong. Live honorably and with dignity. You can do anything you want to do. You're my motherfucking son. Always remember that. Always remember that.

Tears stream down my face I'm having trouble breathing my hands are shaking I'm scared in shock I can't believe this is happening. He stares at me, into my eyes. I'm scared in shock I can't believe this is happening I speak.

I don't want this to happen.

He chuckles.

I don't want this to happen either, but I'm in . . .

I interrupt him.

I DON'T WANT THIS TO HAPPEN.

I'm scared in shock I start to cry I start to sob.

NO. NO. NO. NO.

He stares at me. I look at him I sob I'm scared in shock I don't want this to happen please please please God if you exist save him, save him, save him and I will devote my life to you, please someone anyone stop this please just stop this I sob please please please.

Leonard leans over, puts his arms around me, he hugs me as I sob, hugs me as I sob. He waits until I stop sobbing he speaks.

If you're gonna cry, cry because of all the good times we had, and all the laughs, and all the fun shit we did, and cry because those memories make you happy.

I look up at him. He speaks.

We had good years, my son. Great years. The best of my life.

He stands he takes my hand, I stand and we look at each other for the last time, the last time. He speaks.

It's time now.

I start to cry again.

You gotta leave me. It's time.

I get Bella leave the house as I walk away my legs give. I fall I can't get up I can't move I sit on the grass and I sob uncontrollably sob uncontrollably sob uncontrollably sob. When I can I get up and I walk to my truck and I get inside and I close the windows and lock the doors and lie in the back-seat and I hug my dog my little dog Bella and I sob uncontrollably sob.

Freddie knocks on the window I'm still in the backseat I don't know how much time has passed I'm exhausted, spent, I don't want to move can't begin to comprehend what's happened can't begin to comprehend what's in that house can't begin to comprehend that my friend Leonard is gone, my friend Leonard is gone.

I can't get out of the car. I feel safe in it, feel protected. I can't stop sobbing. Freddie calls an ambulance it comes they remove the body. I can't see it, can't look as they take him away. I sit in the backseat and I sob uncontrollably sob.

Freddie brings me food I can hardly eat. He takes Bella for walks. When it gets dark, I get out of the car go inside. As soon as I step through the door I start crying again I walk straight up to my room I lie in bed and I cry.

It's morning I'm awake I'm so tired I can hardly move. I go downstairs Freddie has coffee and cigarettes. We drink the coffee and smoke the cigarettes and cry together.

We start cleaning the house, boxing up Leonard's belongings there isn't much a few clothes, a few art books, a few pairs of slippers, we throw away medical supplies.

We eat lunch. I tell Freddie stories about Leonard we laugh between tears. We clean.

We eat dinner we laugh between tears.

I cry myself to sleep.

I wake up. Coffee and cigarettes. Freddie gives me the number of a lawyer who set up Leonard's estate. Leonard asked Freddie to give me the number after he was gone. I call the lawyer make an appointment for the afternoon. I go see the lawyer, it's not Andrew the lawyer, it's a probate lawyer. He has an oak desk, oak walls, he wears a gray suit, has a gray-haired assistant who calls me Mr. Frey. He tells me that Leonard has left two trusts. One of them, which is for me, has a significant sum of money in it. I tell him I don't want it, that I want to give it to the institution where we met. He tells me that it is a sum of money large enough so that I will never have to work again, never have to worry about money again. I tell him I don't want it, that I would like him to do whatever he needs to do so that the money goes to the institution where we met. He nods he tells me that the other trust is set up so that a pair of graves in Chicago will always be tended and will always have fresh roses. I ask him how long that will continue to go on. He looks at some papers, looks back at me says the instructions state there is a sum of money in place so that the graves will be tended for as long as the city of Chicago exists. I start to cry again. I sit in the lawyer's office and I cry.

I'm doing the last of the packing, cleaning, the doorbell rings. I walk to the door, open it. Snapper is standing in front of me. I'm terrified, absolutely fucking terrified. I think about slamming the door, but know it won't make a difference. If he is here to hurt me, the door won't stop him. He speaks.

Hey, Kid.

What's up, Snapper?

Not much. You?

You're a few days late.

He shakes his head.

No, I'm not.

Leonard's already dead.

I've known where he was for the last six months. I never would have hurt him. He was a great man, the greatest I've ever known. I'm here to pay my respects.

I step aside.

Come on in.

Snapper comes in, says hi to Bella, gives her a pat on the head. He asks if there's any alcohol in the house. There is a liquor cabinet, I look inside of it, tell him it's stocked. He asks for a scotch on ice and a glass of ice water. I get two glasses, get the ice, pour the scotch, pour the water. I give him the drink he tells me to keep the water. He asks to see the place where Leonard passed. I take him out to the deck. He reaches into his pocket, takes out two cigars, speaks.

Before he quit drinking, he drank scotch, after he quit drinking, he drank water. These are Cubans, they were his favorite. Let's smoke and drink in honor of our friend.

I smile, we toast, light the cigars. Snapper asks me about Leonard's last

days I tell him, he says he wishes he could have been here with us. He asks where Leonard is now I tell him he's being cremated, that I'm picking up his ashes tomorrow. He looks at me, speaks.
I thought that's what he would do. That's good.
Why?
There's something you and I need to do.
What?
Can you get Bella back to Los Angeles, have someone take care of her down there?
Probably. Why?
He tells me why, tells me what we're going to do. We find Freddie. I introduce him to Snapper. I can see fear on his face I tell him everything's cool, that Snapper has come to pay his respects. I ask Freddie if he can take Bella to Los Angeles. He says he's not sure, Snapper takes a roll of hundred dollar bills from his pocket asks him if five thousand dollars will make him sure. Freddie asks why, we tell him, he agrees to do it for free. The three of us go out for a steak dinner together. We order more food than we can eat, Snapper and Freddie drink a five hundred dollar bottle of wine, we leave a huge tip.
In honor of our friend.

end

I teach Freddie how to drive my truck. I give Bella a big kiss she licks my face they drive away.

Snapper and I pick up Leonard's ashes. They're in a box. We put the box in the backseat of the white convertible and we buy an atlas and we start driving east.

We drive across California into Nevada. We drive through Utah cross the mountains into Wyoming. We keep the top down, we drive fast, we take turns at the wheel, switch every few hours. Night comes Snapper sleeps I drink coffee and smoke cigarettes and drive, morning comes I sleep Snapper drinks coffee and smokes cigars and drives. We drive through Nebraska and Iowa and Illinois we drive through Chicago we've been driving for thirty-two straight hours. We switch back and forth one drives one sleeps we stop for food and coffee, cigarettes and gas. We keep driving the Mercedes is a strong car we drive eleven more hours through Indiana, Ohio, Pennsylvania, New Jersey. We drive into New York. We're both tired, spent, it's early morning we're almost there. We keep driving into Connecticut. Snapper knows where we're going has driven past the entrance with Leonard too many times without going in this time will be different.

We approach a wooded drive there's a sign out front. We pull up to the drive Snapper's behind the wheel. He turns to me, speaks.

You ready?

I smile.

Yeah, I'm ready.

Ask Leonard if he's ready.

I turn around, look at the box, speak.

You ready, Leonard?

I stare at the box for a moment, look back at Snapper.

He's says he's been waiting for this day for a long fucking time.

Snapper smiles. We start moving down the drive, through the woods, we come out there's a parking lot to our left filled with Mercedeses and BMW's, Jaguars and Porsches, there's a Rolls sitting apart in a corner. To our right there's a clubhouse, a beautiful, sprawling white building with a columned entrance and a valet station. Spread out behind the clubhouse there's a golf course, we can see sparkling dew on the grass.

We pull up to the valet. A uniformed attendant steps forward. Snapper steps out of the car I step out of the car. I reach into the backseat and I pick up the box. The attendant looks at Snapper, speaks.

May I help you?

Snapper takes a bill from his pocket, hands it to the attendant.

Put it in the lot. Make sure it gets a good spot.

Are you playing golf?

We are.

Do you have clubs?

That's not for you to worry about. Just make sure the car gets put in a good spot.

The attendant nods, gets in the Mercedes, the last of Leonard's many white Mercedeses, and he drives it into the parking lot. We step toward the front door. There's another uniformed attendant at the door. He looks at us we've been driving for the last two days we don't look like we're here for golf. He speaks.

The service entrance is around back.

We step forward. I have the box in my arms. Snapper speaks.

Is this the front door?

Yes.

We're going to walk through it.

The attendant speaks.

Excuse me, Sir . . .

Snapper interrupts.

We're not here to cause trouble, we just need to go through that door. It can be difficult or easy, either way we're going through it. I would highly recommend you make it easy, because if you don't, I will make your life very fucking difficult. Once we're through, you're not going to notify or call anyone, and we'll be gone within thirty minutes. Is that understood?

The attendant looks scared. He nods, speaks.

Yes, Sir.

Snapper reaches into his pocket, hands him a bill.

Thank you.

The man takes the bill. Snapper looks at him.

You normally open the door for people?

Yes, Sir.

Then do it for us.

The man opens the door.

Thank you.

We walk through the door enter a foyer. There are beautiful polished dark wood floors, a mirror, an oak reception table with a huge bouquet, there is subtle flowered wallpaper. A hall stretches out in front of us we walk down it ahead of us there is a large room with couches, tables, chairs, a wall of windows looks out onto the golf course. We walk straight ahead through the room there are sets of French doors we open them walk outside.

It's a beautiful morning, sunny crisp clear. It will be hot later but it isn't now. There's a pro shop and cart station to our left, fifty yards away. Without speaking we both start walking toward it. There's a putting green in front of it, there are three men on it lining up putts. Snapper looks at me, speaks.

Let's follow the rules while we're here.

We walk around the putting green, walk up to the cart station. A young man steps out from the station, asks if he can help us. Snapper steps onto a cart, gets behind the wheel. He looks at the young man, speaks.

We're taking this cart. You can pick it up in the parking lot in a little while. If you try to tell me I can't take it, I'll knock your fucking teeth out. And if you call anyone and tell them we've taken it, I'll do much, much worse.

The young man nods, speaks.

Understood.

Snapper hands him a bill, speaks.

Thank you.

He turns to me, speaks.

You ready?

I nod, speak.

This one's for Leonard.

Snapper smiles, speaks.

This one's for Leonard.

He turns the key, steps on the pedal, we pull away. We drive straight through the course. We drive down the middle of the fairways. We ignore the golfers who are surprised by us, who yell at us, who ask what we're doing. As we pull away I open the box, and as we drive we take turns reaching into the box and spreading the ashes. We put ash on every tee on every fairway on every green. We spread our friend Leonard across the perfect, beautiful green grass of the golf course that he spent his life dreaming of playing, just like one of the members. With each handful of ash we say this is for you, Leonard, and both of us have tears running down our faces the entire time. We spread Leonard's ashes, our friend Leonard's ashes, our magnificent friend Leonard's ashes.

When we finish we pull the cart into the parking lot. We get out, we start walking down the drive that led us here. We leave Leonard's Mercedes in the parking lot, right where it belongs, right where it will stay until someone takes it away. We walk silently, for the first time in a long time we are both without some semblance of our friend. We have left him where he belongs, and where he will stay. When we reach the end of the drive, Snapper takes a phone out of his pocket, calls a taxi service. When he's finished with the call, we sit on the ground and wait. Neither of us speaks, we just sit and wait. Ten minutes later, two cabs arrive. We stand. Snapper looks at me, speaks.

I guess this is it, Kid.

I guess so.

He reaches into one of his pockets, takes out a card, hands it to me.

That's Olivia's business card. I wrote my number on the back.

I feel like an asshole. I didn't ask you about Olivia. How she's doing?

She's good. I'm trying to convince her to marry me.

Tell her I said hi, and that I said you're not as bad as you seem, and that I think she should marry you.

He laughs.

You call me if you ever need anything, or if I can ever help you in any way.

I smile.

I probably won't.

He smiles.

That's probably best.

Thank you, Snapper.

Thank you, kid.

We give each either a hug. We separate. Snapper speaks.

You going back to Los Angeles?

I'm gonna stop in Chicago for a few hours.

Visit your girl?

I gotta tell her Leonard's coming to see her.

He's probably with her already.

I hope so.

Snapper looks at me for a moment, nods, opens the door to one of the cabs, gets inside. It pulls away as I get into the other cab. The cabbie looks at me speaks.

Where you going?

Airport.

Which one?

LaGuardia.

Where you headed?

I'm going to see a friend, then I'm going home.

Thank you Maya, I love you Maya, thank you for our beautiful baby, I love you Maren. Thank you Mom and Dad, Bob and Laura. Thank you Sean McDonald. Thank you Kassie Evashevski. Thank you David Krintzman. Thank you Tobin Babst. Thank you Julie Grau, Cindy Spiegel, Roland Phillips. Thank you Nan Talese and Coates Bateman. Thank you Jenny Meyer. Thank you Mike Craven, Warren Wibbelsman, Elizabeth Sosnow, Jeffrey Dawson, Kevin Chase, Dan Glasser, Matt Rice, Josh Kilmer-Purcell and Brent Ridge, Susan Kirshenbaum, The Motley Crue of Hamilton, Nancy Booth, Eben Strousse, the Boys in the motherfucking GSL. Thank you Nanci Ryder and Lisa Kussell. Thank you Mih-Ho Cha, Noelle Murrain, Megan Millenky. Thank you Dave Massey, Megan Lynch, Larissa Dooley, Justin Maggio, Alex Morris, Feroz Taj, Dave Bernad, Nicole Young. Thank you Brooke. Thank you Lyssa. Thank you United Hudson Grocery and Mary's Marvelous. Thank you Bella and Preacher my little friends, my little friends. Thank you Miles, we're still going. Thank you Lilly, thank you Lilly.
Thank you Leonard. Thank you, my friend.
Thank you Leonard.

about the author

James Frey is the author of *A Million Little Pieces*. Originally from Cleveland, he now lives in New York City with his wife and their daughter.